CONSCIOUSNESS

Consciousness

TALKS ABOUT THAT WHICH NEVER CHANGES

Alexander Smit

EPIGRAPH BOOKS
RHINEBECK, NEW YORK

'*Consciousness : Talks about That which never changes*';
original title: '*Bewustzijn : gesprekken over dat wat nooit verandert*';
edited by Nardy de Nijs-van Aggelen & Philip Renard;
Altamira Publishers, Heemstede, Netherlands, 1990

'*Selected blossoms*'; excerpts from the original title:
'*Bloesems van Sri Parabrahmadatta Maharaj (Alexander Smit)*';
collected and edited by Belle Bruins;
Advaita Foundation, Netherlands, 1998

Translated from the original Dutch by André van den Brink © 2008

Library of Congress Control Number: 2007942583
ISBN 9780979882814

M.C. Escher's "Concentric Rinds" © 2008 The M.C. Escher Company-
Holland. All rights reserved. www.mcescher.com

EPIGRAPH
A DIVISION OF MONKFISH BOOK PUBLISHING COMPANY
RHINEBECK, NEW YORK
WWW.EPIGRAPHPS.COM

CONTENTS

	Foreword by Philip Renard	vii
1.	Your last trump: the 'I-am-ness'	1
2.	The absolute irreversibility	4
3.	About the dog and its tail	11
4.	About freedom which cannot be experienced	26
5.	Singular consciousness	34
6.	The illusion of the 'I'- principle	38
7.	Your want becomes a seeking	45
8.	Bondage is forcing you to seek	61
9.	Consciousness is self-sufficient	70
10.	You cannot hide from perceiving	78
11.	God is formless Essence from which each form originates	83
12.	Your discomfort is your self-consciousness	93
13.	The natural state is and remains undivided	98
14.	The seeking takes place in the sought	103
15.	Life shows itself in a paradox	108
16.	A perfect balance is never experienced	112
17.	In order to be what you are you need not do anything	117
18.	Self-realisation does not need anyone's confirmation	125
19.	What you are cannot be located	130
20.	What do you *really* want?	137
21.	To love is to give—Not to love is to grab	139
22.	The Ever-present	151
23.	Fear of the unknown does not exist	165
24.	Practice makes the living	178
25.	Seeing is being	187
26.	Consciousness is nowhere not	197
27.	There is no precondition for being conscious	207
28.	About 'spiritual autism'	225

29.	Let things tell their story	235
30.	You are consciousness	243
31.	Life is a divine play	249
32.	All knowledge is ignorance	255
33.	Consciousness: your true potential	266
34.	To be free from conditioning is impossible	280
35.	Letting go of the known	285
36.	Knowing cannot know itself	292
37.	The 'person' is the past	303
38.	What you are is not what you seek	309
39.	Relax in conscious being	313
40.	Each vision is a limitation	321
41.	Consciousness is not affected by memory	326
42.	No world without consciousness	332
43.	Love is what you are	336
44.	Desirelessness is your deepest desire	339
45.	Reality is never a problem	350
	Selected blossoms	359
	Footnotes	375
	About the author	376

FOREWORD

by Philip Renard

WHAT IS REALITY? What is man *really* in his original, natural state? What or who, in fact, is the 'I'?

These essential questions form the theme of this book. Since a question about reality cannot be answered at a theoretical level, it concerns something that has to be expressed in life itself. In this matter we have no use for a philosophy, a reflection through a construction of thoughts. The only thing that can bring these questions to a solution is something like *'making the Real one's own reality'*.

Traditionally this has been described by the term 'Self-realisation', which means the realisation of that which one always already is, but which one normally fails to see. This realisation is a subject which is already very old, and which millions of people are interested in, yet few can speak about it from their own experience. Despite the fact that a lot has been written about it, unfortunately authors have often made it into a philosophy, a science or a religion. Thus the relatively small number of texts of those who *did* realize their original nature, in which reference is only made to That which goes beyond all concepts and beliefs, may actually serve as a guide-line. Although in all these texts there is the use of language and, therefore, of concepts, the reader is yet confronted with That which is *before* and *beyond* all concepts, that is to say, with That which he himself is in essence. Such texts often contain a rendering of oral answers to questions of those that are seeking realisation.

The book you are reading now is such a rendering of answers to questions. Alexander Smit is the one who is dealing with the questions. He was born in Rotterdam on 21st October, 1948, and he realized his original state on 21st September, 1978. Alexander speaks only on the basis of his own experience, and he requests those with whom he is conversing to restrict themselves to their own experiences as well. In this way a situation is created in which a real meeting may become possible. In order to be able to transmit anything essential to others, that quality of meeting is conditional. Only thus can such a conversation be prevented from getting bogged down in non-committal philosophizing and leaning on book-knowledge.

What, then, is this 'Essential' that is being transmitted?

In the unbelievably large quantity of ideas, concepts, doubts, feelings and insights that one may have, one factor may be singled out as being permanent, even when all other factors have disappeared, namely the fact that *consciousness* is present there, and that, basically, you *are* that consciousness. Alexander calls the fact that you are consciousness '*the first and last concept*'. At a certain stage this concept, too, will dissolve completely, but for the time being it is still something which can act as a kind of hold, a 'starting-point'.

All other concepts and ideas owe their sole existence to this first and last concept. You are conscious being—even if you doubt it. For, in order to be able to doubt it, you will have to be conscious in the first place. This given fact is so utterly self-evident, that it is being overlooked most of the time. The function of a teacher is to point this out to you, *in* the meeting itself, *in* the presence in which you are included bodily, along with your thinking and feeling. In fact, '*presence*' is but an other word for consciousness. Whatever takes place in that presence or consciousness, the presence itself remains completely untouched. It does not change. *Consciousness is not subject to change*. It does not have any form, beginning or end. It is unborn.

Foreword

That which never changes is the very condition for all that changes. Including all our thoughts and sensory perceptions, which are but constantly changing phenomena, observable without the least difficulty by the never changing consciousness. However, this capacity to observe, to *see*, is not a matter of individual concern. You cannot really speak about it as *'my'* consciousness, not even as *'the'* consciousness, for consciousness can, by definition, never be an object of something else. Consciousness is one. That which makes it possible for the teacher to see is absolutely the same consciousness as that which is making it possible for the seeker or disciple to see.

From this important fact it follows, that the transmitting itself ultimately *coincides* with that which is being transmitted. There is only *one* reality: one unbroken, homogeneous consciousness or *'Self'*, and this may become clear to you, because somebody 'outside' of you—a visible, tangible, living figure—is showing you consistently and convincingly that, ultimately, he is *not* that figure; that he is not this thinking and feeling *'person'* which you take him to be. Through him you are able to see that the *'person'* is actually *not* the one to be liberated or illumined, and that he will never be—and that this is equally true for your own person. For what you are basically seeking is liberation or realisation *as a person*, which proves to be out of the question. In fact, this whole 'person' appears to be nothing more than a collection of thoughts, a social convention.

I do not believe that one can become convinced of the 'obviousness' of this through an explanation about it in a book. The very fact that a visible *'person'* is showing you beyond any doubt that he is, in fact, *not* a person, but Consciousness itself, will cause the credibility of your own person to waver. Indeed, in this very process one will begin to lose all grip as a 'person', and occasionally one may be seized by the feeling to be engaged in some sort of suicide.

For myself Alexander has demonstrated that life from this 'point of view' (which *isn't* a point of view) does not lead to death, even if the person has no longer any leg to stand on. Indeed, the person appears to be absent, yet only then does life reveal itself in all its beauty and fullness. Life itself does not appear to need the support of any such 'person'. Because Alexander is only living from the untouchable, rock-like Consciousness, and as his teaching, under the motto '*First things first*', is directed towards That only, it has become acceptable at a certain point to believe that here is something, that may also be realized by *me*.

After a search of more than twenty-five years, including all sorts of experiences and insights, and after reading the most important books about the Ultimate, I dare say that I was only brought to the heart of the matter through three years of direct confrontation with Alexander. Long before I had learned of such expressions as, 'I am Consciousness only', or, 'This mind is nothing but the Buddha', but never had I seen anybody actually *demonstrating* it. On the other hand several times I had come across people who, after having read everything, had basically become bogged down in an extreme form of cynicism as regards the final *realisation* of these facts—as well as people who, on the basis of an intellectual insight into the message of 'having always been enlightened already', had adopted a pseudo-guruship.

In judging a teacher the question is not how the 'person' of the teacher is behaving, or how he may be considered morally (Self-realisation is something very different from holiness), but whether, in its deepest sense, his *inner* division has really been dissolved. Only such a complete dissolution, that is to say, a total absence of 'person', can help one to see that that which is being enacted before one's very eyes, also concerns oneself. The only measure for a teacher is whether you *yourself*, through the confrontation with him, are coming to clarity. The consistent emphasis on That which is non-divided, non-corrupted and most essential in man (possibly within the capricious context of an acting figure) has been of the greatest importance to me in the teaching of Alexander.

When I say that I am deeply grateful for this teaching, does my gratefulness then apply to the *person* of Alexander Smit? Of course, in a sense it does. But it has also dawned upon me that, in a deeper sense, there is nobody or nothing to be thankful for—that my thanks is only meant for the Unmeasurable which, in essence, I *am*. That this may be transmitted from one 'person' to an other 'person' is a great miracle indeed.

This process of transmittance is an age-old occurrence. The true knowledge in this matter has always been transmitted orally from teacher to disciple, leaving some notable exceptions as, for example, Ramana Maharshi. The oldest recordings about this knowledge are contained within certain *Upanishads* (such as the *Brihadaranyaka* and *Chhandogya*), and are often estimated to have been written around the eighth century B.C. The essential contents of these recordings is exactly the same as what Alexander Smit is transmitting now, namely the knowledge about That which never changes, the '*One-without-a-second*'. The Sanskrit term for it is '*advaita*' or non-duality (from *a-dvi*, *not*-two).

While its contents has never changed and, in fact, *cannot* be changed, the *form* of the teaching may change any moment, and so it does. Alexander's teaching shows much affinity with the Advaita Vedanta of Gaudapada and Shankara, yet his own Advaita tradition as handed down by his teacher Shri Nisargadatta Maharaj may be traced back to the thirteenth-century Jnaneshwar. An important difference with the approach of Shankara is, for example, that Alexander does not see much point in making reservations with respect to worldly matters. Things like monkhood and celibacy stem in fact from the idea that, in order to realize the all-embracing One, some things would have to be excluded first. Apart from that, any such matters have to be judged in the light of the time and culture in which certain counsels were being given.

Oral transmittance means, among other things, that something is being transmitted through the *word*, one of the characteristics of which is its dualistic nature. How, then, can something so dualistic like the word contribute to the realisation of the *non-dual Reality*? Should not everybody in fact keep his mouth shut? Did not Lao Tse say, 'He who knows does not speak, and he who speaks does not know'? Again in the *Amritanubhava* (*VI-11*) it is said by Jnaneshwar, 'How can the power and the greatness of the word ever be described, which (though leading the individual into bondage) ultimately sacrifices itself by taking the individual to his true and rightful position?' In other words, the very thing that contains within itself the germ of inner division or 'bondage' is also the means for removing that division—'ultimately sacrificing itself'.

In our search to be liberated from our bondage we build up concept after concept. In discussions with Alexander a certain concept of ours may be confirmed at some point, only to be negated again completely at some other moment. Only by using the word in such a paradoxical way the very *root* of all concept-making may be seen at a certain point. In fact, each concept or idea appears to be a kind of grip, a trap. Left to your own devices you can only continue to provide new building blocks for the construction of further concepts, and only if you open yourself up to someone who doesn't use such a construction at all, can your own world of concepts fall to pieces.

The unreality of ideas and concepts cannot be made evident through experience or discipline, which are temporary matters that do not go to the root of bondage. This root is traditionally called '*ajnana*', ignorance, and is described as being 'without beginning'. For that reason *jnana*, Knowing itself, is pointed out as the only remedy for dissolving *a-jnana*. Knowing itself will remove all further questions about a beginning, about an origin, because Knowing *itself* is without origin and does not appear to be concealed by anything else.

As a path *jnana*[1] runs via the power of discrimination, by learning to see the difference between the *instruments* of knowing (thinking, feeling and the bodily sensations)—and Knowing *itself*. This difference cannot be made clear without words. The notion that it can also be made clear through yoga, meditation or any other method or discipline, is based on the fact that one fails to see the constant recurrence of the conceptualizing process therein. By the right use of the power of discrimination (which, paradoxically, amounts to a deep, meditative process or *sadhana*) a point is finally reached, where That which is before and beyond discrimination, may actually be seen.

Many of the questions put before Alexander are found at a personal level. Or rather, these are questions brought up by problems lying in the mental and emotional areas. In fact, this is the domain of psychology and psychotherapy. In order to make it clear that, from this angle, it is not possible to gain sight of the 'underground'—Knowing itself—Alexander dismisses most of such questions. This may create the impression that psychotherapy as a whole is being rejected here, but that is not quite the case.

On the other hand what *is* made very clear is, that the very way in which psychotherapy is looking at things—the so-called attitude of 'working on oneself'—carries within itself the impossibility of going beyond its own limits, in other words, an orientation towards the contents of the *person* remains. As a consequence the root (i.e. the presupposition of being a separate entity) cannot be made visible. That is the reason why someone who is interested in the ultimate Truth, is advised to give up the search within the domain of the personality.

However, this does not take away the fact, that there is something like a 'temporary' truth, a squarely facing up to all kinds of emotional knots and entanglements that keep cropping up. When these knots are ignored out of a longing for that which is found to be 'superior', then a foundation for the final research will be lacking. Unfortunately this is happening quite frequently in spiritual circles. For that reason someone who remains too much interwoven with all sorts of unresolved issues, would do well to devote a period of time in facing the causes underlying them. Since any such causes are usually tied up with negation and resistance, it may be helpful to do this with somebody who has already probed into his own negations before, and who has been trained to supervise others in such a research. To this end it is of vital importance that such a supervisor or therapist would at least *know* the natural state himself. From this position he will then be able to help the other to look at the obstructing and confusing elements without condemnation.

The very elements which are usually termed 'negative', and which are mostly hidden under layers of guilt-feeling and other such things, contain a vitality and a creativity that may actually be very useful to us. For that reason it can be said to be very important, that these vital elements are laid bare. The supervisor should offer such a security, that one dares to face even the ugliest of impulses. At the same time he will not have the pretension that this kind of research, at the level of the person, will lead to final liberation. For even at this level one is basically dealing with limitations, the main focus being on the superimposed layers which are to be peeled off and seen through.

Although the process may only concern the 'grosser' illusions (such as the projecting of childhood images onto present situations), even so this kind of supervision may help one to see what one is *not*. At some point the voices of father and mother in us have, unnoticed, become a guide-line in our lives, pushing us to perfection. And these voices, amplified by their apparent counterforce—the demand for total independence—are constantly cutting in on us, because of the imperfections found there. That which at one time used to be a mere witness, has gradually turned into a prosecutor and an accuser. And because we identify ourselves with both the accuser and the accused part in ourselves, the result is an inner discord which, apparently, cannot be stopped. In this discord, in this basic dilemma, lies the real problem of the person.

What one actually needs to see with the help of the power of discrimination is that, in reality, none of the contending parties within you *is* you. If, however, the situation is *not* judged as such, and at some point one is being introduced to such terms as 'the seer' or 'the witness' (as, for example, in Advaita Vedanta), then these terms are likely to be mistaken for one of the contending parties, in other words for the criticizing self-consciousness itself. At some moment in time it is to become clear, that *both* sides of the dilemma are *already* being perceived (and this in a non-condemnatory way) by That which cannot be perceived itself, in other words, by That which does not have any *object*-value. In my view a psychotherapy that points into such a direction, has its place.

The important thing is to perceive the fundamental difference between *two* levels of witnessing, and to find one's true 'ground' for any deeper research. In that case the final objective of therapy would not just be a 'healthy functioning', or (as is current in transpersonal New Age circles) the discovering of a 'superior' (noble) self by a 'process of individuation', but at the same time it would involve an appreciation of the defense character of the person *as a whole*, including its higher or subtler aspects. Such a therapy may well be a preparation for listening to a Self-realized teacher with a ready ear, when the question, 'But, ultimately, who *am* I?', may find an answer there.

If a person is at all interested in realizing the Self, then he would be well advised to stop with the therapeutic approach at some point, because the attention has to be set free, no longer to be focussed onto *contents*, onto *objects*. Therapy is concerned with learning to recognize and see through all the 'grosser' projections. It means learning to embrace the neglected and even detested parts in ourselves with love. But once these have been brought to clarity, there will be room to recognize the 'finer' projection: the person itself. To see, however, that this person merely consists of a series of thoughts and, therefore, of *objects* only, lies beyond the area of 'working on oneself': The person *cannot* do work in order to 'work himself out'.

For that reason the path for realizing the ultimate Self cannot be said to lie in the *continuation* of therapy—even though a temporary investigation into a person's confusion may prove to be quite useful. In fact, the whole issue of realisation lies in a radical *diversion* of our point of view. In therapy on the other hand the entire orientation towards 'oneself', i.e. towards the *contents* of the person, hinges on the need to *improve* oneself. But the fact that one part of the person is believing that an other part needs to be changed, is just one more demonstration of the inner discord. Despite the fact that this process becomes subtler and subtler, it will continue to the last.

Alexander stresses the fact that any form of self-improvement is itself an obstacle to the realisation of our true nature. However subtle the urge for self-improvement may be (for example under the name of 'development' or 'growth'), it still assumes the reality of the person. Only when the whole person is seen to be a bundle of concepts, can the urge to change be relieved. At that point the whole manifestation may be accepted, namely through what Alexander calls, *'Letting it tell its story'*. While all aspects of the manifestation just continue to come up, by looking at them anew, *without wanting to interfere*, the cramp and the vicious circle—essential characteristics of the urge to improve—may actually be seen to consist of one basic 'material', namely Consciousness—the same Consciousness which is seeing or knowing itself. From that point onwards one cannot be in conflict with the seen any more.

Now, why do I maintain here that the relieving of tension and the acceptance spoken of are only possible by entering into a *living* relationship, that is to say, into a *direct* confrontation with a teacher for a period of time, when in fact it may be argued, that such a teacher would only create a *new* dependence? Besides, when it comes to the subject of teachers, all sorts of missteps may be referred to, and the word 'guru' has frequently become a word of abuse.

Indeed, in my own case I was able to observe quite a dose of transference towards the teacher. Over a period of time all the phenomena of dependency put together, both infantile and puberal (i.e. so-called '*in*-dependent'), were projected onto the visible 'person' of Alexander Smit. As to the role of the teacher in this matter, it is to be recognized that there are numerous persons who, thanks to certain psychic powers, hold a position of great authority in their teachership over their followers, and they do not appear to have the intention of giving up such position. That way liberation from bondage becomes like a carrot held out from a stick.

I therefore think, that only the teacher who is giving his teaching from the very highest level, and who is able to demonstrate continuously the difference between the various levels of reality (i.e. between the level of the unchanging Consciousness and that of the changing phenomena), can actually have a non-binding effect on his disciples. For there can only be bondage at the level of the changing person. No bondage is possible at the level of That which is always already illumined, where there is neither teacher nor disciple. It is my feeling that in those cases where a teacher is keeping his disciples in a position of dependency, there insufficient emphasis is being placed on the fact, that *neither* teacher *nor* disciple is a 'person', and that every form of devotion solely applies to That which may truly be called '*the real thing*', namely the Reality which you yourself *are*. As it is said in the poem '*Advaita Makaranda*', 'I am the Power, *on my own authority and absolute*, in which the appearances of world and separate souls, of disciples and teachers, subside.'

The best reply to the question whether one can do without a guru is, I think, Nisargadatta's counter-question, 'Can you do without a mother?' It is an event in time without which one wouldn't be there. The truly opening up of oneself to a Self-realized guru is an event in time, without which one would not be able to realize the absolute oneness of the 'outer' and the 'inner' world. By experiencing a living exception to all the stress coming from 'outside' of oneself—which is but a reflection of the stress 'inside' oneself—the relieving of tension and the acceptance mentioned may become possible. There has to be a tangible manifestation *demonstrating* these. For myself also counts, that the relationship with the guru, with that visible relief of the urge to change, constitutes the only means to get rid truly of *all* gurus, of *all* unperceived forms of spiritual authority outside myself.

What I find special in the teachership of Alexander is, that it is in fact *not* 'special'. It is not exotic, oriental or supernatural in any way. It is very clear that Advaita, which has its roots in India, is not to be transplanted to the West in its oriental form. The essence of Advaita is neither eastern nor western and can, therefore, bear to take on any visible form. Thus no culture or cult has developed around Alexander. What I consider special besides is, that this teaching is being given in Dutch, which may seem a nonsensical remark. Yet how often does it not happen, that obscurities occur due to translators, differences in culture, and so forth? Alexander's way of talking is completely western, modern and simple. Various matters from traditional texts which had hitherto remained obscure to me, were clarified at some stage thanks to a wording totally akin to mine.

The book you are holding now is a rendering of talks with Alexander Smit. In the end it remains but a reflection of the reality enacted in a live encounter. However well-put the texts in this book may be, nothing can take the place of the actual relationship between guru and disciple. Alexander himself wrote, 'He who is serious about Self-realisation will notice that, if one is really honest, one gets stuck at a certain point, and that books no longer offer the solutions one is looking for. Then one realizes that a teacher of flesh and blood is needed.'

———

1

YOUR LAST TRUMP: THE 'I-AM-NESS'

Visitor: You were talking once about the last trump which everybody is holding back, the last card that is held back in the game of Self-realisation, when one is standing face to face with oneself. Could you say something more about that?

Alexander: At first sight everybody seems to have his own trump-card, but in the end it all boils down to one thing: the 'I-am'-awareness, your subjectivity. The awareness of 'I am' is your last trump, it is the ground from which you can form opinions, hold views, have a certain idea about something or somebody, or have a self-image. The foundation of this is the phenomenon that 'I am'.

V: Is there a link between that phenomenon and the ego?

A: The word 'ego' leads to a confusion of speech. The ego was introduced by psychologists to mean the whole personality-structure, the 'I'-structure. But at the root of it there is an almost formless sense of... 'I am'. Nobody doubts that. Even in order to be able to doubt it you have to be there in the first place.

V: But how can this 'I-am-ness' be employed as a last trump?

A: The big delusion *is* this very 'I-am-ness', though hardly anyone gets down to that point. This 'I-am-ness' is what is called *'mula maya'* in Sanskrit, the 'root of illusion'. Whichever way you turn it, some form of self-awareness is there. You could also call it a sort of 'perceivership'. But don't be mistaken! What you want in the end is to disappear, to dissolve in love.

Just look at what you are eagerly longing for. All the things you eagerly want are solvents, i.e. means to disappear in love, your true nature. Whether it is playing the violin, sex, eating or dancing, meditation or football. These things give a sense of liberation, a sense of relief. That's why they are so popular, because there the state of self-awareness is dissolved for the time being—please note: *for the time being.*

As a matter of fact, this 'perceivership' is the same as the self-awareness. Man is struck by a curious fate, for he *is*—and, at the same time, he *perceives* that he is. *At the same time*, which is a peculiar phenomenon. Perhaps one could try and explain this phenomenon in a scientific way on the basis of the structure of the brains etc., but even so! It is inevitable that all such suppositions, all such hypotheses, again, are being perceived.

V: I am still not clear about that trump of yours.

A: The difficulty is that you are stuck with what your senses are dangling before your eyes. Through the play of the five elements —earth, water, fire, air and ether—a gigantic creation is being conjured up before you. As a result of a misunderstanding you have begun to look upon yourself as a *product* of that creation. You were getting consciousness mixed up with its *contents*. It could hardly be otherwise, for until now the only thing you knew *was* contents. Such is the game.

All you can possibly perceive—from the waking to the dream state up to deep, dreamless sleep—is the 'I-am-ness'. With deep, dreamless sleep it is perhaps most difficult to perceive it, for you refer to it as, 'nothing is there'. You bet there is! There is something there, only your search doesn't go quite that far! The problem is not that everything is so terribly complex, but that one is not going sufficiently deep.

(8th December, 1978)

2

THE ABSOLUTE IRREVERSIBILITY

Alexander: It has been quite some time since we met. What have you been up to in the meantime?

Visitor: I stayed away in order to recover a bit. After our last talk it all had become a bit too much for me.

A: Is there anything that kept you engaged? Something about which you would say, 'This is keeping my mind wholly occupied'?

V: I think there is. I have been thinking a lot about desires. And about the 'I-am-ness' you are talking about. I understand this 'I-am-ness' to be the primary fact about me, but it confuses me.

A: In order to desire you need an enormous amount of energy. When your energy decreases, for example, when you grow older, the power of self-consciousness also decreases. The vital energy begins to tick over, even though it does not take away the basic dilemma of one's existence. In other words, the vital energy is withdrawing itself. Just compare it to the inflating of a balloon: A certain pressure is created on the outside material. In the long run, however, the balloon will get elastic, with the result that the pressure will become less. With self-consciousness it is the same. Your body is the scent of consciousness. But, as long as the body exists, self-consciousness will also be there. It is inherent in your 'human-being-ness', you can't escape it. You can never say that self-consciousness is going to stop at a certain moment. There is as much of vital energy in self-consciousness as there is in body-consciousness. And desires are part of it; there is nothing wrong with that.

V: I can understand that. When I am sick, the interest in my environment is considerably less; but as I get better, I am all talks again.

A: When you are in good health, the emphasis is not on one's own body. Consciousness is directed outwards through the senses. Desires are always at the service of body, thinking and feeling with a view to survive. The more they are connected with a supposed 'I', the more destructive their form.

In order to secure possessions you cannot but create the conditions for it. If you have had a peak-experience and you are determined to have it *again*, then you will have to organize your whole life accordingly. That seems pretty obvious to me. You desire to have such an experience again, because your present state is, in fact, intolerable as compared to the peak-experience. This is causing you all the while to face the consequences, namely, that you are growing older, that you may die, that you are finite. The consequence of your being here is that, some day, it is going to end.

In fact, body-consciousness is something intolerable. Though it is enveloped by quite a bit of cultural and social finery, one can easily prick through that.

V: I am wondering what is going to remain then—It all sounds so gloomy.

A: Maybe it does. The things that remain, things that are really integrated—you are not aware of them. It cannot be otherwise, for if you would, it would be unnatural. It would then become a kind of behavioural practice. To practise total negation is impossible.

You either see it or you don't. All practising in this respect is a persiflage of your natural state. The truly natural state is the fullest negation and, at the same time, the total embracement of being.

V: But that is totally paradoxical!

A: They complete each other perfectly. Maybe the so-called primitive people are so 'natural', because they are not able to point to their own 'naturalness'.

V: I don't understand any of this.

A: You see, you can ignore your thoughts, you can ignore your feelings, but you can't ignore that which is most obvious, namely, *that you are*. That is the blind spot that you have. The guru shows you what you really are, which is the function of the guru.

V: What is the function of the guru?

A: Between us, he is the missis or mister who is kicking the last trump-card out of your hands. The last card that you are holding back in the game, consciously or unconsciously. But it is absolutely predictable what your last trump is going to be: It is your great endeavour to escape from the 'I'-consciousness; you are prepared to join in the little games and that's why you are corrupt and corruptible. For that endeavour you will mobilize everything.

V: I once heard that, without a guru, you can't succeed.

A: Don't worry about what others are telling you. What matters now is whether you are open to reason. Your 'I-am-ness' is the 'feeder'. Beyond that you don't know anything.

V: I understand that one doesn't have to do anything for Self-realisation.

A: Maybe—it all depends. What is important is not to rely on all the talk of others. What do you know about them? Do you know what they are up to and where they get their 'knowledge' from? For the moment you may safely leave alone such 'doing nothing'. In fact, quite a lot is to happen first, before you will be 'doing nothing' on the objective side. For at that stage you will have finished negating, then you will have seen that the solution does not lie on that side. Truth is rather to be found within. And nature is most relentless in these things. If you are holding back little aces and trumps even on that side, then there is little hope left for you. You really must have seen enough of it.

V: How can you check that?

A: By asking you about the things you have understood. All the things you get enthusiastic about in the hope to achieve 'something'—your ambitions, your pretensions, your subtle mental constructs...

V: So the guru pricks through them.

A: Yes, that seems quite obvious to me. For your ideas are showing leakages everywhere. The guru is entitled to do so, since you have come to him for relief out of a desire to come to clarity. If you have come for that, then the game, too, may be played. One condition is that the guru himself must have reached the end, and that he himself has covered the road completely. Otherwise it will become a comedy.

V: Doesn't one run the risk of becoming terribly indifferent that way?

A: Not by any means! Indifference brings about the capital sin of running in blinkers. This capital sin is supported by ignorance. Indifference is the absence of any bonds. And the absence of any bonds leads to isolation—*jnana* pushed to insanity. If you don't want any relationships, then nothing is stopping you to go and live in the mountains. But that's not what you have done. You could ask yourself whether or not an indifferent attitude is another way to avoid relationships. The characteristic of the natural state is its naturalness.

V: Then is there nothing to strive for any more?

A: All striving is intentional. Your disappointments will be proportional to your expectations. As soon as the Self is known, one's original striving is no more the same. Once you have seen that all ambition is vanity, that its root is the 'I-am-ness'—the basic assumption—when you have seen that that is vain, an air-bubble, then everything, really everything, will have become empty. Then your ambitions and passions cannot but undergo a change, for *everything* is an interpretation of what you have grasped.

V: So you could say then, that conflict really means, that you want something else than the primary given fact about you.

A: You may say so, but such a definition doesn't solve anything. What matters is whether you *see* it. That alone is sufficient. It is perfectly simple.

V: There is something dreadfully tragic about it, and at the same time something terribly beautiful.

A: The tragedy and the beauty of this discovery are immense. It is the absolute irreversibility. Everything falls into place. Even the body recovers its original sensitivity, for man is an extremely sensitive being by nature.

V: In my day-to-day life all sorts of quasi-realisations seem to take place, perhaps because of my desire to be realized. I also find myself dramatizing things.

A: In the beginning dramatisations cannot be avoided. Just don't pay too much attention to them; they will disappear of themselves. By paying attention to them you will nourish them and keep them alive. The naturalness you are really looking for will happen to you of its own accord.

V: I am asking myself whether I should meditate, observe my thoughts and such things?

A: What do you want to achieve with that?

V: It seems to me to be a useful method to...

A: No! In your present situation it would be the biggest trap you could possibly run into! You *are* the observing itself—No need to go and make yourself sit quiet for it. Never. But if it pleases you, go ahead... You will, however, turn it into a method, and after that into a persiflage. If you want to meditate, then meditate on the one who is meditating: You will soon discover that such a thing is impossible. To observe one's thoughts is useful for certain purposes; you learn how to concentrate yourself properly and so on. But ultimately it leads to nothing. At best you will become a good subtitler. You create the illusion that you are standing *outside* those thoughts—the most dangerous illusion within self-consciousness. It is washing away blood with blood, for the one who is observing is of the same material as that which is being observed. This isn't just a hollow phrase to be used without understanding.

V: In that case, should I forget about meditation altogether?

A: Realisation, real knowing, *is* forgetting, the ultimate spewing of all notions and concepts. Before that you are merely belching. This seeing cannot be achieved by an act of will-power. In other words: Meditation? You *are* nothing but that. The guru may point it out to you, but the *seeing* is up to you.

(20th December, 1980)

3

ABOUT THE DOG AND ITS TAIL

Visitor: It strikes me that much of what is being said here disappears, and that I am left with few ideas. Nor am I able to recall things. But what strikes me most is that you are dealing with people in a very direct way—unusually direct, at least compared to the way in which people 'normally' deal with each other. What I also recall is that all relationships with people would be based on interests.

Today I would like to talk with you about what waking and sleeping really is. I often read that people are supposedly asleep, and that they should wake up from that state. It strikes me that this kind of thing is pointed out in quite a few spiritual books. I do think that lots of people are asleep actually. As for me, I, too, have the feeling that I do not act in a complete sense.

Alexander: I have no idea what you mean.

V: In those books it is said, for example, that in the sleeping state and in the waking state one is equally unconscious. That we are unconscious of things.

A: I am afraid that such a thing isn't possible at all, since I cannot imagine anything to be 'unconscious'. Everything I know is conscious. The precondition for anything I may know is the simple fact of my *being conscious*. Something unconscious simply cannot exist, because everything that exists can only be experienced through conscious being. Therefore, any such thing as 'something unconscious' just doesn't exist.

The division between dreaming, waking and sleeping is extremely thin, as experience is teaching us every day. So, before starting to make big statements about this subject, it seems important to me to investigate the matter thoroughly, especially because no less than a hundred percent of our actions is based on the thinking we tend to do.

V: But isn't there a situation in which one finds oneself to be less conscious of things?

A: You see, the difficulty is that we are assuming things, never looking properly to see whether those things are really true. In any case, to be conscious of something presupposes a background. Whatever you may assert, whatever you may be busy doing, whatever you may remember—there has got to be something which makes it all possible. We had more or less agreed on calling this 'consciousness'. This consciousness cannot be controlled or reduced, it cannot be extended or made conscious even more fully. This consciousness is one's primary given fact, your first insight, the most intimate thing you know. From this intimate knowing it may seem to be possible for you to be more or less conscious of something. But, when you look at it from a somewhat less biased point of view, it will become clear to you that such a thing is impossible.

It is just like dying or waking up. You either are dead or you are alive. You either are asleep or you are awake. It is all or nothing. You can't be dead just a little bit. Similarly in relation to conscious being: You can't be conscious just a little bit.

Now the curious thing about conscious being is, that it is not able to perceive itself. The eye cannot see the eye. Conscious being can never be made into an object, because conscious being precedes any object whatsoever. And thinking or feeling are no exception to this.

In this whole world and outside of it there is nobody to be found who is able to make conscious being into an object. This conscious being which happens to you every morning in the waking state, comes about in a spontaneous and completely effortless way. The difficulty is that everybody has, to a greater or lesser extent, become entangled in the objective world—the world conjured up by the five senses. The point here is to see through the delusive character of both the senses and of thinking and feeling. Not by rejecting or suppressing them, not by a greater or lesser appreciation of them nor by transforming them, but by seeing things in their true perspective. This searching for an opening, for truth if you like, is the real meaning of the word 'philosophy': the love of truth and wisdom. The urge for truth is called 'searching', which is a basic tendency in every human being, both at its highest and at its lowest level. I wonder whether you still follow all of this?

V: I think so. If I understand you well, then what you are saying is that one cannot possibly perceive oneself.

A: If you mean to say one's 'fundamental knowing', then I agree. But I am afraid that, by 'oneself', you mean something quite different.

V: But one can be conscious of other things?

A: Only of other things!

V: Still, one may be analyzing things, for example...

A: That is not the point here. That is left to the psychiatrist. We are not dealing here with the lawful properties of body, thinking and feeling. As a matter of fact, some sensible things may be said about these too. The question here is about, 'What am I?', and, 'Who am I?'

V: That is not true.

A: I beg your pardon?

V: Aren't you also conscious of yourself? Do you, too, not reflect about things? Aren't you, too, involved in yourself?

A: Young lady, please do not project your own situation onto me in order to show me how I am experiencing myself. What you are taking to be my experience is your own experience projected onto me—which has got nothing to do with me. Just like my mother, who always told me to wear a shawl whenever she was feeling cold. What you believe I'm seeing is what you are seeing yourself.

V: I still don't understand. What you are saying is that, at every moment, one is awake. You are quarrelling about words. I have the impression that we are talking about the same thing.

A: Since we attach such great importance to words, we are looking in these gatherings, via words, for an opening towards something living, something that lies *beyond* words. Words are important so long as we don't have anything better. In some way or other we are looking for a meeting.

V: But then, we do have to use the same concepts.

A: The very starting-point of these meetings is that it isn't about concepts.

V: About meanings then...

A: Neither. What I am just trying to make clear to you is that the concepts we use do not convey anything essential. So that we may arrive at the *living* truth, which has got nothing, absolutely nothing to do with concepts. Here we are only dealing with the unchanging essence. Here it is a demolition site rather than a centre for community development. The notions that you are putting forward about who you are and what you are, are not accepted by me. Only the wordless meeting in silence is. For your real depth—the essence—is total silence. There all is plain and clear. There, too, we will recognize each other truly, and I emphasize '*re*-cognize', because you were that silence all along.

V: I can see the bit about the essence, although to me it is much less so when I'm asleep. I just know it.

A: Before starting to draw conclusions it is important to ask yourself what you *really* know. To draw conclusions before investigating matters in depth is a bad habit.

V: But that is my experience now.

A: I go along with your experience, only don't call it a *fact*. Rather say, 'In my experience it is like this or like that', unless you are sure about your case.

V: I am, as a matter of fact. During sleep I don't have that experience.

A: All right. Then, before going to sleep, try to realize what sleeping really means. What I'm saying is: In deep, dreamless sleep something is there, a presence that cannot be got hold of by the image-consciousness that we are used to in the waking state and, occasionally, during dream. Because our memory has been trained to retain *images*—for feedback—you presume that during deep, dreamless sleep *nothing* was there. Yet there was a presence: Consciousness. If not, it would be impossible for you to wake up in the morning and say that you had slept so very well, isn't it?

So there are three states of consciousness that you know of. In the first place, the waking state. From that state we do our reasoning among other things, while the rest is being observed. Next is the dream state and deep, dreamless sleep. You do not know any more states. Do you agree?

V: I do not know the dreamless state.

A: Exactly! If you had said you did, then I would have told you: You *don't* know the deep, dreamless sleep state. You do know it, strictly speaking, as a formless presence, but not in terms of the known. Well, these states are essentially similar because of the simple fact that they can be perceived. Strictly speaking you only know the *images* of the waking and the dream state. As for deep, dreamless sleep, it doesn't have any images, so there nothing can be perceived. There consciousness radiates in all its presence. Therefore, the *jnani* will say that everything is born from that source, and that for that reason everything is consciousness. From that source, out of that essence, the world is born: body, thinking, feeling and whatever you like. That is what we are talking about here. We do not know any other subject. The deep conviction that all this is true, added to the impossibility of identifying oneself with any object whatsoever, is called illumination. Not because I say so, not because I'm trying to convince you of something or other, but because you can see it. All questions coming up from that source are welcome now—other questions are not.

A: (to an other visitor): Is this clear to you?

V: I think so. I think what she means...

A: Don't try to help her. I'm asking whether it is clear to *you*.

V: Yes, I was able to follow it.

A: By comparing your thinking to hers?

V: No, by listening.

A: Well, what did you discover from what was said here?

V: That it is actually true—that for me, too, there are two states which apply. For me this is linked up with the fact that I can't get at the deep, dreamless state, because I can't get at the waking-state-without-thoughts either.

A: Who is telling you not to think during the waking state?

V: Well, I don't know.

A: Have you ever had a night's sleep without waking up? A peaceful night, when you didn't have any dreams, at least according to your experience?

V: Yes, I have.

A: Right. How could you know then, that you had been sleeping so peacefully and well all night, if there had not been a presence to tell you about it? As you didn't wake up all the time in order to become 'conscious' of the fact that you hadn't been awake, how could you have known that you had been sleeping so well? There *has* to be a background.

May I just ask you what you were doing on the 3rd of January 1963?

V: I wouldn't know.

A: Yet not even for a moment do you doubt the fact that you existed that day, do you? We really do know this deep, dreamless state, only not in terms of the known.

V: If I get this right, then what you are saying is that, each moment, you know what you are experiencing, that you are conscious every moment.

A: That you are conscious every moment—that's for sure. *What* you are experiencing rather depends; but you are conscious, with or without images. The advice I am giving you here is: Don't let yourself be hypnotized by what those images are trying to tell you. For, if you don't see things in their true perspective, then you will fall a victim to them. Stay with the heart of the matter, for that is what you *are*.

V: But that's of no use to me whatsoever! Every day I've got to live my life! If I am not happy with the way my life is going, with who I am and what I am and feel, then I just have no use for this. And that is my experience every day: I am just not happy with it. If I have to stay like this for the rest of my life...

A: What do you mean by, 'Stay like this for the rest of my life'? Apparently you are not happy with the image you have of yourself. Now, all the things that could possibly be good or bad about you were absorbed by you from your environment: Your mother who believed that you were to be brave always—and nobody is capable of being brave all the time—and now you have to be brave again, because your boyfriend believes that that is how 'it' should be. But it is a difficult life-task to please everybody, and to please oneself is probably impossible.

The problems are sure to be found at that level, but not the solutions.

V: What I hear you saying is that, each moment, one should be happy to be alive, always being content with everything as it is. But there are times when I just don't like the people around me.

A: We don't have to anything, nor is this an issue about liking things. Likes and dislikes are conditioned reflexes, determined by whatever you may have learned to like or dislike. All that is only the surface—your parents, your environment, your school etc. A world that is the same to all doesn't exist. The world is more like an image that you have created for yourself. If only you take a close look at what you like now and what you used to like as a little girl years ago. I just presume that you are not playing with dolls any more and are making sand-pies all day long. That's what you liked to do in those days.

What you like or dislike about the world is your *particular notion* of it. The problems *in that world* can only be solved by you. Those solutions must be at the base and not at the surface, otherwise you are like someone who is going to pamper a sick tree in the garden by cleaning all the leaves with a washing-glove. In an exceptional case this may be necessary, but in this case it is the roots that need watering. You have to go to the roots, for that is where the disease is—*Provided* you do want a fundamental solution. If not, then there is a whole world waiting for you full of compensations.

V: I suggest that we start right now.

A: We are dealing here with nothing but that.

V: No, because right now I'm not dealing with it. I'm not busy thinking—Right now I'm busy feeling.

A: Before you can think or feel anything, there is conscious being as the precondition for those thoughts or feelings. That source is the antechamber of everything else.

V: But isn't thinking an acquired habit?

A: That is not the issue here. I don't reject thinking. Thinking has its place within conscious being. But anything you are saying about the essence, the source, from the level of thinking is from hearsay, second-hand. It is a different story when you are looking at your thinking from the source itself. There is nothing wrong with that.

What is needed is to shift one's centre of gravity. Now the centre of gravity is 'in the world', in 'thinking' or in 'feeling', but just try and turn it around.

The senses are naturally inclined to take an outgoing direction, which is how it should be, otherwise we wouldn't be able to survive one more day in this world. But he who puts his centre of gravity in this world is only asking for chaos and trouble. The world will continue to create troubles for you, unless you know its delusive quality—which is one hundred percent. That is why all *jnanis* emphasize the realisation of that which you really are. After that the so-called world will not be a problem any more.

V: So one should move from the source to the mind.

A: It is not a question of your moving towards the mind. It all happens of itself as you begin to see the true perspective. At present the centre of gravity is so close to your mind, that things only seem to become clear to you in terms of thinking. You are so much accustomed to measure everything with the mind, that you draw everything that appeals to you to yourself, and everything that you dislike you push away from you. But the essence, the immeasurable formless Being, can never be measured by your standards. On the other hand it is quite possible to talk about the mind from the essence. You can talk about any object, so why not about the mind, which is as good an object as any other—nothing more and nothing less. That is the reason why I can freely speak out all the things that occur to me. The mind functions perfectly by itself and naturally, just like eating and drinking and digesting and going to the bathroom. It is a natural movement.

V: Who is telling me that you are speaking from that essence? Is it possible to speak from the essence at all?

A: I am telling you. There is nothing *but* the essence. Each thought or each feeling is a gift from that essence.

V: But how do you know it is coming from the essence?

A: It is the unconditional condition for everything.

V: Maybe the essence, too, is an acquired habit.

A: Maybe, maybe. I am telling you that that is certainly not the case. The essence is the precondition for all that is acquired. If you are interested in it, then there is the possibility for you to see whether it is true. If you are not, then don't bother and stay away! But for goodness' sake, don't make it into a game. All that I'm doing is giving answers to your questions at your request, because we are seeking to have a meeting. If you like it, then investigate it —Don't make it into a game.

V: I find it difficult, because you are not taking things easily.

A: Nor do I intend to. Otherwise we will only get down to the ordinary chit-chat and superficial bother. It is not a question of democracy here. For in that case we will start to exchange views and that is not the purpose here.

V: Yes, but...

A: No, I am not going to be agreeable to you. If you don't like my words, then you may leave right away. You have come here to listen to me, isn't it? I didn't come here to listen to your discourse.

V: Tell me, then, what this essence is, what is important about it! Tell me where I should look for it.

A: What I am trying to get across to you all the time is that you may be looking for it, but that you will never find it; and certainly not on the conditions you have made for yourself and for me.

All searching is preceded by the first insight. That first insight is the fact that you are. That you *are conscious*—nothing more and nothing less. All your searching is preceded by the essence. In other words, that which you are searching for *you already are.* The way you are now busy dealing with it is like a dog that is running after its own tail. By agreeing to your propositions, by listening to you, I'm just pushing you a little bit, so that you go running after your tail even faster. Then I am trying to break through the circle by not accepting your opinions. Yet you insist on getting drunk by spinning round and round, and next you are surprised about the giddiness you have and how all this has come about.

What I want to make clear to you is that *what you are, you can never find,* you can never make it into an object. This whole search is based on illusion. You are searching, because you believe you can find 'something'. Here it is made clear to you that there is nothing to be found—which means that you stop searching. Perhaps that is not what you want. Perhaps you want an alibi in order to continue with all sorts of nonsense for years to come. Maybe you hadn't come for that in the first place.

Truth is so unbelievably simple, so obvious, that one almost always tends to overlook it. However, as long as you are not really convinced, you have no other option but to continue searching. You could also quit, angered even, or with a subtle air of, 'I think I've got the point now'. But, as long as you haven't seen the point completely, you will have no other alternative but to continue to search in some way or other.

V: I just think that people's actions do not proceed from that essence. I just don't agree with you.

A: As you like. Last time we were talking about your origin. You will remember that we were discussing this union of your parents to which you owe your existence, do you? Everything has come from that union. There is a word in Marathi which means something like 'womb', literally meaning 'bed of consciousness'. Conscious being is the precondition for everything you know, including your previous and your next lives, if you happen to believe in such things. The fact of your being conscious now, of consciousness being there, is the only capital you have. For the rest you have no leg to stand on. That discovery is without any concession, you can't fiddle with it. You are free, unbound, formless conscious being itself.

By way of gift you are sitting here as a body, which is the scent of your conscious being. That is the nice part of it. But what are we doing? Out of ignorance we are making it into one big mess, mistaking the form for the real thing. When we die, the form is left behind, whereas the formless does not disappear. For where should it go?

Just see the beauty of it and be happy. Don't be fooled by delusion, by the illusion that you are just a form. The Sanskrit word *'maya'* means 'that which is measurable'. But the immeasurable cannot be measured by the measurable.

V: It seems to me that what is being said here is just too simple.

A: Yes, it is simple. But normally we insist that things should be complex. I am quite willing to tell you a complicated story with a lot of Sanskrit and difficult words in it, but then you will complain again that it is so difficult and 'oriental', and that it is not suitable for the West—as if consciousness would be interested in 'East' and 'West'.

In the battle to keep up the 'I'-structure you have grown more and more clever, and so you got yourself from the frying-pan into the fire. You fell a victim to your own constructions. Indeed, you are not able to see with singularity. You are seeing everything in a criss-cross manner and always through the spectacles of your own, particular views or self-image. You have learned to experience the world after your own particular fashion. The more you begin to discover the true perspective, the clearer things will become.

However, I understand very well that my explications are of no use to you, except that they might stimulate you to look with more depth and more love. My advice is to stick to one thing only, to that which you really know, your immutable focus. Remember that you cannot know anything without being conscious, that consciousness is the precondition for everything. The clearer the insight, the more chance is left for the liberating action to take place. It also applies to these talks. If it helps to clarify matters for you, then here is your place. But if you are only making constructions of what is being discussed here, repeating them elsewhere, then these things are of no use to you. The real issue here cannot be conveyed or contained by any construction whatsoever. To repeat it always means *not to understand* it. In true understanding—not in repeating—total clarity and silence remain. Never a construction, never a formula. Not even the construction of a non-construction.

When you are really convinced, not a single question will remain. And this conviction, which means true freedom, does not need anyone else's confirmation.

(4th January, 1982)

4

ABOUT FREEDOM
WHICH CANNOT BE EXPERIENCED

Visitor: You once said that Self-realisation is really nothing but detaching oneself from the idea that one is attached to something. You also said: Prove it to me that you are attached and I will make you detached. At that time you were speaking about the fact that real freedom cannot be experienced, that real freedom is free from the *feeling* of being free. You also said that the act of perceiving is taking place without any effort. Could you say a little more about that?

Alexander: Even when you are very tired, the witnessing of your tiredness goes without any effort on your part. The same applies to happiness and other perceptions. You are the effortless witness, the perceiver of all that happens, under all circumstances.

V: Is it the purpose to be constantly aware of such perceiving?

A: You are already aware even before you realize it.

V: If I accept that and...

A: No, no. You can't just accept it on my authority. It has to be crystal-clear to *you*, otherwise you will land into the sphere of religious belief.

V: Suppose I really see it, then I won't need to do anything further?

A: The precondition for the contents of consciousness is conscious being. This may lead to a confusion of speech, because, in Dutch, 'consciousness' is treated as a noun, and there is the risk of qualities being attributed to it. The attributing of qualities to conscious being is not proper, for, after having investigated the matter with due discrimination, one will realize consciousness to be without any qualities. Qualities are always on the side of the *known*, that is to say, on the side of what is being perceived. And whatever can be perceived is subject to change and is, therefore, not the unchanging, indivisible 'One-without-a-second'. Even without Advaita scientists are coming to this conclusion. Psychologists discovered pretty soon that nothing can be said about consciousness. On the other hand some things may be said about the *contents* of consciousness. But whatever is said about it is, again, the contents of consciousness, so on the side of the *known*. That is what psychology is about. Structures of thinking may thus be described and put in order.

Psychology is taking full account of this fact. Psychology is the study of behaviour. But studying behaviour is itself also behaviour. Whatever it may be, any perception of thoughts, feelings or objects, presupposes a background. Without a background it is impossible for anything to appear. This background is also called 'emptiness', 'space', and sometimes '*akasha*'.

In the use of our language the word 'self-knowledge' is quite frequently giving rise to misunderstanding, because there we try to investigate our thinking and feeling from a self-image, from an 'I'-structure (the identification with body, thinking and feeling). This is, in fact, impossible. An 'I'-structure cannot investigate anything and doesn't *know* anything. An 'I'-structure may at best be perceived. How is that perception possible? Through the space, the availability in which it is possible for it to appear. Once the 'I'-structure has disappeared, space and availability remain. This applies to all forms of perception.

For convenience' sake I will here call the awareness in that space 'singular consciousness'. Of course, this is just another term, again being perceived within that space. In this space where perceptions become possible, perceiving is aware of the changing of events such as light or sound. The changes in this space occur at such a high speed, that we have the experience of a solid continuity. In other instances the changes are taking place at an extremely low pace like the changes of day and night, of the seasons or, if you like, of a lifetime. The continuity experienced by us is, in fact, nothing but the succession of very rapid changes. But it always has space, availability, as its basis—even in the atom. We are inclined to ignore that aspect, yet it does exist. Since it is the basis of creation and manifestation, everybody is searching in his own way for union with this emptiness, the singular consciousness. Naturally it is sought for at different levels, but the basic movement is the same.

We can see this most clearly in sexuality and love, since these are spatial and make for space. It is hardly possible to do any thinking there, because there, for the time being, the pairs of opposites are nearly dissolved. Such an experience refers to our essence. The same applies to extraordinary sports performances, where some kind of union takes place as well. Similarly with music, dance and many other activities. The emptiness is also present during deep, dreamless sleep, which is why everybody likes sleeping. And, as you know, a disturbed sleep causes fatigue and irritation of the physical mechanism. In other words, here too, the balance and the alternation of events apply.

In the same way a kind of standstill of the projecting mechanism occurs, whenever a much coveted object has come within one's reach, particularly after much of painstaking effort has been made. The object in view has been attained, the standstill lasts for some length of time, and we experience a happiness, because we have been successful. After which we again project a new objective for ourselves. What eludes most people is the fact that the happiness is not dependent on the object, but on the projecting mechanism coming to a standstill—in other words, on the emptiness. For that reason the pursuit of objects has to be continued all the time. These forms of activity create a sense of union of the perceiver and the perceived. It occurs to me that everybody is seeking that—union. Of course, at different levels, still the basic movement is the same.

V: Why is man seeking this?

A: Because his original nature *is* space, emptiness, availability and consciousness.

V: Isn't that a construction of ideas?

A: Every construction of ideas is preceded by consciousness, which is able to perceive the construction. First there is the space. Within consciousness the construction appears. No construction or formula is able to enclose consciousness and, by definition, every description will be the reflection of a fragment. Consciousness cannot be squeezed into any formula or concept whatsoever. How will a part be able to contain the Totality? On the other hand the Totality can certainly contain the parts. As a consequence it is impossible for the 'I'-structure to become transformed into singular consciousness. In fact, thanks to the very absence of the 'I'-structure the Totality stands revealed. Such an absence of the 'I'-structure manifests itself as serenity at the level of feeling, as clarity at the level of thinking, and at the level of the body as equilibrium and health. When this state which, of course, is a temporary one, is not claimed as being 'I', then there is that freedom which does not 'feel', which cannot be 'experienced', but which *is* experience.

The motor of the search is the non-experiencing of an equilibrium by us, the field of tension of the pairs of opposites. All spiritual seeking is based on one's being-out-of-balance, a lacking that is felt and which is restored through balance. In a *real* investigation, however, you will discover that the sun rises at dusk. The *feeling* of being-in-balance is still a balancing.

V: Are you striving for a constant peak-experience?

A: If you would have a constant peak-experience—which is impossible—you would explode. A peak-experience is only possible in relation to its opposite, a valley-experience. You wouldn't know what 'green' was, if you were totally surrounded by green. You know green only as the opposite of other frequencies. Actually, man is being misled by the pairs of opposites and, as a consequence, he doesn't see their basis. This is the cause of all suffering.

What may be comprehended is that the pairs of opposites are perceived within consciousness, which is the bearer of both. Just like the *yin-yang* symbol of ancient China in which the positive and negative aspects are borne by the emptiness. They can only manifest themselves *within* that emptiness.

V: The emptiness you were speaking about, could you also call it 'silence'?

A: You may give it any name you like. But the *naming* of silence is not silence, the *naming* of emptiness is not emptiness. We mistake the word for the thing. No doubt you've heard this before, but apparently it hasn't sunk in sufficiently deep. You may call the absence of sound 'silence', but that doesn't give you the *knowledge* of silence. Moreover, how do you want to perceive silence? You can only perceive sounds. In fact, strictly speaking silence doesn't exist.

Experiments were made by locking up people in a completely sound-proof room. After a couple of hours these people became completely crazy because of the rushing sound of their blood circulation and the beating of their heart. Total silence doesn't exist, neither physically nor mentally. Only movements and the changing of objects may be apprehended.

V: What actually is the purpose of these meetings?

A: Somehow or other we have gathered here, because of certain interests on the part of the speaker and the listener; otherwise this combination wouldn't be possible. From the side of the speaker there may be the need to express himself, acting upon the impulses of those that have come to see him. The people react to the impulses of the speaker and thus an exchange of energies begins to take place which, so the speaker hopes, will lead to clarity. In India this kind of gatherings is called '*satsang*', which means, 'meeting with the holy ones'. But the correct translation is, 'meeting with clarity, with the pure', the meeting with that which is without any friction.

In the first place it means that there is no *must*, because a meeting implies the absence of any compulsion. As soon as a 'must' or a 'will' arises, there is no more question of a meeting. A true meeting, even between two persons, is only possible when there is no must. Compulsion always means friction. So to be meeting and to be without any friction is one and the same thing.

At the bottom of your heart you are the friction-free, ever-meeting self. But this clarity appears to be soiled by all sorts of things. Thus the idea comes to your mind that you have to start *doing* something in order to change that situation. It means that you are dissatisfied. In other words, you go in search of clarity, a solution, relief, *moksha*, enlightenment. But what you do not see is that all searching for enlightenment etc. is a self-maintained mechanism. You are busy thinking, that is to say, busy with concepts, in order to solve self-made problems, which is impossible. You cannot solve problems through thinking, for thinking *is* the problem. How can a sword cut itself? How can blood be washed away by blood?

Therefore, what you have to begin with is to see that there *are* no solutions. For, together with the hope for a solution as presented to you by the various teachers in the supermarket of awareness-raising, you are keeping the vicious circle intact, while failing to look at the problem. Your search for a solution, your whole investment in enlightenment, is nothing but one big defense mechanism to prevent you from *seeing* the problem. You are only looking at the solutions, and there aren't any. You are not interested in problems, only in solutions.

The hope and the belief in solutions is created by the mind which, of all things, is the creator of the problems! Such is the movement, and along with that movement you will be buried! Each attempt to reach a solution is the avoidance of the problem. And most of us here have come for a solution of their problems. Many people that come here have already been all over the place—with Krishnamurti, with Rajneesh, with Muktananda, etc. They have tried all sorts of things—*hatha yoga*, meditation, therapies—but it didn't help them to solve their basic dilemma. Don't get me wrong: I am not saying that you shouldn't practise *hatha yoga* or meditation. If you like these things, then by all means practise them. But it will not solve your basic dilemma. Of course, a supple body is better than a stiff one, although in the end the body is going to become rigid anyway. I have nothing against dying except for the fact that, next day, one has become so rigid!

V: So you don't see any solution?

A: I don't see any problems and, therefore, no solutions either.

V: So we cannot do anything?

A: You have to see clearly that all doing, all striving, all exertion or all movement towards a solution or goal, is the negation of the problem. Problems and solutions always go together. Where there is no problem, there isn't a solution either.

Realize that all your toiling, all your 'working on', your ambitions, your endeavours and your meditations are leading you nowhere. They only distract you from that which is urging to make itself clear to you. By not doing anything—not by 'doing nothing' as yet another solution—but by really not doing anything, an opportunity is given to body and mind to manifest themselves at their natural basis. That does not mean any 'special sensation' nor a special state of consciousness; no 'higher' or 'lower', no *moksha*, no enlightenment or non-enlightenment, for all these are names for something which cannot be named. It is a freedom which cannot be experienced.

(18th February, 1982)

5

SINGULAR CONSCIOUSNESS

Alexander: Realisation is to perceive really and totally, that you are not attached to anything. Bondage, when looked at it this way, is believing oneself to be attached to things. When you are dead-tired and let yourself drop on the bed, you are, without the least effort, a 'perceiver' of the fact that you are dead-tired. So there is something in you which is standing 'outside' the tiredness. In a sense this applies to all situations. You are the perceiver of things from the moment you were born up to the moment of your death. It may be that we don't remember all sorts of things, yet a gap in one's memory doesn't mean a gap in one's existence. When you say that you have become 'conscious' of something, then this very fact is already preceded by consciousness. The condition for the contents of consciousness is consciousness itself. The confusion lies in the term 'consciousness', which gives you the notion of an object. However, no qualities may be attributed to consciousness. Consciousness is not an object and can never be objectified. Every object is preceded by consciousness.

Visitor: But we are here to discover that and, apparently, that isn't possible.

A: It isn't, strictly speaking. However, much may be seen through thorough investigation.

V: At times I am so terribly aware of my loneliness... My only desire seems to be to attain to true happiness which, however, doesn't seem to happen.

A: Man carries a curious fate: He is a witness and, at the same time, a suspect of himself. It causes him to become estranged from himself and from others. At the same time he is trying, via this split relationship with himself, to come to some kind of singular consciousness. This leads to disastrous results. The outcome cannot be different from the given datum. In all of your eager actions lies, at the end, the expected recompense—the singular consciousness: *That* is the motor of your seeking. The seeking stops as soon as you have become ecstatic, when you wish to be drowned in that ecstasy and want to continue it. This, in turn, keeps other mechanisms going.

What I want you to understand is that this kind of things can only be solved by a thorough investigation. And not through an attack or an adjustment from your split condition. You are in search of singular consciousness, because that is your true home. But you know very well that you can't have peak-experiences all the time. You know very well that, during a performance, there is a difference between the moment the curtain goes up and the moment the curtain falls. It is not the same. Look for that which never leaves you. Self-realisation means breaking through the vicious circle of seeking; the finding is up to you.

V: I think I'm able to grasp all the theory of it, but it's the practice which makes it so hard!

A: There is no difference between theory and practice; only in your mind there is. In reality all is simultaneous. Don't create unnecessary problems. Don't let yourself be hampered by such thoughts. Such thoughts do not work for you, they hamper you. Once a thing has been thoroughly seen, practice will follow spontaneously. Therefore, first see, and then the 'doing' will follow of itself. And if the 'doing' is not following, then all sorts of things have not yet been seen at a deeper level. See what your true stability is, for without that stability you will not be prepared to face your self-consciousness and accept it.

V: How can I judge whether you are enlightened?

A: What a question! You will never know it, because to you enlightenment is an idea, a concept. Only if you are prepared to drop all ideas about enlightenment, then there is a chance that we will really meet each other. Don't occupy yourself with that sort of questions; they are totally unimportant and a sign of defense. You are wasting time by collecting information and comparing behaviour. There are no measures and criteria for judging whether someone is enlightened. 'Enlightenment' is a concept and merely refers to something living and stable.

V: Actually, I don't know what I am looking for with you. You are telling us things and referring to something I can't get at.

A: You don't want to hear at all what I have to say! I have been telling you repeatedly, that the problem you have is a basic dilemma, namely the desire to die and the will to live.

These two are simultaneously pushing themselves forward within you. On the one hand you would actually like to be dead, which you are afraid of, and on the other hand you want to live, which is what you are equally afraid of. You want to be dead and live at the same time, which is impossible. This dilemma manifests itself each morning when you wake up. You want this, but also that. This is your basic dilemma: the apparent choice between two impossibilities. For the one excludes the other. That is the dilemma that is to be solved. Dive very deep into that situation. You are being pushed forward by forces you do not know—towards life, towards death, towards sex, etc. You will have to find a centre inside yourself; you have to centre yourself. From that centre within the dilemma will resolve itself, never from the outside. Even if you will be thinking about it for years on end, or for the rest of your life, you will never be able to find a satisfying answer, because this is a fundamental fear. No concept about life or death is able to contain even the slightest bit of reality. The mind is asking for a solution, but the solution does not lie within the mind.

Existence shows life and death to be each other's opposite. To live means not to be dead; you simply can't be dead just a little. You are either alive or you are dead. If there is no life, you are dead. Even when you are half-dead, you are still living. Either you are asleep or you are awake. The moment you know that you are awake, you are no longer asleep. Go by your own experience and don't live on second-hand information. Make a thorough investigation as to what is really true, and the result will be peace, serenity and energy. It is up to you to do it.

(12th December, 1982)

6

THE ILLUSION OF THE 'I' PRINCIPLE

Alexander: The idea of having been born implies as a logical consequence the idea that, some day, you will die and disappear. The sense of being 'somebody' leads one inevitably to the notion of being 'nobody' some day. The one notion invites the other. We have reduced existence to a collection of ideas, but concrete life is not an idea nor can it be grasped. Life cannot be comprehended. Only concepts can be comprehended. All mystics came to the understanding that life is incomprehensible. Existence, life, cannot be made into an idea. Besides, the identity which you take yourself to be, being based on an idea as well, is totally deceptive. And that deceptive identity is your suffering.

The illusion of an 'I'-principle may be seen through by the power of discrimination in combination with intelligence and inner strength, which causes it to lose its power immediately. For at the base you will find that such an identity cannot exist at all and, as a result, any crisis will thus be eliminated. To assume an identity means to squeeze things into a concept and to identify yourself with it.

Visitor: This inner strength, can it be drawn from the practice of *hatha yoga*?

A: Possibly. But the best source of energy is love. Most energy is drawn from love. Ultimately everything is done out of love.

Love is at the heart of your existence. This you know very well intuitively, yet you complain that you have no contact with it. Yoga or religion is to make contact with that source of love, to re-establish the connection with your real nature. In fact, religiosity, worship, and Self-realisation, have one thing in common: the dissolution of the fundamental dichotomy.

Maybe you are saying that you are in search of the origin of your real nature. But you can only say so, because you think yourself to be disconnected from it. As a matter of fact, this *idea* of being disconnected from your original nature *is* the basic dichotomy. And all religions and yogas are seeking to repair that apparent split. I am deliberately speaking of an *apparent* split, for in reality nothing *has* been split. It is self-consciousness which is responsible for this misconception—not Consciousness, but *self*-consciousness, the 'I'-principle. It is that which is creating the illusion of *you* being there, of a *personality* being there. In the West the dissolution of this dichotomy is called '*Unio Mystica*', and in India '*moksha*'. Both terms, however, are referring to absolutely one and the same principle. He who has not dissolved this dichotomy imagines himself to be in trouble.

Man is deeply religious by nature. He is aware of being separated from his original nature through his self-consciousness—via body, mind and feeling. It is a process of awakening. The awakening of self-consciousness is the cause of the separation. The way back is through yoga and religion.

V: Then what *is* the dichotomy?

A: It is the tension between the self-consciousness and your true nature.

V: What is the cause of that dichotomy? Why did self-consciousness separate itself from the real Self?

A: This is one of the most absurd questions you could possibly ask, because you are now taking for granted that, before this dichotomy occurred, there existed an 'I' which identified the Self with body, mind and feeling. Such a question is absurd, based as it is on pre-conceived ideas.

V: Orientals have a greater leaning towards the inner world as have westerners towards the outer world. It looks like the oriental has proved himself capable of creating a non-material world?

A: No, don't be mistaken. The so-called inner world is just as material as anything else; it only manifests itself at a subtler level. It is important to keep in mind that the consciousness we are talking about here, ultimately constitutes the sole reality for the *contents* of that consciousness. Whether its contents consists of more subtle layers or of concrete materialism, it doesn't make any real difference to the one, unchanging Consciousness. This conscious being alone is the catalyst, which is making things possible. You have to understand clearly that the essence of what all paths to liberation, and Advaita Vedanta in particular, are saying is: That real nature, that divine principle, is *consciousness itself.* You, though, as an identified being, are confusing consciousness out of ignorance with something other than what it is. Now, a thing cannot be anything other than that from which it has originated. And all things originate from, sprout in, are perceived through, and disappear again in that conscious being.

If we now take a look at the so-called western man who engages himself in nuclear physics and all sorts of in-depth research, then he is ultimately arriving at the same staggering conclusion. And it cannot be otherwise, for truth is truth, in whatever way you find it.

The problem is that we have acquired certain notions about consciousness, thereby mistaking the expression or, in other words, the *contents* of consciousness for ourselves. But the truth is, that only consciousness *itself* constitutes our unchanging Self, and that no reflection about consciousness can hold the ultimate Truth. We have come to believe that we are what we see, and we do not realize that we are the means *by which* we are able to see: As a manifestation, as a body-mind-feeling, we are one of the many expressions of consciousness. But as to our origin, as to our essence, we cannot be any different from anybody or anything else. Differences are only possible with regard to form. Each leaf from a tree is the expression of the One, and, in essence, it is not different from us. Only the form is different. Of course, as human beings we have infinitely more possibilities for expressing and manifesting ourselves than a leaf from a tree.

Our self-consciousness causes us to find ourselves in trouble. If you want to solve that in a fundamental way, you will have to be at the source, at the root of the delusion—*mula maya*. The water at the source of the river is pure, but it is no longer so at the mouth of the river, because of all the rubbish and poison of the world. One technique for going back to the source, to the essence, is yoga; Advaita Vedanta is an other, Zen yet an other again, etc. Wherever you penetrate as far as the heart of the matter, you will find the same thing there. Maybe concealed by codes you don't understand, maybe disguised by countless conventions; maybe hidden by cryptic texts or by a secret restriction; maybe protected by all possible and impossible means. But ultimately you will clearly see the universality of all. *'Tat Tvam Asi'*: 'That thou art'—Consciousness itself—*not* the *contents* of it. Whether you like it or not is of no importance, for consciousness doesn't take any interest in your countless opinions. He who wants to know the truth is not going to shrink from anything that is not to his liking, from anything that is not in correspondence with earlier views. Such views will have to give way to the truth.

In a sense Advaita is ruthless as far as the investigation is concerned; yet truth stands the most critical of tests. That is a fact. Don't get me wrong: This is about *absolute* Truth, not about relative truth.

The lotus flower is the symbol of Advaita Vedanta. The lotus grows out of darkness and mud through the water towards the light, and next there is the unfolding of a lovely flower above the water. The lotus flower is symbolic for existence in the world. Having been born in water, having developed in water, it does not become wet itself. In other words, man may live *in* the world, but need not be *of* the world. Such is the state of a Self-realized human being.

Self-realisation is expressed through action as well. Once the essential thing is seen, practice follows as a matter of course. Such practice is the natural outcome of Self-realisation. Thus *doing* yoga' is changed into *'being* yoga': The connection has been made—You have finished. The way in which you will express yourself afterwards will remain a surprise, because each bird is known by its own note.

V: Would you say, then, that there are no problems at that level?

A: It is only at the level of body, mind and feelings that problems occur—not at the spiritual level.

V: Do you mean to say that there are no problems at all? Life in this world is bringing with it the unavoidable troubles of being at the mercy of the elements, of problems—is it not?

A: I am not saying that there isn't any opposition or resistance! While everything is expressing itself through opposites, what I am referring to is a condition which is *free* from all such opposites and troubles. Again, at the level of the body, mind and feelings there will always be opposites and problems. But what I'm saying is that, once you have realized what you really are, the so-called problems of this objective world will no longer be insurmountable.

V: My feeling is that you are not saying everything that you've got to say.

A: Let the impulse come from *you*. Don't wait till something is going to happen from my side. From my point of view I have nothing to say. What is it you want to know?

V: I still think that, despite the fact that you contradict it all the time, there is more than one is able to see. Thoughts, for example, also exist, although one can't see them .

A: If you didn't perceive your thoughts, then how do you refer to them? There is an infinite number of matters we simply take for granted, never stopping to realize whether it is actually true what we are saying about them. What we should understand is, that we are not talking here about anything magical, about UFOs, or any such things. As long as blood-pressure had not been discovered, nobody was suffering from high blood-pressure. As long as cancer was unknown, nobody died of cancer. Formerly you just died. Formerly—and now I am speaking of the very long ago—one didn't even see the connection between copulation and the begetting of children. Then, at a certain stage, through the power of human discernment, one came to see the connection. The knowing, the 'being aware of something', the cognizing, is responsible for the way in which we read the world. Suppose we didn't know anything about all those atom bombs being aimed at us. Then we just wouldn't be afraid of them. The knowledge of them creates the fear. Thinking creates fear. All that belongs to the domain of the mind.

V: I understand what you are trying to say, but I don't agree with the idea that things don't exist, as long as one isn't thinking of them or isn't aware of them. They sure exist!

A: They only exist as thoughts, not in reality. The world is a presentation of the mind; a 'real' reality is not to be found. No one has the same experience of the world; everybody is living in a projected world of his own, created by fears and desires. What the 'real' reality is remains unclear. Just now you are working at your own fears and desires only—not at some given 'world'.

At best you are working at a world of your own creation. The knowing of a world merely proves the existence of the *knowing*—not of a 'world'. The moment you become conscious, you create a world based on opposites: good and bad, light and dark, etc. However, these do not have any 'real' reality. When you denote something as being ugly, 'beautiful' arises along with it. In presenting a solution, I also present a problem. Thus all opposites are linked indissolubly to each other. In fact, all thinking takes place by means of opposites, without exception. There is nothing that can be done about it. Life and death, warm and cold, enlightenment and ignorance—there is always an opposite. Everything has its opposite, for you can only think in opposites. If not, you couldn't have a frame of reference. The naming of things is necessary in order to survive. What I want to make clear is that we attribute names to things that we do not really know. Only realize that they are names, and that the name can never be the thing itself.

(18th December, 1982)

YOUR WANT BECOMES A SEEKING

Alexander: Most of us are in search of something special, something extraordinary, something worthwhile. However, in order to be quite clear and open from the start during the meetings which we will be having with each other over the next few days: This is not about something extraordinary. There isn't anything extraordinary either about you or about me. This seems to me to be of great importance, because it has become customary in circles of people who are seeking 'the spiritual', 'the higher', that there ought to be at least something special about the speaker. Still, I may not be able to prevent the people who have come to see me from perceiving something special about me or about the things that are happening here, but then such pleasure is entirely theirs. I am telling you this, because it is common practice to create and keep up a kind of atmosphere that has nothing, absolutely nothing to do with what we are dealing with here. The issue, therefore, is not about anything extraordinary; rather about something natural, something quite self-evident. The moment you believe or are getting the idea that I am 'special', a separation is born which may lead to curious complications. At the same time, if, for various reasons, you do prefer to make me into something I'm not, you run the risk of missing the very point these meetings are dealing with. In order to get a clear insight into what is being said here, it is important to begin at the beginning. That beginning is the fervent wish of each man to be special. He does not want to be ordinary, which is one of the many movements of seeking. Of course, this seeking for 'the other thing' is always a seeking for something that is different from what is now. In other words, there is no acceptance of one's primary given datum. It is a matter of cutting into two, a splintering of that which cannot be split—a split, a division.

Man is generally not aware that his entire seeking implies a wanting to be different, to be something special, in contrast to what he meets with in the workaday world. Man is a curious phenomenon, in search of food, clothing and shelter and, when these desires have been fulfilled, in search of respect, fulfilment and love.

Why are we meeting here during these days? No doubt because somewhere inside your being there is a feeling of want. We go to meetings like these with the idea that you can get something out of it, something special, something quite unlike everyday life. Something that is different from the ordinary. Fed by the daily experience of commonness and shallowness, by the feeling that one's life isn't anything special. You have an idea that there is something different to be found from your day-to-day life. You call it liberation, *moksha*, *nirvana*, enlightenment or God, and in doing so you place all these things outside of yourself and outside your daily life.

So there is a want. If I may invite you to go deeper into that which you are seeking or into that which is your want, then we may be able to come to a discussion.

Visitor: You are saying: There is nothing extraordinary about man. But I can't accept that. I see the mass of people and I know that I am also part of it. Still I think that there is more than that.

A: Why do you think that there is more than that?

V: That is my feeling... I'm not sure about it. I would like to discuss it further.

A: Anything more than you can see for yourself is borrowed, if not stolen. What is now, *is*—The rest is a fabrication, a mental projection. But that you cannot accept. Because you can't accept the grey ant-hill of everyday life, you invent colours. Just like someone who sees himself steadily growing older, but continues to live with the images of twenty years ago and flirts with it. But that is not going to stand in the way of the laws of nature. You just can't accept the course of life. For that reason you go in search. But of what?

V: Of happiness.

A: Are you not happy now?

V: Reasonably happy.

A: 'Reasonably happy' is not happy. 'Reasonably happy' is related to reason. Reason cannot be happy.

V: Fair enough—I'm happy.

A: Then why are you here?

V: I like it here.

A: The word 'happy' is derived from 'to happen'. When something 'happens'[2], then you are 'happy' for a moment. For example, you see a beautiful man or woman and you think: If only I could spend the evening with that person! And there you are standing at the railway station in Utrecht and, sure enough, the person in question is standing right there. Then you walk up to him and you say, 'I have the irresistible feeling that you are the only true one for me.' And then this person says, 'I wish I could say the same about you!' Well, in that case you will be unhappy, because things didn't 'happen'. For, if that person would have said, 'This is what I've been waiting for for the past three months', then you would have been happy! Then you would have been in the seventh heaven, forgetting that you were in search of enlightenment and the higher concerns of life. In any case, such is the happiness of the world, and it is wonderful.

V: All right, I understand what you mean. But I have become suspicious even of happiness.

A: What you want is quite natural: To escape from those movements that hurt you. When you are doing fine, you don't want to escape from those movements at all, then you want to embrace them. In fact, you are employing your whole thinking and feeling for squeezing the things of life in the mould that you think most suitable. You are like the person who goes to pick up the autumn leaves, paints them green, and then wants to stick them back to the branches. Such a person would appear a bit odd, to say the least, wouldn't he? But is it any different from your own efforts? You are always busy avoiding the unavoidable. You swim like a salmon against the stream. Even though you have seen hundreds of times that it's of no use whatsoever, still you keep on trying. That propelling force I call the strategy of hope, the movement of seeking. As you look at your life with love, at your endeavours, your promptings, your motives, your encounters, then ask yourself the question: What did it lead to in the end?

The answer for most people will be, that they have come just as far as where they started out. Indeed, a bit more discouraged, but certainly not happier. So, then, ask yourself the question: What have I *really* understood about myself?

V: I guess I'm looking for a situation, where I will be able to react in a perfectly spontaneous way to whatever circumstances I may happen to meet in my life.

A: Is that the want you feel? You do not know how to react to situations. You want to be spontaneous. That, of course, is already a spontaneous reaction to a situation. Your want is what you wish or do not wish. When you are looking for a partner, there is a want somewhere. If you don't want a partner, then there, too, is a want somewhere. Not wanting is also wanting. You want something or you don't want something. Both movements are wants being felt. To begin with: Do not condemn this—neither your wanting nor your not-wanting. Look upon it as a given fact. It is a given fact of life. You are not free to want something or not to want something. It is simply a matter of fact. You want something or you don't—fair enough. Know that it is a want you feel, nothing more. Perhaps, after a few days, you don't want what you first wanted—fair enough. That also is a given fact. Observe the movements of wanting and not-wanting without getting trapped, without condemning.

You will have to start somewhere, so start without condemning, right there where you are. Perhaps up till now you have been using all sorts of systems such as yoga and meditation in order *not* to have to face your wants. Perhaps your entire seeking has become just that. In other words, you want to get a balance, an equilibrium. You want to be centered. Just get this right: Someone who is happy no longer needs to *become* happy. Someone who is free no longer needs to *become* free.

I will tell you an interesting anecdote. During the fifties there was a great teacher living in South India. His name was Shri Krishna Menon. Besides his role as a teacher, he was also a public prosecutor, and in that capacity he used to have contacts with the prisons on a fairly regular basis. Sometimes he had to stay the night in a cell, because there was no place in the hotel and he could not get home in time. Next day he could just walk out of his cell, unlike the prisoners. He saw it and realized that man's position is really quite similar. He can step out of his so-called imprisonment any moment. But some prisoners prefer to stay in prison, even when they are released. Only those who really feel imprisoned choose freedom. Both are part of our world.

What we want to point out here is, that all movement towards a goal, all seeking, arises from a not-being-in-balance. You are hungry, for example. Then you go and have something to eat. Now the balance is going to be restored. Maybe you've been eating too much; then you will have to wait for some time. You are out of balance and a process of recovering is active. Whether it is about a full stomach or an empty one, something is out of balance, and because of that the movement is set going, and you know it.

This mechanism which restores its own balance, not only concerns the body, but also the mental areas such as thoughts and feelings. Of course, this subdivision is only a way of speaking, because, in reality, the subdivision of body, mind and feeling constitutes an undivided unity. What we can see quite clearly is, that everything is moving towards a natural equilibrium. We are not dealing now with the *way* that is employed to bring about such equilibrium. The way in which is not the point at issue now. Never condemn the way in which this equilibrium is restoring itself, never condemn the means. There is no essential difference between someone meditating and someone visiting the pub. In fact, it is exactly the same thing. What people are doing is to restore a balance, nothing more. It isn't a disaster in any way, except when you begin to condemn it. This balance-seeking movement takes place at an individual, international, and at a universal level. It is a basic given fact. If you do not make friends with this movement, it will turn against you.

One of the most important frictions within you is, that you have separated yourself from that which is happening to you, and from that which you experience. For example, when you have become terribly angry, so much so that it actually terrifies you, then you *are* the anger—at least for those few seconds. However, almost immediately after it happened you say, 'I should *not* have been angry.' Right after the fact you deny or tone down what actually did happen. For a moment you were total anger. So much so that it got you completely terrified. You were beside yourself with anger. But were you *really* beside yourself? Were you *really* terrified? In any case you were a witness of what happened. So there was something in you that was *not* terrified, something in you which was *not* beside itself. How could that be? And yet, a few seconds after the anger, you are saying, 'I should not have been angry'. Then you look upon the anger as something that is separate from you. That is more or less what we are doing with everything. If we pay a little attention to these things, then we will clearly see where the split is being made, where you start to divide life.

All right, you become angry—There is nothing but this anger. You feel this enormous energy coming up. That is what you are then. Be a witness, be aware of what exactly is happening. Remember not to divide yourself, not to make a fragment of yourself. You are complete, not a fragment. Life is something complete—Don't make a separation in it.

In nature and, therefore, in our own lives too, we find that everything is moving towards an equilibrium. Such is nature and we are no exception to it. Don't have the experience of yourself as being separate from what is actually happening. You are part of the totality and the totality is part of you. But perhaps somehow you started to experience yourself as being separate, as someone who doesn't really belong, who stands detached from the whole. With the idea in the back of your mind that you are in control, that it is *you* who is making things happen. The notion that it is *we* who make things happen and who are in control, is expressed through our speech, for example in such phrases as,

'Do you think we'll keep it dry?' As if it's *you* who is controlling the weather. Or as in, 'Are you letting your hair grow?' As if it's *you* who is making your hair grow. Our language is full of such expressions, giving the suggestion that it is *you* who is controlling the course of things in nature. But nature controls itself, including man.

What we are proposing here, what we are pointing out here is: Make a halt, a stop, a break. For we are in danger of being carried away by the basic movement of the self-restoring equilibrium as if by a cyclone, and in particular by identifying ourselves with it. This is not only happening in our own comfortable little lives, but also in relation to one another and, if you like, in the world as a whole. This beginning, this coming to a halt, this break, is an invitation to have a closer look at how things are put together, because those 'things' are situated on the objective side. However, the majority of us does not wish to look at how things are put together and, as a consequence, we just continue to persevere in all sorts of silly little solutions and narrow views, both in relation to ourselves and in relation to our environment.

For this break, for this coming to a halt, a number of ingredients is required. In the first place courage, and in the second place commitment. Some form of wanting to know passionately, of wanting to get an insight into it. But most of us are afraid, preferring illusion to reality, preferring to stay in misery and trouble, in short, in what's 'familiar' to us, rather than venturing into anything new, anything untouched. So in order to face your own life a huge dose of courage is indispensable. Buddha, Jesus and Shankara were no weaklings, they were not men without will-power. I don't put these men on the stage to mirror ourselves by their example, for the days of Buddha, Jesus and Shankara are gone forever. Perhaps they would be startled, perhaps astonished, if they were to return to our times. But even if they would somehow have expected it, they would certainly say: 'Look at what has become of the living truth. It has turned out just the same as it always has.' Nowadays things are no different from the days of Buddha, Jesus or Shankara. Although the manifestation has assumed a totally different outlook, little has changed in essence. Even now man has the possibility to choose: truth and veracity, or delusion and lies.

V: But then, how are we to move forward in modern times?

A: In the first place, accept that there isn't any 'forward'. 'Forward' suggests that there may be something else than what there is now. It is a subtle strategy in which you deny what is. It shows that you want something different. That is acceptable at the level of the world and the forms, and that force is responsible for many changes, but when we project it onto the immaterial, spiritual level, we get into trouble.

Why are you not satisfied with your life? Because that situation, your own life, does not know any joy. No liveliness, no sparkling scintillation. You are basically living like a zombie, a living dead. From that condition of deadness, that coma, you begin to dream and fantasize like someone who is living without any warmth, affection and bodily contact. Such a person will begin to have dreams about such things, which is quite natural, for nature wants to have those things in balance. But then, if you are severely conditioned by some form of religion, then you may begin to think that you are bad, that it is not good what you are dreaming or thinking about, that you are responsible for what you are thinking and dreaming. And in such a situation there is no place for seeing anything, no place for feeling anything.

In India the approach we are trying to discuss here is called '*jnana*'. Shri Krishna Menon sometimes called it 'the art of perceiving'. Of course, not only perceiving with the eyes, but *totally*, with one's entire being.

V: It is sometimes said: Be satisfied with what you have. Is that what you mean?

A: Such a thing is bound to lead to *dis*satisfaction, for you haven't got anything. Life is showing you, that everything may be taken away from you. You haven't got anything—You *think* you have. We even speak of *'having'* someone to love. Freedom and love is to see and know from head to feet that there is nothing in the whole cosmos that is yours. The body and the brains with which you think out everything, you owe them to the love-play of your father and mother. From that union you are born. Your whole being—body, mind and feeling—is a gift of love and union, of energy and life-force. But when you take a look at how you experience yourself, then it looks like that which was created in love and pleasure and union, is to end up as a sad, dull and deathlike phenomenon.

You see, we are stuck with so many everyday trivialities and, at the same time, with so many basic problems and troubles. Just how do you want to get at the basic problems in the face of all those trivialities that take up all of your energy? When a mountaineer wants to climb a high mountain, but his equipment for climbing even a simple hill is not in order, then how is he going to reach the top? Your equipment for everyday life is not in order. While climbing the spiritual mountain half-way you are already dying from cold, hardship and misery; you are being hindered by the unnecessary ballast which you had taken with you on your journey. Once more—if it is to be said at all—*begin at the beginning*. Every journey begins with a preparation, and amongst so-called spiritual seekers there are but few to be found who do just that.

I will tell you a story about how these things were dealt with in former times, when the world hadn't gone mad yet. In the eleventh century there lived a young man in Tibet, whose name was Jetsun Milarepa. Milarepa was not only a great yogi, but also a singer and a poet. In his youth he had learned sorcery as a result of various misfortunes and miseries. For example, in the end he was able to destroy the crops by dropping big hailstones from a sky that was completely clear. And these skills were just what he needed in order to take revenge for what many people and close family members had done to him. He had been doing quite some mischief, so much so that things were getting altogether out of hand. He reflected deeply on his unhappy life and decided to go in search of a guru in order to find relief and liberation.

To cut a long story short, he found his guru in a most peculiar way. However, in order to receive instruction from him he first had to build a house on a spot which the guru had pointed out to him. After months of labouring in the thin Tibetan mountain air, Milarepa had reached the top of the house. Just at that moment his guru came to take a look and said, 'I'm not sure... but, as I look at it now, I would prefer that you move the house three meters to the right, for there it will have a better view.' As you can understand, Milarepa was staggered at what his teacher had to say. However, without any further delay he pulled the house down and started building again. After four months the teacher came by again and said without hesitation, 'I'm not sure... but I don't think you quite understood what I had told you. The house is standing far too much to the right, and it should also come a bit forward.' By now Milarepa's heart sank. Couldn't his guru have said so earlier? However, he finally plucked up all his courage and started all over again. Three months later—he began to get the knack of it—the house was finished. Then, again, the guru came by. 'Well', he said seriously, 'I'm not all that happy with it. Pull the whole thing down and put it up a hundred meters further on—and add another floor on top for any guests that may be coming.' Now Milarepa was really getting fed up with it. But, anyhow, he built the house. This house, too, he had to demolish and after an interminable lot of ordeals he finally received instruction from his guru.

The story wants to make clear, that it is a serious matter, this whole business of enlightenment and liberation. In olden times the disciples were put to the test endlessly, and sometimes they were treated quite cruelly, until they proved to be prepared to overcome obstacles. Ultimately in order to overcome the greatest obstacle, namely that of the ego. After having stood all these ordeals and tests, and only then, they received instruction from a master.

Nowadays the situation is no different, although it will often take a different form. The tests and ordeals are a training to strengthen one's basic equipment and to see whether one is really serious. But most of us do not take this enterprise really seriously.

V: You could say that the whole point of this *jnana*-approach is to take note of...

A: That is what you've *heard*, but not what you have discovered for yourself. *Before* you start to take note, you *are* already aware.

You are a witness *already*, before you start to take note. Don't make these things into a formula, into some magic phrase. Don't lean on second-hand statements of other people, but see for yourself whether it is true.

When you wake up in the morning a world appears before you, whether you like it or not. Whether you are projecting it or not. Even though you do not know how, there is a *knowing* that a world appears. You *know* that you are walking, but not *how* you are walking. You *know* that you are thinking, not *how* you are thinking. It just happens. And all you can do is to put a name onto that which you cannot grasp—that of which you *know* that it happens, but not *how* it happens, to which, however, no absolute reality may be attributed. Of course, you may give it a name. But you do not really grasp it.

V: When you know all this—that you are conscious—then there is nothing...

A: That is not what is being said here. All that is being said now is, that a world appears before you, and that you can identify yourself with it. But *how* the world appears, what that world really is, of that you do not have any true knowledge. *You are*—whether you like it, or not. We know ourselves to be in a very ambivalent situation, a dilemma from which we don't seem to be able to extricate ourselves. This dilemma derives its *raison d'être* from the notion of '*I am*', and the consequence that, one day, that is going to end.

This knowing that you exist is sometimes agreeable to you and sometimes it isn't. One day you enjoy existence, next day you don't and you wish to be dead. There is an ambivalent movement going on which manifests itself in the dilemma, 'I want to live', and, 'I want to be dead'. I want existence and intensification and, as its opposite, extinction and dissolution. In this basic dilemma many a one will recognize himself.

No doubt we are trying to make all this bearable by thoughts of heaven and reincarnation and so on, yet in the inmost recesses of your being, there is a doubt somewhere; you are not sure. In fact, in the deepest corners of your being there is uncertainty and fear. That is why I reach you the beginning and not the ultimate end. You must start exactly there where you are. From the given fact that you are probably just being afraid and that, after all, you just don't know. You see, all of this is really quite natural; it is part of life, part of the manifestation. There is nothing bad about it—it's just a given fact.

V: Are you never afraid?

A: What a question! Of course I am. At the level of the body there are reflexes and conditionings which see to it, that I'm not run over by a car and put my manifestation in danger. Do you think that, when a tram is coming my way, I won't jump aside, just because I discovered myself not to be this body? Of course I would—I'm not an idiot!

Many people who come into touch with spirituality and yoga and Vedanta like to talk about the *idea* that they are not the body. However, most of them do not act accordingly. Such people I call 'arm-chair' *jnanis*—chatterboxes. We shall see, when such people have to undergo an operation, or when they are invited to pass through the gate of death, or when they discover that they have a serious illness—What will they say then? We shall see... Talking is easy. When you've just had a good meal, it is fairly simple to have a good discussion on the benefits of fasting and strict dieting. When you are enjoying a wonderful relationship, it is easy to say that, when you're on your own, you feel quite comfortable as well. When you've just had an orgasm, then sex doesn't seem all that important. The need for things comes to light only, when you want them badly. For example, when you find yourself in a concentration camp or when you're being kidnapped. Or when you stand face to face with death, or you're getting five months of solitary confinement. Then only it will become clear as to how matters stand.

Once upon a time there was a man in India, who was living in a quiet village. This man who was getting on, claimed that the world did not exist. Now, in this village they had heard such things before, and out of politeness no offence was taken at it. In fact, the people didn't mind at all. Whenever the man started to talk about it, they nodded politely and after a while they went their way in order to get back to their work. This man, however, who didn't have much to do, started to discuss these things more and more frequently, and finally the villagers began to get annoyed about it.

One day they decided to go and do something about it. During the villagers' meeting it was decided to dig a pit of seven meters deep, two meters wide and three meters long. And so, when the man was seen again standing talking about the non-existence of the world to a rice-seller, they caught hold of him unawares and threw him in the pit. For a whole day and a whole night they left him that way. Since the man was not married and didn't have any children and but few friends, he didn't go missing. The following day some villagers went to see how things stood.

'Well', they shouted, 'does the world now exist in your pit or does it not?'

'No, it doesn't!' the man shouted, 'the world is unreal!'

'All right', the men said, 'in that case we shall leave you a bit longer in that unreal pit of yours.' The next day at exactly the same hour they came to have a look, and again he replied, 'No, the world is unreal.'

'All right, one more day in that case!' the men said.

After two weeks he said in an enfeebled voice, 'I will not tell it any more.' Then they helped him to get out of the pit, and quiet was restored to the village. Henceforth the man from the pit led a silent and sober life. He spoke little and, because he didn't parrot anything or anybody any longer, his real nature became more and more apparent and true. In the end he met with a guru and became enlightened. After which he never spoke a word again. Nobody ever heard from him.

Be on your guide against parroting. Don't just repeat other persons' words. All parroting is the concealing of shortcomings, a lack of originality, a want of the real. In the end the trick behind it will be exposed. In fact, there are three tricks: boredom, loneliness, and the fear of death. These are the basic tensions, the dilemmas. Pure boredom, loneliness, and the fear of death—the great unknown. There are but few who are prepared to face these three obstacles, for it requires courage, passion and intelligence to face your own life. The word 'intelligence' means: the ability to read between the lines. It requires a centre, a steady, unchanging point from which you are looking: a centred being. Without such centeredness you are like a house that is being swept away by the all-consuming force of a cyclone. But deep within the cyclone, deep within your own being, there is a centre, which is totally still and untouchable. That is your true centre. From that stillness, from that centre you can live. That centre is ever pure and untainted, in that centre there is neither movement nor experience. That is the centre from which everything is born and in which everything will die: your presence, your being. That presence cannot be imagined, for it is the precondition for all thinking, feeling and living—the still centre of the cyclone. Life as a manifestation is a total paradox, an apparent opposition that is perfect. The centre, your being, is the unchangeable within the changeable. The manifestation is the visible side of God, your being is the invisible side.

(18th December, 1982, morning)

8

BONDAGE IS FORCING YOU TO SEEK

Alexander: What is the reason for your coming here?

Visitor: In the first place the curiosity whether here I will be getting to hear something different from the School for Philosophy. I have discovered that my wants are of my own making. Would you like to say something about that?

A: The fact of our wanting 'more' or 'different' in our daily life is born from the experience of the pairs of opposites. If you pay a little attention to it, you will discover that experience is only possible through opposites. Light and dark, happiness and unhappiness, beautiful and ugly, good and bad, and so on. On the other hand the natural state is really experience-less. No happiness is experienced there, for happiness is the opposite of unhappiness. The natural state cannot be sensed or experienced. The natural state is conscious being. It is often defined as 'nothing'. 'Nothing' is a combination of not-anything, no thing, no object. In English you say *no-thing*, not anything. Nothing is not something vague, not something misty, for even that would still be an object. Anything vague remains an object, however vague or misty. What we generally call 'nothing', as a reference to our inmost being, is really total awareness. As long as the vision within yourself is not clear, you cannot but continue to seek. It is a compulsion, a must. Even if you would like to stop, you will still continue. In whatever formula you may put it, you will continue seeking, your restlessness will not have gone. And that becomes your want. In other words, the seeking is a supplement to the want *experienced* by you.

What it all depends on in the end is yourself. The greater your dedication, the greater your response, the more intense the answers of your teacher will be. Be only satisfied with the very highest, the very clearest. He who seeks will find. All depends on you, not on the guru. For the guru is perfectly satisfied, even with your dissatisfaction. The quality of the disciple is the quality of the guru.

V: This morning you said that everything is consciousness, including body, mind and feeling. You also said that thinking precedes feelings. In my experience feelings are detached from my thinking.

A: We can never experience two things at the same time, strictly speaking. You always experience only one thing at a time. This you can learn to perceive quite well through the exercises of *hatha yoga*. There is an exercise in *hatha yoga* which is called 'shavasana'. *Shavasana* is often translated as 'relaxation exercise', but it really means 'dead man's posture' or 'corps posture', because the body lies like a dead one. The reason for such translations as 'relaxation exercise', 'relax posture' etc., may be, because in the West we would find the other names scary. In the dead man's posture attention is focussed on contemplating the body after first having tightened the body carefully for a couple of times—this in combination with correct breathing. But the contemplation is what it is really about. For example, attention is directed towards the ears, and is being focussed completely on listening. Then, after a while, you shift your attention, for example, to the places where the body is making contact with the floor. Now the special thing about this exercise is that, each time you shift your attention to an other sense-organ, attention is making a jump. At that very moment attention is in a kind of no man's land. It happens very quickly, almost unnoticeably. That is why you have to be so attentive and do this exercise in a quiet environment. But because the focus of your attention is naturally on everything that moves, the no man's land escapes your notice. If you do this exercise regularly, you will discover this happening. Practise for three months and you will succeed at least once. That way you can learn to see that your attention can actually manage only one thing at a time, never two or more—remember that. It may appear to be otherwise, but it isn't. It is an optical illusion that you have got used to and which you have never noticed. In reality sensations follow each other successively.

V: This morning you were mentioning three things: boredom, loneliness, and the fear of death. Would you go a bit further into that?

A: There comes a moment in the life of every human being, when he will ask himself the question, 'This life, what does it really mean?'

The very simple-minded put this question to themselves as do the quick-witted and complex minds amongst us—indeed, the great minds who are at the height of their thinking and power. Ultimately every man will find himself in a situation, where he is putting this question to himself, because he does not know what to do any more with the situation which he sees himself confronted with. Three basic movements or, if you like, standstills, may then be observed: boredom, loneliness, and the fear of death. There are still more, but during these days let us limit ourselves to these three phenomena.

V: Is one aware of this boredom at all?

A: What you are not aware of doesn't trouble you. As opposed to boredom stands diversion. The Dutch word *'vermaken'* (to divert) has a number of meanings: to alter a garment, to bequeath an inheritance, and to divert in the sense of 'taking pleasure in'. According to my private dictionary the meaning is: to make a diversion, to divert a thing from what it is. We go and see each other in order to divert ourselves, in order to give ourselves a break. Our entire social life is based on diversion. Being alone is badly suffered on the whole. Even most hermits and yogis have some form of company, often an animal, or, as the word indicates, a companion.

This 'being alone' is very much of a taboo. Not seldom do we hear that you should be able to be 'on your own', thereby more or less indicating already, that you are not able to do so, or that it is actually being experienced as something uncomfortable.

V: But in your innermost being you *know* that you are absolutely alone, don't you?

A: Yes, in your innermost being you know it. Maybe you also know it with your intellect, and maybe you even feel it. But to be *really* alone without any conflict is of a totally different order. That is why you will see to it, that you are never going to be alone. If necessary, you'll even go and live with someone you *don't* love for that matter, or with a parrot, a monkey, or a goat. In the worst case you make it your goal to be alone.

Nowadays we have the so-called 'LAT'- relationship, 'living apart together', the modern solution for being isolated. Seeing each other when you feel like it. Being on your own... until it begins to feel uncomfortable. Then you go and see each other again. It all has to run somewhat synchronously with the partner, otherwise it is going to be a failure after all... These attitudes are visible in our society. If we go back to the source of it, we come out at an attitude of mind which is motivated by the avoiding of these three existential, inescapable facts: boredom, loneliness, and the fear of death. The avoiding of these three basic facts I call the strategy of fear.

He who wants to make the journey inwards, should not at the very outset start off with prepossessed standpoints and judgements. Look upon these three phenomena—boredom, loneliness, and the fear of death—as a given fact, and don't do anything about it. Because doing anything about it is in hundred out of a hundred cases a strategy of fear in the form of running away or embracing. Why do you want to go away? Because it's hurting. Why do you want to embrace something? Because you have an idea that it is going to give you happiness. You always want only one side of the matter. 'Pleasant', however, is leading irrevocably to its opposite, and vice versa. Inside every man there is a potential killer and a potential saint. We all represent both the lowest and the very highest. The majority of us are somewhere in between. So the question is: Is it possible to look at yourself and at the world exactly as they are? Without wanting to change anything about them? That is going to be the problem. For what does it mean in practice, in daily life? You don't know anything apart from daily life for that matter. It means total awareness, without inner condemnation, for condemnation is indicative of an inner dichotomy. Please note that I say 'condemnation' and not 'judgement', which is something quite different.

V: But then, how do I know what is good or bad?

A: In your being there is a knowing which is not based on thinking, a compass that is always active, indicating the right direction. For example, when you are telling a lie, then there is something within you that knows that you *are* telling a lie. The discrepancy between the known lie and the known truth shows itself in a tension that may simply be measured at the skin. Outwardly it may look as if the truth is being spoken, but the body, and particularly the skin, is receiving a signal. In other words, the split situation causes a tangible tension.

Such knowing is a *pure* knowing. It never lies. You—the person—may want to lie, but something inside you *knows* that that isn't right. You know the oscillations of that compass without the least effort. It is an *inner* knowing, a deep sense of truth. However, contact with that inner sense appears to be disturbed by thinking and feeling, and sometimes even by the body. Through the strategies of fear that have become operative, you shout down your own compass. At that point it is essential to make a halt, otherwise you will become destructive. Meditation is such a halt. Meditation says: Stop and *see*. With what? With something that is different from thinking and feeling. For thinking and feeling *are* perceived and cannot, by themselves, see anything. You can perceive thoughts and feelings, but thoughts and feelings cannot perceive *you*. Thinking, therefore, is *not* seeing. Thinking is thinking. Thinking enables us to build an airplane and get in it so as to arrive in New York at a certain hour. The fact that trains connect properly, that traffic lights function properly etc., all that comes from thinking. Thinking has its place. But inside, deeper than thinking, you *know*.

Has it never struck you that, when you meet a person for the first time, you cannot but get a certain definite impression about him, a tiny little shock, something very intuitive? When, ten years later, that person did something good, or rather, something bad, you will often say to yourself, 'I knew it'. It is a knowing deep from within, from that which is without any projection. That 'deep within' never lies. Thinking does. Thinking is one big lie. Through reasoning thinking can twist what is straight and the other way round. But deep within you *know*. That knowing is not thinking. How often isn't it that you say, 'Somehow I *knew* it'. It shows that something in you was quite sure about it, but that you let yourself be fooled by the mind with its ability to dangle things before your eyes that prove to be lies. You acted *against your own better judgement.* Please note: You acted on the authority of a confused thinking.

Thinking appears to disturb the natural state to such an extent, that techniques are employed to let the thinking mind explode or have it disappear altogether. Therefore, that which is essentially a wonderful faculty, now becomes a threat to oneself. These techniques which are used to let the mind explode or stop, are not seldom applied by people who are themselves not capable of overseeing the overall complexity of thinking and mind. So by and large things are not getting any clearer this way. On the contrary, the majority of those who applied themselves to these techniques—originally meant to serve quite a different purpose—become more confused thereby, not to speak of any excesses.

Those who come into contact with yoga, Zen or any other techniques and ways to liberation, and who become actively involved in them, often lead a confused existence. Their daily life is not seldom a chaos. Now, don't try to lay the blame for it on yoga or Zen; rather look at the way in which you yourself are applying yoga or Zen, otherwise you would be doing them a serious injustice. On the whole yoga and Zen and other beautiful traditions are not used properly.

The essential question remains: What is the meaning of this whole search after liberation and enlightenment, which is now beginning to take on massive proportions? What are you really doing with it? Is it an intellectual affair, 'arm-chair' Zen, 'arm-chair' *jnana*? What is it that you actually do not want to face?

V: What I do not want to face is the fact that I'm living now, and that, one day, I'm going to die. Deep in my heart I do want to face it though... I want to be able to die...

A: Actually, that is what is happening every day: Each moment everything is dying a certain death. All is dying and renewing itself. Every seven years you have got a completely new body. The old body has died, each cell has been replaced. Where has the body gone from the time that you were four years old? That body has altogether disappeared, is dissolved, renewed. It has got a completely different form. Nothing is left of the body of when you were four years old.

V: I have been doing some serious and deep thinking, and I now know that a chair and a human being are the same. I know it with my head, still I don't experience it that way.

A: That doesn't surprise me in the least! A chair is really something different from a human being! Only at the very highest level the chair and the human being are perceptions within conscious being, and ultimately they are Consciousness itself. But the chair will never ask itself that question nor will it ever be able to find out, whereas man does have that possibility. The chair will never know the answer, because it cannot ask the question, but man will find an answer, because he is able to ask questions. Indeed, both the question and the answer are made of the same substance out of which this whole world has been created, namely consciousness. The second point is: Who told you to experience things that way? Rather look at what *is*. What *is* is what you are seeing *here*, right now. Life is being enacted before you, everything is happening to you. If you project it forwards, you call it 'future'—that which is being 'forwarded' to you. The more you organize and push at the mental level—where there *is*n't anything to be organized—the more energy you lose in futilities.

Let us listen once more to a statement made by a Zen master: 'You need not push the river—it flows of itself.' If you realize that even the behaviour of three atoms is totally unpredictable, then how are you to predict the behaviour of three billion atoms? We are one whole of forces of elements and atoms. How can a part grasp the whole? How can a particle direct the whole? How can a particle contain the whole?

(18th December, 1982, afternoon)

9

CONSCIOUSNESS IS SELF-SUFFICIENT

Alexander: An 'I'-structure cannot comprehend anything, which is due to the simple fact that an 'I'-structure is perceived, and anything perceived cannot know or comprehend anything. To comprehend means always to hold, to make it into a concept. Existence is beyond all concepts.

Visitor: I understand what you mean, but I fail to see it altogether. It is not a reality to me. I know that, in my daily life, it just isn't like that; it is more of an idea to me, but not a reality I am living. What is creating that idea?

A: Thinking. What you have to see clearly is that thinking is the *contents* of consciousness. Consciousness is the basic material, and this basic material is neutral. Within that neutrality an 'I'-structure is projected. This 'I'-structure is being perceived, but the 'I'-structure *itself* doesn't perceive anything. It is in no way instrumental in the knowing or even cognizing of anything.

V: But the 'I'-structure is there all the same. After all, you too manifest yourself, don't you?

A: I do not manifest myself. Through the union of the sperm and the germ-cell a body was formed. Out of that a life has developed which may last for 36.000 days. *That* is what is manifesting itself.

V: But is that energy not following certain laws and taking a certain course?

A: It certainly is, but 'I' am not that.

V: But it is something specific to you. It is *your* consciousness.

A: I can't detect any identity or personality in it, let alone an 'I'. Such a so-called 'I' which you want to persuade me of, derives its right to exist from consciousness—not the other way round. I cannot find anything personal in conscious being, at best the awareness of 'I am', in a specific body, made complete by thinking and feeling.

V: Which is manifesting itself specifically in *you*.

A: But so it does in plants, animals, and in other human beings.

V: In that case the awareness is still specific to you or to me, isn't it?

A: I can't detect any 'you' or 'me' in it. All I can see is consciousness, which has manifested itself in the form of people, animals and the things that are present here. There is no room for a 'personal identity' in it.

V: But surely, we all do believe in our ego—Isn't that enough proof?

A: That is just what I am trying to make clear to you: That it is precisely *that* which is the delusion—the belief in an 'I'-structure.

Egotism. That is exactly the trouble as far as the manifestation is concerned. That is the cause of all suffering.

V: I can see what you mean. But in the meantime this 'I'-structure is there all the same.

A: Why don't you stop sticking to conclusions without first having looked at things properly? I am telling you that, in reality, such a thing as a personality or an 'I' cannot possibly exist.

So many times you have been to India, haven't you? You have seen so many people there, thousands and thousands of people, in all forms and colours—all sorts, from the healthy to the dying. Perhaps there you also saw dead people lying in the street. Now, in the case of a dead person there are four things to be noticed: The body is rigid, the vital breathing has gone, the body-heat has gone, and the heart has stopped beating. When the body-heat is going, death is approaching. The vital breathing fails and then the body becomes rigid. Now, what exactly has left the body? For the body as such is all but complete. The whole body is more or less still intact. The nose, feet, hands, eyes—everything is still there. All the things which the living person may have got excited about or pleased with are still there. Yet none of the things that were valuable to him are now no longer of any relevance to him. The body is dead, and now nature is going to celebrate, because in nature one thing is living on the other.

But what exactly is it that has left the body? What makes the dead man dead? There is nothing visible to be detected there. The clairvoyant will say that, at the moment of passing away, or shortly after that, a subtler body may be seen above the physical body, the two being connected by a silvery thread. But, later on, that also disappears. You could say then, that the light—the invisible side of the manifested, the formless—has left the body.

The innermost being has to be unchangeable. If it could change, then it wouldn't be unchangeable. Then it couldn't be the

'One-without-a-second'. Anything with a form, however subtle, has somehow to be subject to change within time and space, which are forms as well. That is why one's innermost being has got to be unchangeable and formless, for only the formless cannot change. Consciousness is formless, colourless, without taste and smell, and so on. Consciousness is making all things possible through instruments which we call 'senses', and which lead to experience. Since it is consciousness which is making perception possible, consciousness itself cannot be perceived. Thus at death the possibility to perceive is withdrawn, for consciousness needs a form to manifest itself, to become manifest.

Please listen carefully, as this is one of the most difficult things about it: Consciousness cannot but manifest itself through *form*. Form, therefore, is consciousness become manifest.

V: I'm not sure I understand this. I once had the distinct feeling of being jealous...

A: We are not talking about jealousy now. You must stick to the subject.

V: Is the energy like that of jealousy a neutral energy?

A: You don't want to budge, do you? As you wish. The self-creating equilibrium at that level will see to it, that everything will be set right. An energy like jealousy has been aroused, and it will have to go somewhere, since you refuse to accept it and look at it.

V: But why am I not putting that energy into happiness instead of in jealousy?

A: If the self-creating equilibrium is requiring you to do so, then it will happen that way. In any case, don't imagine that it is *you* who is doing it.

V: Then why is it that a certain equilibrium is required of *me*?

A: Because of the fact that *you*, against your own better judgement, keep on identifying yourself with the objective world, with the world of objects that are continuously colliding with one another. In fact, nobody is requiring *anything* of you.

V: But someone else would react differently!

A: Are you someone else? Of what interest is that to you?

V: But, then, isn't that something specific to *me*?

A: Aha, you want to go that way again. No, not to *you*. Each human being reacts in his own way.

V: So all are not equal?

A: Of equal value, but not equal. The manifestation is making that clear to you. Inequality is everywhere. No two things are the same. The only thing in which we are equal is consciousness. Consciousness is only manifesting itself, expressing itself through form. The expression wants to survive and enjoy itself as long as possible. The form wants to form, manifest itself, wants to show itself and be seen. Jealousy means surviving and wanting to be seen. If not, how would you keep your husband or wife at your side? These are all survival strategies of the manifestation. In our culture it is even commonplace to believe that, if you are *not* jealous, you do not really love the other person. Those conditionings are aimed at survival. Everything in the manifested world is aimed at survival. So also the ego, the self-consciousness that knows that its improper position is a threatened one. The same applies to points of view, emotions etc. and, of course, in the first place to the body itself—the body being the most important one, since it is the basis for everything else. The entire health care up to the practising of *hatha yoga* is at the service of this surviving, which is the body's nature. When you are going to the tropics, you first have your vaccinations to ward off any deadly diseases. Also you don't drink water in the tropics without boiling it first, otherwise you may risk your life. All that is quite natural and completely acceptable. Why do we live in houses and not in the street? Because, if we would be living in the street, we would thereby reduce our chances for survival. Your house, your clothes, everything is at the service of your survival. You stand a better chance in a proper house than in a dampish porch. So, in essence not much has changed as compared to olden times. Things stand pretty much the same. Everyone wants to live at the physical level and, as to the emotional and mental levels, the same thing applies.

V: Have you never looked upon yourself as an ego?

A: My God, what a question! Somehow it has always been obvious to me that *my* experience of reality could never be absolute. That *my* views could always be set off against those of others. Whatever I started out with, in the end I always was left with the question, '*Who am I ?*'

Feelings and mental processes are naturally there, but an 'I'-structure is nowhere to be found. The notion of an ego has always been foreign to me. I could never understand how one was to get rid of the ego, for I've never been able to find one.

All started with conception. The fruit of that conception developed, and after birth it developed further, being kept alive as a body by its environment. *I* didn't do anything. Even now this body is being fed by the earth and by the people around me. I myself didn't contribute anything to it, I had no essential part in it. I have recovered myself in a state of consciousness. In a perfectly spontaneous way, without the least effort. It wasn't an act of will-power—no action on my part. I know that I am part of the whole and the whole is part of me. But I fail to see, how I could possibly put myself forward as something static, as something permanent, for I don't see any ego or any 'I'-structure.

This phenomenon, this body, will last 36.000 days at the most. It has a temporal and illusory value of about one hundred years. How did such a structure come into existence? Purely as a result of the union of our ancestors' energies. Through conception—the basic concept—this phenomenon which manifests itself in body-mind-feeling, has come into being and so it became visible. Conception put the energy into motion. This three-dimensional illusion has a life-term of about one hundred years. With the growing of awareness one becomes conscious of oneself. It is the same for everyone. Consciousness is finally conscious of itself.

V: And an 'I' is projected into that?

A: I can't see how such a thing is possible. But those who manage to do so seem to meet with troubles as a result of it, most of it in the form of suffering and sorrow. The suffering and the sorrow are introduced the moment a fragment is being projected onto the whole and one finds oneself identified with it.

V: Of late I don't see any point in asking any more questions. Each time a question crops up, the answer follows instantly. At the same time things are not altogether clear to me. Yet by asking questions I don't seem to get any further.

A: Still it is important to ask questions. The seeming burden of the pairs of opposites is easily carried in clarity. Let yourself be carried by the light. Tradition means the transmittance of the living light, not of book-learning and trifling information, valuable though these may seem at first sight. In the end you will have to let go of any such book-knowledge. The desired effect of these meetings is perhaps, that you will gradually come to steer by your own inner compass and not by the compass of 'what the books are saying'. The wonderful thing about a living experience is that you never need a reference for it at some other place: It is yours. As such a living experience is not a matter of memory. Of course, there is nothing against books, but as your inner and outer life begins to become really clear, you will lose your interest in books.

V: What do you mean by 'lose your interest'?

A: 'Interest' comes from the Latin inter-*esse*. Inter means 'between', *esse* means 'being'. Here *esse* stands for consciousness, inter for that which stands in between, the veiling. When the veil has gone, no longer anything will stand in the way of being to be what is: *conscious being.* Then you will have lost interest. Consciousness is sufficient unto itself.

(18th December, 1982, afternoon)

10

YOU CANNOT HIDE FROM PERCEIVING

Visitor: This afternoon you said that it was important to ask questions. I have a question. You said that your tradition was the transmission of the living. You also said that the living is not to be found in books and that, in the long run, one loses interest in such literature. Would you like to go a little deeper into that?

Alexander: The presence of the living is always a threat to the dead, the static, to that which has got stuck. The living always poses a threat to what is institutionalized, the established, the status quo. For what is static, fixed, institutionalized, becomes superfluous the very moment when the living enters. Then the 'talking about' the living appears somewhat superfluous. Those who know their true nature become silent and acquire an unprecedented, tangible depth. Even in their movements and sounds there is something silent.

Indeed, the living is, without exception, a threat to that which has got stuck, to the reflection, the false. In history it may be observed that, whenever anything truly profound and living presents itself, the form in which it appears will be destroyed or eradicated before long. Good examples of this are Jesus and Socrates, because both were a threat to the static. Jesus had no problems with the whores and the publicans. The really heavy cases were the Pharisees, the men of learning, the scribes, the priestly class. They represented institutionalized truth, whereas

Jesus represented the *living* truth. He did not live according to the scriptures.

In the world you can see that, each time a person is accorded a really living truth, the institutionalized religions and organisations will defend themselves tooth and nail, the simple reason being that institutions and organisations are not very tolerant of the living. The living is the opposite of the dead, that which has got stuck. The living will always pose a threat to apparent certainties. You can judge from an organisation's defense, its urge to fight, and from its missionarism, how dead and static it has become.

V: Yesterday you said that all things derive their value from their opposite. Everything is complementary. Then how are we to get any notion of our being, if we do not know what *non*-being is?

A: Non-being is not really the opposite of being. Opposites can only be perceived within being *itself*, within the presence. Non-being is a supposed condition. For example, the absence of something is called 'nothing'. 'Nothing' is a combination of not-any-thing. But such non-being is, really speaking, an unimaginable situation, because no imagination can do without 'being'. Non-being is actually something unimaginable and, therefore, cannot be experienced. For instance, when a painting has been removed from the living-room without your knowledge, maybe you will say on entering the room, 'Oh, I see that the painting is no longer hanging on the wall.' But, as a matter of fact, such a thing isn't really possible, for you cannot perceive the *absence* of a painting. Of course, everybody will understand what you mean, but in reality that is not possible. You cannot perceive the absence of an object. However, because of your memory you will be able to tell as a matter of course, that there is something missing in your latest perception of the wall. So, in fact, you are looking with your memory rather than with your eyes.

Now back to being. What you truly know is being, because knowing takes place within being. The opposite side of knowing is not-knowing. Being, however, remains. You don't know non-being, strictly speaking, nor *can* you know it, because in order to know it you will have to *be*. So, strictly speaking, there is only *being* or, in other words, *knowingness*. The interpretation *within* being, or *of* being—knowing—is the *known*, which is always found on the objective side. Absolute Being is the only thing which is not on the objective side, and it can, therefore, never be known. Being and non-being may be compared to life and death. Life is what you know, and death is what you do not know; the moment you come into contact with it, you disappear. It is exactly the same with non-being. As soon as non-being becomes possible, you disappear. So you can never come to know non-being. On the other hand Being also can never be known, because that, too, is not an object. Rather, it is that which makes the objects possible. The knowing of being appears within Being itself, but, as an experience, the knowing of being will always be an object.

In the same way you cannot know silence. Silence is the absence of sound. What remains, then, is the absence as compared to the situation which took place just prior to it. Again, this comparison is made possible through the memory, for silence as such cannot be experienced. Only sounds can be experienced. Besides, in reality you can never have *total* silence. If you have total silence, you would probably go mad. Thus silence and Being have something in common. The presence is always there and, within it, the knowing becomes possible. Then only follows the interpretation, which then becomes the explication.

As soon as something is coming into manifestation, it must express itself in multiplicity, in duality. Thus there will always be *two* sides to the matter, as with a sheet of paper, which must necessarily have a front and a back side. As a matter of fact, these two sides of the matter are a frame of reference for us in order to be able to lead our lives, otherwise you really wouldn't know the front from the back.

The only thing you *know* is, that you *are*, thereby introducing the fact that, one day, 'it' will end. In this you can't have any choice: It is a dilemma. Thus, whilst you cannot be *non*-being, *being* also seems to present problems or, in any case, it has its consequences.

As we were discussing yesterday: Feelings go proportionally deep. If you are feeling ecstatic, then you will move towards its opposite proportionally deep, for the two always go together. As you are not quite capable of accepting either one, you lead a greyish existence. The apparent choice is either to embrace life or to isolate yourself, isolation meaning even more greyishness and dullness. For the price you pay for isolating yourself out of fear of life—namely, the fact that you don't want to be involved any more—is equally huge. Anyway, it is a fact of life that, when I am sitting here, I cannot be standing there, and vice versa. Thus, in order to see things clearly, it is important to observe *both* aspects, *both* these tendencies: the embracing *and* the isolating of a certain situation. Such observing is a different form of taking distance, which is not born from any reaction or wanting to fly, but from the desire of wanting to *see*. And in order to be able to see, you must first be calm about these tendencies.

With the first second of your waking up you can see quite clearly, that you are asked to commit yourself to that which is newly presenting itself to you. A world appears before you, and something is wanted from you. Maybe you can still remain lying down for a while, yet something is urging you to make a choice between embracement or isolation. In fact, this process is continued for the rest of the day: isolation or embracement, embracement or isolation. There is anger: embracement or isolation? There is joy: embracement or isolation? There is something you don't like: embracement or isolation? All the time something is wanted from you. You can observe this movement between embracement and isolation quite clearly, if you pay a little attention to it. The fact that you can *see* it means, that you are *out* of it, for both embracement and isolation are happening on the *objective* side. From the witness, that perceiving, you cannot hide, nor can you embrace it. That witness is the still centre, while the movements, the tendencies of embracement and isolation, are the storm. But deep within the storm it is calm. The centre of the cyclone is still. Such is the paradox.

The real witness is never involved in the event: he is witnessing. Therefore, all he does is *seeing*. The witness is the centre of all events, of anger and joy, of illness and health, of birth and death. Nothing escapes this witness: he is the centre of the world. But you make a suspect of that which the witness is witnessing. That is where the split begins. That is where the trouble begins, the confusion and the storm. Somehow or other you are creating a witness-suspect relationship with yourself. Ultimately, however, there is only one thing: the witness. The rest is an interpretation of thinking and feeling.

(18th December, 1982, evening)

11

GOD IS FORMLESS ESSENCE FROM WHICH EACH FORM ORIGINATES

Alexander: The secret of existence is expressed in the union of man and woman, in the merging and impregnation. We thank our existence to that merging, brought about by the sexual energy. From that union we are born, and because of that we know the world and ourselves. All things would be unthinkable, if that union would not have taken place. The consciousness of the world and of ourselves is stored in the seed-consciousness. The form is already determined and is only waiting to develop. From the seed of a tiger only a tiger can come, from the seed of an oak only an oak can come. The potential form of a man or of the oak or of the tiger is contained within the seed. The sperm cell is the active pole and the egg cell the passive, awaiting one. The egg cell is the receiving factor, the sperm cell the active one. Antonie van Leeuwenhoek saw sperm cells for the first time under a microscope and discovered countless little tadpole-like creatures moving around rapidly and dynamically. All on their way to the top, all heading for one goal: impregnation, new manifestation, new form, growth.

This seed-consciousness is analogous to ourselves, for in our behaviour we are not much different, once we have taken the form of a human being. We all want to reach the top, improve ourselves, higher up, pursue objects, attain to perfection, and so forth. This is the essence of the seed-consciousness as it manifests itself. The sperm cell goes up towards its aim—which is the magnetic action—and is out to survive and manifest itself. It wants to express itself. Similarly we, too, all still want to be the best, the most clever and the fastest one. This seed-consciousness contains the form of the body with all its movement and manifestation. It is already embedded in the sperm cell, just as the scent of a flower is already potentially present in its seed. That is why I say that the body is the scent of consciousness, as translated through the five senses.

The body, or the consciousness of the body, is maintained by the vital breathing and by food. The five elements—earth, water, air, fire and ether—see to it that the consciousness of the body, and along with it that of the world, is sustained. A sick body is the result of the five elements not co-operating properly, in which case something is disturbed. This play of the five senses makes the manifested consciousness possible. If one of the five elements is disturbed or cut off, consciousness withdraws itself from the body. Then one speaks of death.

He who has grasped this will never be able to say that he is the body. The body can never be the ultimate reality. Billions of bodies have been populating this earth and will be doing so. Perhaps the most important fact that needs to be grasped is, that we are *not* the body, for all suffering and sorrow stem from the notion, 'I am the body'. Strictly speaking, the body is a form like any other, a composition of elements held together in a miraculous way by forces we do not understand, but which are a given fact all the same.

Visitor: Are you now saying, that the consciousness will disappear along with the body?

A: Because you experience your body as the reality, you reason out everything from the standpoint of the body. But the Absolute can never be measured by such a limited thing as the body. The immeasurable can never be measured by the measurable. And if anything can be measured, then surely it is the body!

V: I can't understand how the consciousness will fall off along with the body.

A: When consciousness falls off, the body falls off and vice versa. The two always go together. The consciousness which you think you experience, is an image-consciousness, for you always speak in terms of images. You always need to have a picture for everything, which is one of the five modifications of the mind. The world that is known to you is made up of images, imprinted by the five senses and held together by an other modification of the mind, memory. These five senses and the power of imagination together with memory conjure up the body and the world. Through fascination and un-centeredness you take the world to be something other than it is. Here at these meetings we are taking exactly the opposite direction, towards the only thing you can never know, since it has no form: your essence, your real nature. All the rest is images, thoughts, feelings. This means that the waking consciousness and the dream consciousness—the only states that are known to you through images—are alternating states that belong to the mind with its five modifications, namely memory, imagination, sleep, right knowledge and wrong knowledge.

In Advaita Vedanta the world is said to be *unreal*—not non-existent. It does exist, but as a product of the mind, and therefore it is not the ultimate reality. As a matter of fact, the world derives its reality from consciousness. It exists in a real sense as a three-dimensional play. The Indians have a beautiful word for it, '*lila*', the divine play, the play within conscious being, the play of the five elements. And as long as these elements are playing, there will be consciousness. This conjuring-world will disappear when the play has finished.

V: When consciousness disappears, where does it go?

A: Where *should* it go? As far as you are concerned, it rather depends on what you believe in. Energy is always seeking a form. If you believe in those forms—and believing is a form of energy—then consciousness will take on the forms that you wish for or that you are afraid of. Until the illusory quality of all this is seen through. Then consciousness goes home, disappearing within itself and of itself. That is why the *jnani* is not afraid to die. The whole problem is that you mistake the form for the reality and the ultimate. You have learnt to experience the universal consciousness—which you *are*—as individual consciousness. But that is a delusion and untenable. Moreover, delusion is maintained by delusion. Do not try to wash away blood with blood. The truth is that in consciousness not an atom of individuality is to be found.

V: Is it then reabsorbed into the whole?

A: There *is* nothing else. At heart that is what all religions are talking about. If you go and search for it, you will recover entire pieces of it. But religions have occupied the place of the living, and religions have become static reflections of the living.

In Europe Self-realisation is called '*Unio Mystica*', the absorption of the individual into the universal consciousness. Now, don't think there are *two* 'consciousnesses'. Consciousness is one. To *be* that oneness is yoga, that is religion. The connection made anew, the connection with the essence which had been cut off.

V: I am quite able to follow what you are saying, but to experience it seems pretty hard to me.

A: Who is to experience it?

V: I can reason it out.

A: Reasoning can only be done intellectually. Reasoning through feeling is not possible. But this isn't about a certain way of reasoning. Reason, *ratio*, is only a very small aspect of the mind. We are not dealing here with thinking, we are dealing here with seeing. That seeing will reveal itself to you—no thinking is involved.

V: In that case I wonder how you can still be doing your work in daily life?

A: Is there anything apart from daily life? Why put up all those separations in your life: theory, practice, daily life... That way there is no end to it. Moreover, here it is not a question of your putting anything into practice in daily life.

Such a question is born from the notion of a 'doer'. Who is there to be doing anything anyway? Once the delusion of an 'I'-structure is seen through, who is there going to be left to do anything about what? If you can see this, not as an idea, but as a reality that is experienced by you as such, then—and only then—all will happen of its own accord. Then each thought, each feeling, each gesture will be an expression, a translation, a geste of that truth which you will have realized in your innermost being. If not, then the truth has not really been integrated, in which case it remains 'arm-chair' *jnana*.

One thing is certain: There won't be anyone left to 'do' anything with it in any way, even though it won't keep you from doing all that is natural and necessary. In any case, an illusory figure like the personality or the self-consciousness can only make illusory movements.

Discover your real nature and be still with life. Do not imagine that, when 'it' happens, you will stop breathing, or that you won't have your chocolate spread any more.

V: Can you speak of an 'I'-structure in the case of a baby?

A: In the case of a new-born baby there is hardly any 'I'-structure there, though potentially there is one. There it is merely a question of eating and drinking, space, warmth, etc. There the primary dynamic is existing and living. After some time, because of the changing of objects, the little child begins to project time and causality, and it begins to imitate its parents and the environment. Next come 'tomorrow', 'yesterday', 'later' and 'now', etc. In short, the child begins to construct a world, which is how it should be. It is something perfectly natural, for how could it live otherwise? Next an 'I' is projected into that which was first experienced as timeless, open, spatial, unlimited and free, and then only the 'I'-sense arises. As such that needn't be a disaster. However, later on several 'I'-structures begin to develop, opposing one another, and clashing with each other in a desire to survive. Thus the need arises to have rules, morals, ethics, 'sin', etc., in order to regulate all those interests. Next a mental world arises in a world within a world.

Now, if anyone is saying, 'I can't do anything with these data', then he is telling the truth. For indeed, he can't do anything with it: Everything is 'doing itself'. Only *Being* is.

V: You haven't said anything about love yet.

A: Is that what you want—talk about love? You shouldn't talk about it at all: You *are* that. To talk about love is hypocrisy.

When you love somebody very much, then it may just happen that you are simply being swept off your feet. You just can't put into words why you love somebody that much, for everything you can think of doesn't seem to carry any weight. And indeed, it doesn't, because love goes beyond all ideas and notions. Thinking cannot reach there at all, not any more than feelings; they seem ever inadequate. So, when two people love each other deeply, it is often quite still. Love is sufficient unto itself. Each word would disturb.

However, you are not able to love somebody at all, because you haven't accepted yourself. You have yet to face the fact that your being *is* love. Everything in this world is *self*-love. Each form wants to live and survive, from the micro-organism up to the elephant. Why? Because everything loves itself perfectly. Even an 'I'-structure wants to survive. And, physically speaking, a disease is nothing but a war going on between two or more organisms fighting each other life-and-death.

In Indian philosophy there was a classification of four species of life. Briefly it came down to the following:

In the first place there is the unanimated realm of minerals. There the atoms are attracted to each other and move ever closer to one another: suns, moons, planets, and so on. This is called '*annamayakosha*'. Next is the realm of plants, where the atoms are closer to each other and inter-action is taking place. This is called '*pranamayakosha*'. Those atoms appear to us in the form of plants. Then there is the realm of animals, '*manomayakosha*'. The atoms of it form bodies which we perceive as animals. And finally, there is the human form, '*vijnanamayakosha*'. It is the intelligence-body, the atom endowed with reason and with the power of discrimination. All these different structures are living from and on one another—minerals, plants, animals and human beings. They all exist by the grace of one another.

The Indians in North America used to address plants, animals and trees as brother and sister. They spoke of 'brother bear', 'brother tree' and 'mother earth'. The Indians perceived this very clearly. I once heard a story that may not be correct from a historical viewpoint, but it is interesting all the same. It tells something about the word 'Indian'. The story relates how Columbus, when he discovered America in 1492, believed himself to be in India, since he met with people there who, as he put it, 'were living in God'. For that reason he named them, in Spanish of course, '*Indios*': 'Those who live in God'.

Of all the manifestations only man is capable of attaining absolute freedom, because man is possessed of reasoning power, discriminating power, and the possibility of self-reflection. These three faculties distinguish him from the animal. Look at the dog: Even though you treat the animal ever so badly, he remains faithful. Perhaps that is why some people have got a dog instead of being married. It is said sometimes, 'He has a dog-like devotion'. A five-year old child can easily lead a horse, even though the animal must be at least thirty times bigger. We are capable of taming the most ferocious animals and we go to the circus at a fair price to see whether it is really possible. Perhaps you have a sneaking hope in your heart that the animal will turn against its oppressor, and yet...

It is written in the *Ashtavakra Samhita* that, if one takes part in the play of life as the knower of the Self, then one doesn't have anything in common with the people who live in the world like a beast of burden. In different translations you even find it said that people who do not realize anything, are no different from mammals. If you do not know the Self, you live like the simple animal. It also eats, mates and sleeps. In that case you are not making use of your human beingness.

V: I would like to come back again to the subject of death. When you die, is it the essence which remains then?

A: Surprising how you jump from one subject to the other! It won't be easy to come back to death though. However, I'm telling you: The formless state to which you will return when you die, will remain—Your consciousness will disappear.

V: So my consciousness will not continue to exist?

A: Consciousness *is* not yours.

V: But why this creation then?

A: It is God's little gesture. Why? Why? Why? This is one of the most illegal questions you can make up—for various reasons.

In the first place, because you are seeking an explanation for something that cannot be explained. And if you *would* have the explanation for it, it still isn't going to get you any further, for things will still be the same. All you are doing is to put different names to things that you can't understand, while imagining that you *do* understand them. Who knows, whether all is not being enacted according to laws that we aren't even aware of?

Secondly, you cannot say anything about your real essence, because whatever you may say about it, will be measured by laws and terms that are necessarily bound by limitations, and which, therefore, cannot get at the real essence.

In the Bible the blame is laid at the door of woman in the story of Creation, and with that belief half the world is living even today.

V: So God is the formless essence. But then, why is this world as it is?

A: Which world? Your world or the world of Ronald Reagan or of messrs. Van Kooten and De Bie[3]? Try to understand once and for all, that no independent world exists apart from your viewpoint. Everybody is living in a private, projected world of his own, including all images, fears and desires. What you truly are is formless essence, the natural state, which *you* will never be able to know. *That* is God. That's why in India you are said to be God, equal to the gods. What's more: First *you* have to be there, and only *then* can there be gods. This is not a matter of blasphemy. It is blasphemy when you turn God, who is formless essence, into an image. He who discovers that God is living in his own heart, sees the same in everybody else. The Hindus grasped this well. And is it not written in the Bible, 'Thou shalt not make an image of the Lord your God'? But we are slow learners indeed.

(18th December, 1982, evening)

12

YOUR DISCOMFORT IS YOUR SELF-CONSCIOUSNESS

Visitor: Does a person who knows his natural state, escape the natural laws that hold good for this world? And is there, according to you, a possibility for man to change?

Alexander: Looking at it objectively from the level of the world, naturally there are laws which no human being can escape. If the organism is losing too much blood, it is put into danger. Even the one who knows his natural state cannot escape it. No mortal being escapes the laws of nature. However, it is man's specialty, as distinct from the simple animal, that he can make use of a very highly developed discriminative faculty. Man is equipped with *vijnanamaya-kosha*, the body of intelligence, which enables him to avail himself of the wonderful power to see in between things. He does not merely and exclusively live by the lines of force as indicated by nature. Man is capable of more than that, which makes him so interesting as a phenomenon as well. He is able, to a greater or lesser extent, to make or break his own destiny, which is also what he wants. He can express himself in the world and, at the same time, he is also an expression himself.

I am reminded of an interesting story about a king and how he thought he could decide his destiny. This king took a very great interest in magic and fortune-telling. For that reason he had gathered around him a great number of fortune-tellers, magicians and astrologists who, as to their wisdom, were well-matched. The king would ask for their advice on a regular basis, and on such occasions he would listen attentively. One of the fortune-tellers was outstanding because of the great precision with which his predictions and interpretations used to come true. And so it didn't take long before the king was listening to him only. One sunny day the king called him by his side and said, 'I want to discuss a serious matter with you.' The fortune-teller looked at the king importantly and said, 'Please, do not worry, sir, you may ask me anything; you need not be afraid.' For a long time the king looked in front of him thoughtfully, and then he asked somewhat unexpectedly, 'When will I die?'

'That is quite a question', the fortune-teller said bewildered. 'Anyway, I will find out. Please allow me three months and I will give you the answer.'

Three months went by, not without anxiety, and the king became more and more impatient. Finally he couldn't stand it any longer and called for the fortune-teller.

'Well? How does the matter stand? Do you know it?'

'Well', the fortune-teller said, 'do you really want to know it?'

'Don't wait any longer, man!' the king burst out, not without annoyance.

'Three more weeks', the fortune-teller replied.

'Humph', said the king, 'that's not too much.'

Then, all of a sudden, the king turned round and said with a strange smile, 'And what about *you*, my dear fortune-teller, how long have *you* yet to live?'

'Me?' the fortune-teller asked, his eyebrows somewhat raised. 'Another thirty years to be exact.'

Then, all of a sudden, the king took a sword from under his robe and shouted, 'I will prove that your predictions are worthless!' And in one stroke he cut off his head. With astonished eyes the head of the fortune-teller rolled through the hall of the palace. Three weeks later the king died.

This story makes it clear, that the fortune-teller was right and not right at the same time. And with many things in life it is exactly like that. Man can express himself in and on his environment, yet at the same time he is and will always remain part of that expression himself. If he would use his faculty of seeing for learning to know himself, it would mean immense progress. It would offer enormous possibilities for the happiness and well-being of human beings, animals and plants, in a word, for the whole of creation. But although enormous changes have taken place and a lot of very hard work is put into changing man's fundamental attitude with respect to himself, it nevertheless would appear that man is making very little use of this capacity as yet. The result of it is destruction and aggression, despite the fact that change and improvement, too, may be perceived, both on an individual and collective scale. Such a fundamental change in man's attitude towards himself has become a pressing need, and is certainly no longer a matter of luxury or of leisure activity. Individual ignorance leads to individual destruction, collective ignorance will lead to collective destruction, unless man—that is you and me and all of us—is going to change fundamentally.

V: In any such event the shock incurred may be necessary and functional.

A: It is not unthinkable. One cannot have a clear picture of all the natural laws. But what one can see clearly is, that you cannot exploit the earth, as has now been happening for the past two hundred years, without taking the consequences. Nuclear tests, which are still going on, disturb the natural balance, acid rain is threatening the woods, and jungle forests all over the world are cut down at high speed. In Nepal a complete landslip is taking place due to foresting—land which radiated its beauty untouched for thousands of years, is disappearing purely through ignorance, greed and wastage. The forests are the lungs of this planet, and the earth is a most sensitive organism. What the consequences will be of such uncontrolled behaviour, dictated by greediness and ignorance, is yet to be estimated.

V: Do we not all have a hand in it?

A: One more than the other. But let's not busy ourselves with the question of who is to be guilty and why. Too much time has already been lost on account of that. The important thing now is to act with intelligence. As was said earlier on, all our actions and motivations are based on a number of motives—in fact, on one motive only, namely fear. This fear moves in many directions, this fear takes on many forms. Three of them we will discuss during the days that we are gathered here. They are: the fear of death, boredom, and loneliness—the unbearable burden of being alone and the loneliness resulting from it. As long as our actions are based on these three pillars, our behaviour will continue to be unintelligent. Thus we remain a victim of circumstances and accidentals, of narrow-minded ideas and reactions; of futilities, petty philosophy and New Age babbling. As long as fear is the motor of our existence, we cannot but act the way we do: in a destructive, petty- and narrow-minded way, scrappy and divided.

The fear of nuclear war directly refers you to your present existence. The dilemma of your life is intensified by it. In the event of a nuclear war you will lose everything that you know and have, what you are and what you are not. Including your whole life. Not many people are prepared to face this issue. The whole point of the present time, in contrast with the past, is not to run away or to lose oneself in strategies of fear by applying methods, theories and philosophies. For these very strategies stem from the basic dilemma and from one's inability to see what *is*. They spring from the given fact that you exist and that, at the same time, you actually do *not* want to exist. Please note, 'at the same time'. That is the dilemma. That is your discomfort, your trouble. That is the discomfort of self-consciousness.

The given fact that *you* exist and that you are not really able to love it, is unbearable. The reason being that out of that love—which *is* yourself—and out of yourself you have made a concept, an idea, an image. It is not a live experience. As a 'person', along with your environment, you will never be able to conform to all the images which you have built up for yourself out of fear. This illusory figure is forever busy fulfilling its own requirements. And the poor body has to run like a Pavlov-doggie in the tracks of this illusory figure in the form of objectives and motives for obtaining enlightenment and relief and fulfilment. Indeed, all the things you do, including the quest of your self, you do for a purpose, with a motive. You are never without a motive, innocent, guileless. You are always out for something or other—*goal*-oriented. For that's what cheers you up. But it is a cheering-up which you derive from a promise that will never be fulfilled.

This is what I call the strategy of fear. Each approach is based on a strategy of fear and, therefore, destructive and an act of aggression.

(19th December, 1982, morning)

13

THE NATURAL STATE IS AND REMAINS UNDIVIDED

Visitor: You once said that consciousness is conscious of itself. Thinking and feeling would not disturb that state. What do you mean when you say, that identification is not really possible?

Alexander: When it is a question of identification, then a separation appears to have been effected there where this is not really possible. Identification is an optical illusion. In reality you are never identified, it only appears to be so. The separation is never real, it is a mirage, a fata morgana. No one is really ever split. Thoughts come and go naturally, and the same applies to feelings. But the natural state remains undivided, there are no changes in it. It is not split, it is non-dual.

This primary given fact is always present, it never leaves you. After that opinions arise, which derive their light from consciousness. Next concepts and beliefs are formed. The constant factor within the changeable is your primary given fact. Focus the attention on the constant factor of everything as the point from where to unravel things. Realize your primary insight. Then consciousness will be conscious of itself without any effort. The beauty of it is unprecedented.

V: Could you tell us where thoughts are coming from, and why they come and go? And what is the constant factor you are referring to?

A: I am not interested as to where thoughts are coming from and where they go to. Yet they, too, originate from conscious being, are perceived in it and disappear in it. Don't occupy yourself with unsolvable questions; all it produces are unsolvable answers. Consciousness is ever present in the presence and the absence of the image you have made of yourself. The only thing which you cannot see, however, is consciousness *itself,* whereas that which is illumined by consciousness can be seen and is perceived by you. See what it *is* and it will lose its illusory quality. See the false *as* false and the Real will remain.

All things in the world have got an existential as well as a time value. In chemistry and biology these secrets have already been revealed. No need to hammer at an open door. Everything happens according to laws. The more laws you know, the more unpretentious you become.

V: You are saying that man is the constant witness of all that happens. According to you everything is following a natural course. Does not all become rather dull that way?

A: Dullness and boredom are approximations. These approximations are susceptible to change. Boredom is also a sign of intelligence. The simple animal doesn't get bored easily: A cow may be looking at the same things for years on end without much problem. Man gets bored more easily, because he is more intelligent. The more intelligent a man, the easier he will feel bored. Intelligent people can see through situations more easily, and thus things become predictable to them. This accounts for the drabness and dullness of existence, for in that case the recurrence of events is anticipated well in advance. Then repetition becomes boredom.

To the child, however, repetition means to meet the familiar. That is why children all over the world are saying 'pa-pa' and 'mama': two times 'pa' and two times 'ma'. It is the repetition of the familiar. It is always the interrelation that is being sought, and it is found in repetition. Re-peating is the re-calling of that which is in danger of becoming concealed. To learn is to repeat. To the child, but also to the adult, it is a constant re-gaining of the familiar. That is why making music, playing and working, saying one's prayers and one's *mantra*, as well as the changing of the seasons, is an indefatigable repetition. To the adult repetition usually means boredom, because in the long run all stimuli become a habit. Then repetition no longer has the function to familiarize as it has with the child.

The ability to see everything anew and fresh is a *gift* of Self-realisation, never the aim. It is a looking back in wonder. To see all things anew does not mean that memory is failing, but that the mechanisms of the discriminative faculty of thinking along with its greedy motives have made themselves redundant.

Life is sufficient unto itself, without motives and ulterior purposes. A situation always implies a possible approach, and your approach, your attitude therein, is of the utmost importance. With that you can make or break everything.

V: This witness that you are talking about, is it a kind of observation-post from where everything is being perceived? How should I picture it?

A: To a lot of people this being-a-witness, this perceivingness, presents many unnecessary problems. Simply be conscious of the fact that you are, nothing more or less. Don't make yourself into an observation-post, for that is precisely the way to create a subject-object relationship with yourself and, from there, a witness-suspect relationship. In that way you are introducing a split, there where there is none. Then you will be busy all day observing your own thoughts and feelings, and you will only be paying the wrong attention to them. In the natural state it is not a question of any observation-post being there, but only (the experience of) pure seeing. What you perceive is made possible through memory. The witness is your still centre.

V: I realize that hope, belief and love are quick-sands, but in real life I experience them as life-giving forces. Do I fool myself?

A: Hope, belief and love, as ideas, are always quick-sands. He who builds his life on these ideas will experience their stifling effect. There is a saying, 'Man lives by hope', and so it is. Most of us need the strategy of hope in order to move forward. Still only those who are in distress are in need of hope. If there would be no more hope, then this would have a crippling effect on the majority of us. Almost all religions have used hope as a strategy to lead and mislead the people into certain directions considered right by the leaders. The same applies to politics. Thus for centuries the mind has been trained *what* to think, but not *how* to think. Hope for a life to come, hope for a hereafter, hope for better circumstances, hope for a better life. This has been the driving-force of humanity for ages. Hope for a cookie, when you've been a good boy. In fact, the strategy of hope is only applicable to people with a poor discriminative faculty, to people who cannot be made to move in any other way, the lazy man who will not seek for himself, but who wants to be led by the hand of some daddy.

The strategy of belief is more or less of the same calibre. A strategy of laziness, indolence and naivety. In metaphysical realisation it is nothing short of a disaster. It is an unwritten law in Advaita Vedanta, that you never accept anything on the authority of your teacher; that you never accept anything, just because he says it. Belief is something different from faith. Faith is blind. Faith has *got* to be blind, otherwise it wouldn't be faith. A 'seeing faith' doesn't exist. Faith is always blind. Faith feels its way along.

The most dangerous of all strategies is the strategy of love. A lot of misery has been wrought in the name of love, usually well-meant, but coming from sheer ignorance. Concepts such as belief, hope and love—as concepts—are always a strategy, a form of politics. A way to steer things into the direction you want them to go; in order to have it your way, somehow or other; in order to command respect, to win love and affection, and for the realisation of your interests. A strategy which you once needed as a child to get your way, or to win the love of your parents and your environment. All these mechanisms have their seat in the body, in your memory, and they are brought into motion whenever a situation similar to that of the past occurs. That is how you become a beggar.

Although Advaita Vedanta is hardly concerned with this kind of strategies, it is not unthinkable that such intricate, often destructive, self-repeating mechanisms may be stopped through intensive self-examination and loving introspection, as well as through a good deal of courage. But that is not the *purpose* of Self-realisation. In Advaita Vedanta that is not the goal.

Advaita Vedanta concentrates itself on the 'One-without-a-second'. It wants to know what the *true* Self is. In fact, psychological complications and social complexities ought to be treated by the 'qualified' experts. However, these people are often living in darkness themselves. The fact that, nowadays, these subjects are also being discussed amongst Advaitic circles, is caused by the inescapable fact, that modern man not only greatly identifies himself with the body, but with the areas of feeling and thinking as well. With the result that, in contrast to the past, psychological problems are being emphasized rather than Self-realisation.

A great exponent of Advaita once said, 'It is not difficult to find the truth, but it is impossible to please everybody.'

(19th December, 1982, morning)

14

THE SEEKING TAKES PLACE IN THE SOUGHT

Alexander: The fight against disease and the precautions that are taken to prevent one from falling ill, are without any doubt strategies for survival. Everything in nature wants to live, from the smallest micro-organism to the biggest animal you can imagine. Within the body a life-and-death battle is taking place in order to allow a greater organism—the body itself—to continue its existence. Millions of factors are required and are connecting with one another in order to have things function properly. The fact that everything is functioning as well as it does, is a miracle indeed. Nowadays the possibilities for survival have increased even more and, along with it, the number of vital questions and the opportunities for full development. One basic fact remains though, which is that everything in this world is based on the force, on the dynamics of life and of survival. Not only physically, but also emotionally and mentally.

Psychologically speaking we can see, that the psyche is putting together an 'I'-structure which wants to survive, and which wants to continue itself. It may be that, in the history of mankind, this has not always been the case. Perhaps then it was more a question of group-consciousness or, if you like, of tribal consciousness. But even so, as a group, as a tribe, it wanted to survive. Along with the 'envelopment' of the individual, of the self-consciousness, and of its continuation, to have an 'opinion of one's own'—a specific way of looking at things that is altogether conditioned—has become important in an unprecedented way. Of course, such an 'opinion of one's own' has been distilled entirely from circumstances, from second-hand information, and so on. Yet it remains a remarkable phenomenon, that man wants to have an opinion 'of his own'. The forming of an opinion, this 'wanting to have an opinion of his own', this specific way of looking at things, is also responsible for the fact, that we select friends who hold views that are similar to ours, while our enemies are those whose views do not agree with ours.

And then there is the façade of tolerance, usually for the sake of a proper appearance, which is often nothing more than the civilized recognition of division. In this way we acknowledge each other's views, while fighting the views of others, when these do not coincide with ours. In all sorts of ways: through daily papers, magazines, (tele)vision, politics, religion, and so on. As such there is nothing to object to, because man's inclination to belong to a group with the same vision is something quite natural. However, there is a snake in the grass, which is that we become so incredibly identified with what we call 'our' view, 'our' opinion, and 'our' ideas that, in the long run, we will no longer be fully alive to the reality at all, blinded as we have become by purely mental gymnastics. Such routine identification makes us stupid, crippled, insensitive and aggressive and, when the conflict comes to a head, we are prepared to cut each other's throat.

This is a given fact that we may come across anywhere—it is not the particular view of the speaker. Because of the fact that views mainly occur within the thinking mind, it is difficult to see through them. Of the three combining forces of body, thinking and feeling, thinking is the most subtle one. And, being the subtlest of the three, it is the most difficult one to see through. Not in the last place because we want to see through it by using thinking *itself*. However, thinking cannot see through anything, for thinking *is* being seen. Thinking doesn't see anything of its own. Each thought is being perceived within something *other* than thinking as such. Thinking is only an *aspect* of existence.

No doubt thinking is necessary. Yet thinking cannot solve your existential problems for the simple reason, that thinking *is* creating the problems. The problem faced by man is neither thinking nor feeling, neither his body nor the world, but the measure in which he is identified with these. The whole problem is one of identification: man's fundamental dichotomy.

In language we come across the word 'holy', which is derived originally from 'being whole'—not split. Of course this has nothing to do with the so-called saints, thrust upon us by religion. To be whole, or to be holy, means to be one, undivided, non-fragmentary; a mind which is not split. The word 'individual' also denotes the same thing, namely 'un-divided'. Today the word 'individual' is particularly charged with the sense of having an identity with opinions and ideas and ways of one's own. Whereas my meaning of the word 'individual' is someone who is *undivided*, of one piece, not divided into body, mind and feeling or, in other words, not *identified* with body, mind and feeling.

By their very nature body, mind and feeling want to manifest and survive themselves. This is observable; you can't have any moral objections to it. For example, such a deep-rooted urge to survive is expressed quite clearly in the case of suicide. Whenever anybody wants to put an end to his life, he has to take very drastic measures. He cannot simply jump into the water. The bulk of the body has to be made heavier by means of a millstone or some other heavy object, otherwise the body will begin to swim all the same, despite the resolution of wanting to die.

Life wants to manifest itself, and everything stands at the service of that manifestation. That is how matters stand, nobody excepted. Of course, you may just try to run away from this given fact, but in that case it is bound to raise its head at some other place.

A woman who, for instance, identifies herself with the idea of womanhood being enslaved by a men's world and, therefore, with the need to be 'liberated', will identify herself with the world of feminism. On the other hand a woman who prefers to follow a different model and who identifies herself with that model, for example, through a stylish and modern look, will probably feel more at home with fashion shows and aerobic dancing. Both, however, are forms of manifestation based on the notion of, 'I am this', or, 'I am that'.

Visitor: I have the idea that most of us have a feeling that life isn't worthwhile, not to speak of any destructive feelings and frustrations. With the acceptance of existence, does one stand a better chance to survive?

A: One could well imagine that, the moment when all is clear and there is total acceptance, there would no longer be any reason, any motive left for being afraid in the event of one's passing away and disappearing, for to die is to disappear. The organism of body-mind-feeling might well respond favourably to it. You could possibly become very old that way. But the reverse is not unthinkable either.

There are people in psychiatric asylums who become very old, probably because they do not share certain concerns with us, in particular those of this world. The same holds good for monasteries and for prisons as well, because, obviously, everything is terribly regulated there, very sober, and so there are few stimuli that would break up the organism. By the way, I gather from your remark that you have a sneaking hope of standing an even better chance for survival, once you have attained 'the insight'. Am I guessing right?

V: Yes, I reckon so.

A: You must be careful so as not to fall into the trap of hope's strategy again, the hope for 'better', for 'different', etc. The only thing which is required of you is to realize how, through your own strategies, you are constantly blocking yourself. Don't rely on any path, method or strategy in this matter. In the end this whole 'searching for' is... a survival strategy that is maintaining itself. Existence is everywhere: no need to search for it! The seeking takes place in the sought. Don't be fooled by the thinking mind which is always after 'better', 'faster', 'more efficient'. Your whole thinking as you experience it now, is trained for defense and is at the service of your defense.

V: Looking at it from your point of view, we must be real big oafs by coming to you, instead of going for a walk in the woods and enjoy nature.

A: Enjoy your true nature. As long as you haven't solved the little riddle of your existence, you cannot but go and search for that which you believe to be seeking. Even going for a walk in nature is not going to give you any joy. You might even see the trees as an invitation to hang yourself.

There are two kinds of people, broadly speaking. One very big group has found an identity for themselves already, is more or less content with that, and will hardly ask themselves any questions. An other group, much smaller in number, is vaguely anxious about themselves, living in a shadow of disquiet and dissatisfaction. These people are wondering: Is this all there is? What is the sense of being born, of living for a while, and of dying a nobody? What is the purpose of life? Who *am* I?

To that group of people I am addressing myself. The first group of people is already happy, and is already walking in the woods, even though they don't see the wood for the trees. That you would all be real big oafs is quite a different matter. I can't detect any identities and, therefore, no 'oaf identities' either.

(19th December, 1982, afternoon)

15

LIFE SHOWS ITSELF IN A PARADOX

Visitor: How will I know that my seeking, along with the construction, 'I perceive that I am perceiving', has come to an end? For that is what's running through my head all the time... You once said, 'Just see whether it is true that you are the effortless perceiver.' But, then, that too is being registered again, and then I think, 'Now I'm perceiving it.' And that observation, in turn, is also perceived by me, and so on and so forth.

Alexander: So you would like to know when that is going to stop? When you won't be thinking about it any more?

V: Yes, I would.

A: It won't be clear to you as long as you are thinking about it. For in that case there is a thought feeding an other thought, and then you will find yourself in a vicious circle. Sometimes very drastic measures are required to break through that circuit. Certain schools of Zen specialize in it, and so do certain forms of *jnana yoga*.
    It may well happen that a teacher will tempt you to develop all your concepts along one particular line—for instance via logical reasoning—so that, in the best of cases, you are left with one basic concept to satisfy the intellect. For example the thought, 'I am the witness.' Then the teacher will leave you to sink, to settle

down into that thought completely, in the idea that *that* is the root of your existence. So you're feeling quite happy, as you have the idea that all is going quite well with you, and that you have almost grasped the matter. And then... one fine day, the opposite is penetrated so deeply into you, with such power, that the two opposites have become equal. Occasionally this may lead to the sudden insight that is sought for. In a sense the world has disappeared then, as the two opposites, being under high pressure, have collapsed into one. Henceforth you are forever free from all useless thinking, and clarity remains. That is what may happen through Zen, through certain forms of Tantra, as well as through some specific forms of *jnana*.

V: It seems to me that such a thing cannot be brought about by oneself.

A: Quite true. That is why in the East, and in the past in the West as well, the guru has got that function. It is the job of the guru.

A different approach, although based on the same principle, is that you get a response from the teacher, which will act as a direct opposite to everything you are communicating to him. Normally we like to see that the latest discoveries regarding ourselves are confirmed by someone else. Usually this is the teacher. In such a case the teacher uses the strategy of the opposite, so that your 'own viewpoint' becomes unsettled. For, more often than not, the things which you get to hear from the teacher, are made into a certain viewpoint by you, into a concept. Until you get enough of it, realizing that no single 'view' fits existence. After that it will no longer be possible for you to employ any viewpoint whatsoever, whether it is to confirm your existence or to deny it. Once such a situation is created by the guru, clarity remains. In India there are known to be 139 such ways for making it clear to the disciple what he is. Each teacher has got his 'own' kind of way.

Then there is yet an other approach, which is one of total surrender. However, many disciples have great difficulty with this approach, because the surrender goes as far as their fear. In an age like ours, where reason takes a central place, it may be that total surrender is asking a bit too much.

V: You are talking about 'surrender', but surrender to what?

A: To the guru. But, especially in the West, this has become a delicate question. Automatically there is the thought of a Jim Jones[4] etc. Despite all that, total surrender is a very special path. In India this approach is known as *bhakti yoga*. When you are able to love somebody with all your heart and being, then it will no longer be difficult to love the rest of the world as well. Love, total surrender, is a form of suicide, a form of eliminating yourself. Elimination of your false self-images, to be sure. Even in 'worldly love' you see the wonderful phenomenon of love conquering everything.

Listening, too, in the true sense of the word, is a form of love. Maybe the most important point of these meetings is the quality of one's listening, and the love that one is able to show in listening. To listen is to open oneself. To the majority of us applies, that we need a lot of words before we understand. Whereas, ultimately, a good listener has no more need of words.

At some stage you will notice, that you no longer need to *think* any more about those so-called spiritual subjects whatsoever. For, then, a deeper sense of understanding is born. In the face of such true understanding, any interest in spirituality and freedom that is prompted by thinking, will have disappeared completely. Then real freedom and spirituality are born.

I don't encourage anyone to become spiritual or religious. You can't 'become' religious and begin to live 'religiously' anyway. Life *is* religion. Life is religion, because life *is* not split, but whole. As a 'person' you just cannot become religious or practise religion—It is a façade! Again, you can't *do* yoga. Yoga and religion mean the same thing: to join what is divided. But reality *is* not split. That is why each form of 'treading the path' is the putting up of a façade.

If you identify yourself with such spirituality in all its crazy forms, you will become an enjoyer of yourself. An enjoyer of states of mind, of states of consciousness. Then you are feasting on your own state of mind: You are about to reach a climax, but that isn't giving you any *real* satisfaction, for all that only consists of ideas and fleeting patterns. Then concepts and ideas will force you into even more sophistication, still higher, even *more* absolute, even *more* holy... Obviously these are going to lead you nowhere, because the consciousness that you really *are*, remains unmoved in the face of all such *tours de force* of the intellect.

At the same time those ideas *do* transport the mind; they absorb you, and they deceive you. Whether the trick is used at the mental or at an emotional level is irrelevant—in both cases it is equally absurd.

In fact, someone who knows the natural state—and, as a matter of fact, who doesn't?—is an embarrassingly *normal* person, unacceptable to the environment who is ever keen on something extraordinary, something 'special'.

If spirituality is attended by extraordinary matters such as miracles, rapture and special powers, then it is accepted, then it will receive public approval. But what's more ordinary than life? Life is the most ordinary and, at the same time, the most curious thing you know. Life shows itself in a paradox.

(16th March, 1983)

16

A PERFECT BALANCE IS NEVER EXPERIENCED

Visitor: I understand that you prefer not to speak about social issues nor about problems dealing with relationships, or any such things. Nevertheless, could you offer a solution for the enormous problems in the world and in society? What scope does the individual have in it?

Alexander: A possible solution for the problems in society is, in the first place, to be totally free from any interests and greed oneself. A co-operation may be established at the very moment when two persons or parties have the same goal in view, but without the 'I'-structure having any interest in it. As soon as no further personal interests are involved, 'it' happens of its own accord. Even on a minor scale this may be observed. When personal pressure is off the kettle, everything may be accomplished in a spirit of true relaxation. Then, in a sense, everything is accomplishing itself.

Whenever personal interests are at stake, any relationship will be cumbersome and heavy. A relationship then becomes an unwieldy institution, devoid of any lightness. But if the presence of a deeper awareness of freedom appears, then the magic of the relationship will automatically return. The magic in a relationship will disappear, because there are obstacles standing in the way of relating to one another. The deeper awareness causes the obstacles to evaporate. Once a relationship is made static as a result of interests, greed, rights, and the assassin of the 'I'-structure, you know yourself to be in a cumbersome and heavy movement. The art of being in a relationship with persons and things is that the flow—which is the one characteristic of being in a relationship—is not made static. This is asking for alertness and attention. The awareness in freedom is not to be mistaken for just doing what you feel like, which is considered to be the highest form of freedom by many people.

It may be that, in such matters, it is more difficult to find one's way these days, since any frame of reference in the form of parents who may serve as a role model, or an educator, a vicar or a parish priest, has more or less fallen away. On the whole one is no longer looking into that direction and, as a consequence, people nowadays have to sort things out for themselves. Perhaps for the first time in history man stands alone in this respect, despite his many congeners. Anyway, while living one's life, one learns how to live.

V: Doesn't a lot of misery derive from the fact that everybody, as an individual, is trying to attain to individual freedom?

A: Individual freedom doesn't exist, because the individual, as we have created it, doesn't exist. It is a delusion. All so-called complexity is the result of the sexual energy and its manifestation. The continuation of the manifestation is effected through the sexual energy. Suppose there wouldn't be any more sexuality for the next hundred years, then all of the so-called global problems would be solved literally within a hundred years' time. In other words, there wouldn't be any more people left; the whole 'world' issue would be solved. He who has fathomed the mystery of the sexual energy, has fathomed the mystery of existence. He has understood everything in the true sense of the term. If my father and mother had not been there, and they had not had that union, then the manifestation of me as you are now seeing it before you, would not have been possible—at least not in this form. That seems pretty obvious to me. And this holds good for all of us. The mystery lies with conception.

V: Still, as individuals we are all different from one another, aren't we? How should I deal with that? What is my destination?

A: To dance the dance of life: That is your destination. You are the remembrance of your parents. Your body resembles that of your parents, it is the remembrance of them. The mystery has become manifest in you, and it is dancing its little dance. Life is dancing itself to its very end—such is its nature.

V: But in the mean time the body is there, acting and living its life all the same, with all the consequences of it.

A: What do you want me to do about it? The world becomes manifest in the form of the pairs of opposites. Pleasant and unpleasant go hand in hand; in fact, they are inseparable.

V: Pleasant and unpleasant may go hand in hand, but when you've got to live with a very troublesome person by your side, then I find that actually quite hard—It certainly isn't pleasant!

A: Have you come here to complain? Suppose everything would be pleasant, then you wouldn't know what pleasant was. You wouldn't have a frame of reference, and so there wouldn't be anything to compare it with. Pleasant and unpleasant go together. If everything was tiresome, then you also wouldn't be able to recognize what tiresome was. The pairs of opposites themselves make you aware. That is how matters stand. They always go together, inseparable. That is why truth has to be looked for beyond the pairs of opposites. You can be conscious of something only because duality is there. You just cannot escape it. And you can't escape it because of the simple fact, that there is no escape from duality. If you cannot accept duality, you are swimming against the stream.

Duality, however, is born within non-duality. There nothing is left to be divided or to be split; you can't go any further. If you do not want to accept duality, that is to say the world of name and form, you will stay at the level of a puling child that isn't getting another biscuit—the child that is crying, because the vegetables on its plate are encroaching on the potatoes, without any clear partition being left between them... with the result that dramas are created about such questions as to whether the gravy that is to go with the hotchpotch should or should not be poured into the little hole at the centre of it. All of that turns out to be highly important then. For the child it is perfectly all right, yet for an adult all that may seem somewhat infantile.

If you could really see that your existence—which includes everything—is the sexual energy made manifest, that everything is dancing its little dance: in death and in life, in children, in flowers, and in animals; in clouds, and in seas, in planets and in whatever you like, then what would *you* want to change in it? Do you have any hold on reality? You are like the ant that lifts itself from the ant-hill, calling out, 'Hey, God! Do you want to box?'

V: Do you mean that we ought to strive for harmony instead? That I do recognize, for within me there is a permanent quest to achieve harmony.

A: To strive for harmony—and for certain people this may be a hard nut to crack—is for those who are living in a deep coma. The natural state is perfect already. To strive for harmony is turning the world upside down. Maybe there is a tendency towards peace and amity, but the reality is turmoil and war. What you want is harmony, but it never is going to be harmonious. For life proves to be a movement which is seeking for a balance of its own accord. Perfect harmony and balance, if at all possible, would be your death. Indeed, the bigger the fluctuations, the more intensely conscious you are. Because of the opposites.

There where everything is harmonious and in balance, there one will eventually fall asleep through a lack of life. Too much of harmony is always dull and boring. You have to be a fan of it. Nothing bores you as quickly as harmony and balance. It is precisely the fluctuations which make life interesting. And it may well be that, when you will have reached this so-called balance—which is more likely to be a standstill and a false certainty created by thinking—you will then have manoeuvred yourself into a crisis, as you have left to one side the shady side of yourself thanks to your models of harmony. Mechanisms like body, mind and feeling want to survive and to continue themselves *by nature*. The self, *of its own accord*, is looking for a balance *already*. If you have been eating too much, then the mechanism will want to take rest. If you are eating too little, then the mechanism will go in search of food. If you are in balance, then you won't or will hardly be aware of the mechanism.

In fact, a perfect balance would never be experienced, because in that case there are no more opposites. What *may* be experienced is the *temporary* absence of the pairs of opposites. Then your true nature comes to light just for a second. On the other hand the condition of being *out* of balance is experienced as an alarm-signal in order to restore a certain balance. To seek a balance is to bring the opposite poles into equilibrium. Based on the experience of the pairs of opposites something within you may be telling you: 'I want this', or, 'I want that'. But what you do not see is, that all happens of its *own* accord: There *is* no 'I' that is able to, or that is going to restore anything. You are the perceivingness of all perceivable processes. Everything is looking for a balance of its own accord.

(23rd March, 1983)

17

IN ORDER TO BE WHAT YOU ARE YOU NEED NOT DO ANYTHING

Alexander: Why do you come here? What is the use of coming to listen to these talks according to you? Meetings such as these become a habit, they soon become an institution, thus easily defeating their objective.

Visitor: The purpose of my coming is that I want to reflect on what is being discussed here. What interests me most is what true consciousness really is. I understand from your words that it is one's very self. That all of us have come from one big whole and are speaking from that whole; that consciousness manifests itself in human beings as thinking, feeling and acting... That one can choose, and that there is an energy which may become condensed or dilated... Do we actually have a choice? In fact, I get quite confused by the things which I'm hearing from you.

A: If you don't mind, let us first go back to the question as to what consciousness really is. The difficulty, when you want to describe the heart of the matter, is that you are always making use of limited means. To describe consciousness is only possible in terms of the known, and in fragments. If you would make the effortless effort to see and to understand truly, then you would be able to see that everything you know or may know is perceived every moment without any effort. This manifested consciousness manifests itself in everything. As soon as you go and do something with it, as a particle of the whole, as a 'person', as an 'I', then you are dividing that which is whole. Then one part is trying to comprehend the other. That way it becomes a jugglery. This jugglery, too, is perceived, and then you wonder what you can do about it. Well, nothing. It is doing itself. In any case, what you can see is, that without the least exertion you are perfectly effortlessly aware, conscious of the manifested world. When you have seen through the habit of interweaving yourself with everything that moves, suffering ends. If there is anything to be done at all, then this is the only thing you can do: To be what you are, and for that you don't need to do anything.

Whoever attempts to grasp consciousness by words or concepts will, sooner or later, be left empty-handed. And since you *don't* like to be left empty-handed, you are filling conscious being with delusion and nonsense. With descriptions, philosophies, explanations—always necessarily in terms of the known, of things perceived by you. Yet long before you set out to describe conscious being, conscious being was there already. Eventually you will discover that the very substance by which you are attempting to describe consciousness, consists of nothing but conscious being.

Take a sheet of white paper. Is it possible to write down anything on the paper without the white background? The words need to have the paper, but the paper doesn't need the words. It's the words that need to have a background. So the contents of consciousness needs to have consciousness in order to manifest itself. The paper is white, but the characters are black. You wouldn't be able to see white characters on a white sheet of paper. Such a contrast is necessary in order to get the message across. Words want to communicate something, to refer to something. The contents of consciousness is needed for consciousness to express itself. That is how the manifested and the unmanifested are connected. A film is best projected on a white screen. The images are moving, but the screen remains unmoved and is not concerned with the film. Yet it is indispensable. It leaves the screen indifferent as to what is being projected onto it, the screen only makes it possible: The screen is the availability. And of course, there is the light-factor. Without the light even the screen would not be visible.

V: But then, what does it mean 'to experience'?

A: Even before you have made a concept of what it is 'to experience', experiencing is already there. It is each man's basic given fact: awareness. Some call it consciousness, cognitiveness, or knowingness: These are all words for the same thing. All things pleasant and unpleasant are sensations, and they only become possible through awareness. Take away awareness and all is gone. If you are not aware of something, then it also doesn't exist for you.

When you go to see a doctor and tell him, 'I have got a pain here', you can only say so, because you are aware of that pain and are able to locate it. But the awareness itself you are not able to locate. Even a baby is able to scratch at the exact spot where it is itching. That awareness is the fundamental given fact of existence. Even in order to be able to doubt it, awareness has got to be there already. Nothing is possible without awareness. It is your only link with so-called reality. Within that problems occur, as well as happiness, listlessness, boredom, power, rapture—in short, everything. As soon as awareness falls away, the world falls away. We do so many things, still all those things are simply and solely possible because of that awareness.

What is important for you to see is, that awareness isn't a problem. What seems to be a problem is *becoming* aware. Man seems to be entangled in his sensations, in his probabilities. Somehow or other he has got himself involved in awareness' contents. Just consider a current situation: You are meeting with an other person, in fact, quite a beautiful person. And you are totally overcome, you are overflowing with feelings. A mysterious happening is taking place. Now, how do you know all those things? Because you are conscious of them. But for you the matter doesn't end there. Somehow or other, something is there within you—your self-consciousness—that is completely or partly being carried away by the event. Whether it is happiness or anger or depression, it makes no difference, because all such movements are essentially the same. Only the one is charged positively and the other negatively.

As long as experiences are pleasant, you say, 'I'm so happy. Ah, what a blessing! If only I could stay this happy!' But as soon as you have an uncomfortable experience, a feeling of frustration, then at once you want to get rid of it. However, happiness and unhappiness always go together. That is also the reason why you're stepping into a trap, when you get all ecstatic when, for example, you've just discovered something interesting about yourself. So, then you have discovered that, and immediately you go into ecstasy. The ecstasy as such is not a problem at all, if only the matter ended there! But you are transported by it. You are carried away by it. *You* appear on the scene and at once, immediately, there is the identification with this 'you'. The ecstasy or the pleasant sensation is not the problem, whereas the identification with the 'person' is. If only you could see things in their true perspective as manifested consciousness, then everything would be just fine. But out of sheer habit you will go and establish yourself completely in this 'you', thus making the identification complete again. However, whatever goes up must also come down, for such is the law. In fact, there are two forces: The one pulls you up, and the other pulls you down. And then there is the devil to pay! The whole point is to let all the movements within the manifestation—both positive and negative—tell their story from your centre of awareness, your silent centre.

Take for instance jealousy, a destructive force. All right, you are totally jealous. A huge shot of energy throws you off your centre, at least so it seems. Then, ten minutes after the event, you say to yourself, 'I should not have been jealous', because you were trained to react and label such an emotion as being 'no good'. Yet the fact is, that you were conscious of an enormous jealousy. So you can't very well get away from it. Everybody saw it, including yourself! Now, in order to go on wriggling your way out of it, you need to play a good many tricks. Therefore, just look that jealousy straight into the eyes and stop running around it. Don't try to change it or to excuse it in any way. Just be that jealousy completely...

At that very moment, however, you will have to pay full attention, for then attentiveness is what you will need most. In that instant of enormous jealousy there is no longer any separation between you and this jealousy: At that moment you are that jealousy. But then, the next moment, you're saying to yourself, 'I should not have been jealous', or, 'I'm now learning to accept it', or, 'I'm already making good progress', etc. Now, what is being said here is: Stay right in the essence, and just look from the essence at what exactly is happening there. So even more stepping back than you have ever done before. And you can go back much further, for there is plenty of room in that awareness. Awareness is the very space in which everything appears.

The question, therefore, is: Are you capable of being aware, meaning here and now, consciously of what is happening, without wanting to change, deform or transform it?

Here we have come to a point which is of great importance, as there is a lot of misunderstanding regarding this phenomenon: Looking at it from the standpoint from where the conflicts occur, you would argue that such centeredness is a matter of practice. You would swear that such centeredness could be acquired, or in any case be stabilized. However, this is something you cannot practise. If I may invite you to look in the manner just indicated here, then it would appear that you could actually practise this centeredness. That you could actually teach yourself to live from this centre. But that is a standpoint, a viewpoint, a conditioning. It may appear to be so, but that is not the reality.

The ground of your existence, that from which everything originates, this silent, imperturbable being, is ever conscious of itself. With or without problems. That conscious being is always there, even when you are supposed to be unconscious, which is impossible. All the movements which you call 'life' are perceived within that still, conscious being. But there is not a 'somebody' there, who is perceiving something. The 'person' who is supposed to perceive something, is the perceiving itself, which is not an activity, but perfect silence. This seeing does not exclude anything, whereas thinking does.

When you are walking down the street, for example, you can observe that there are certain sounds that are not pleasant to you, which is not unthinkable in a big city. Now, just compare it to when you are walking through the city, and you are in love. Then you would be walking quite differently through the same city. Is the street different? No, everything is the same. Is the traffic less hectic? No, even more hectic than usual. Are the sounds different? No, everything is the same, and yet... It is because *you* are different: your attitude is different.

Just walk down the street and hear the sounds, allow them. Listen as if you were hearing them for the first time. Allow life to be, don't resist what is. Accept the primary given datum, then you will feel that something is changing in favour of life and of you.

It is your particular vision which makes that something is nice or not nice, good or bad. By realizing that, you are not going to be changed into a zombie or a softie, but you will recognize yourself to be the one who is causing the problem. Even so, it may well be that certain sounds will still be unpleasant, that they do grate on your ears, but it's no longer going to be a drama, rather a simple given fact. But the way your perception is now, you will always be running behind the reality. Your life is one big fight against the natural laws and against the so-called reality as it appears to you. Life happens to you. All you can do is to be available. That availability is the natural state, as receptive as a womb—feminine.

The point is this: Can you be exactly what you are, without wanting to change or maim or interpret it? The reality which is happening to you, can you take it exactly as it is?

V: I really don't know.

A: Just see how much preoccupied you are—how full of prejudice. With notions that have got nothing to do with the reality. That's what's making you suffer—It is your own doing. The reality is there all along, but it is being veiled by ideas and concepts of your own to which you apparently prefer to give your attention instead. As a result it would seem as if you are not capable of seeing the reality—natural existence—which is there without any friction.

V: Should I then surrender myself to the moment itself?

A: There is no such thing as 'surrendering to the moment'. That is a myth. Just *because* you are conscious being, the moment surrenders itself to *you*. But you refuse stubbornly; you say no, you fend off. Everything in nature is pressing to reveal itself to your mind's eye, but you shut yourself up in a cocoon of self-images and delusion—of, 'It is this, and not that'... Such is the mechanism of the discriminating consciousness which you appear to be identified with. You are swimming like a salmon against the stream.

V: It is very easy for you to talk like that, but even so, those conditionings are playing a very important role in it. Besides, to me the breaks in the awareness you are talking about are a bit of a problem as well.

A: In awareness no break is to be found whatsoever. In attention there is, but not in awareness. Life is not enacted by fits and starts. It is one continuous whole from the moment of conception until death. And indeed, conditionings do play a role, but nothing more.

V: The phenomena that appear before me—am I also part of them?

A: As an appearance, yes. That is how you appear. But what you are is the awareness itself, and that at the same time. That is the factor which is making it all possible: the conscious being, the ever effortless one. And this constant, effortless awareness is the perspective we are discussing here; it's the reference, not the happening itself. Realize that life, including your appearance, is presenting itself to you, that it is a happening without any effort. A divine manifestation which expresses itself in the pairs of opposites. That is how God looks at himself and sees that it is good.

(30th March, 1983)

SELF-REALISATION DOES NOT NEED ANYONE'S CONFIRMATION

Alexander: Most of us are interested in Self-realisation with side-effects such as a specific experience, becoming happy, or a certain goal. Very few people are interested just to disappear, which is what Self-realisation implies: the total disappearing of the known, and in the first place the disappearing of the personality.

Visitor: If it happens 'just like that', then you can't do anything for it? After all, it is always the 'person' who is seeking?

A: Quite right, it is the person who is seeking. But there is no relation whatsoever between the personal and the Absolute.

V: How odd.

A: It is odd, because it doesn't fit into your mental picture.

V: That applies to almost all the things you are saying.

A: I am trying to make it clear to you, that consciousness cannot be located, in no way whatsoever. It's absolutely out of the question, whatever you may do. It cannot be located anywhere. And because it cannot be located, you have an uncontrollable need to mould it into a concept. The moment you mould it into a concept and begin to live by the conviction of that concept, there arises a horrible discrepancy, which is untenable in the long run, and which will lead to suffering. And this suffering, again, will lead one to search for the source. The absurd thing about the whole story is that, in the end, you discover that consciousness actually never left you, but that, all that time, you thought it had, as in some horrible dream. Such realisation is always attended by some sort of laughing and crying at the same time, because then you see the absurdity of the whole problem. Each time when you get dangerously close to yourself, you begin to rationalize, casting things into a mould. You will begin to introduce ghosts, and ethereal and astral matters, and God knows what. You will be looking for recognition in the form of words and concepts and symbols. If you could only see what the real issue is here, you wouldn't read one more book on the subject. Why read? To see your doubts confirmed?

Self-realisation and the clarity that goes with it, does not need anyone's confirmation—absolutely nobody's. Such confirmation can never be given to you by someone else. And if at all it is to be given by someone else, then it would mean a vote of no-confidence as regards your own realisation. For that reason a guru will never tell you: 'Now you are enlightened!'

It is *you* who will ultimately prove to be the measure, which, again, will prove to be no measure at all. But—and this is happening over and over again—one is always looking for the confirmation of that about which one is ultimately *not* sure. What you are sure about does not need any confirmation whatsoever. Whenever you are not living from your own experience, from deep down, you begin to rationalize. Then you start to read books, search, and do all sorts of things. But as soon as Self-realisation, that clarity, is totally there, then you won't need anyone's confirmation. Then you fall under the free ones.

Self-Realisation Does Not Need Anyone's Confirmation

Nobody can confirm Self-realisation for you. No Ramana Maharshi, no Nisargadatta, no Krishnamurti, no Rajneesh. Nobody. The irony of the story, the absurdity, the paradox, is that, ultimately, you are your own measure, and that that isn't a measure any more. With that your existence ends. With that you have dismantled yourself, though not destroyed. With that the whole illusory figure has fallen apart and the real thing is born.

V: That does not come about through seeking?

A: The seeking proves to be the big obstacle in the end. Still, you can't stop seeking. Therefore, seek in the right manner. Look for teachers who confront you and put you into trouble, never for teachers who confirm you.

V: How do I know that I'm fit for this path?

A: You don't. The people whom I think to be unfit are turned away by me. If they search sincerely, they will certainly find somebody who can help them to take the right direction. This path is not for one and all.

V: How will I know who I really am, if I can only know what I am *not*?

A: What you are cannot be located. At the same time it is there, life-size, as your essence. But it can never be located. You may be able to locate an object, but not consciousness. Where could consciousness be located?

V: Are there any dangers on the road to Self-realisation?

A: There is only one danger, which is the threat of losing your life. And you will mobilize everything to prevent that. The guru cuts off all the escape routes; that is all the work he does. The teacher may put the question before you: What are you busy doing? What effect did the search have on you? Has the clarity come? Did your teachers and gurus give you enlightenment? Where do you stand? Those are the basic questions. 'Who are you?' 'What is consciousness?' 'Why are you here?' They apply to everybody.

You need to give yourself completely. Therefore, one basic question is: Are you prepared to give yourself *completely*?

V: I really want to know what I'm not.

A: Everything that can be made into an object is what you are not. What is preventing you to be who you are, are your investments. If you want to realize what is being said here, then you will have to stop making any more concessions. Accept everything that may come on your path. But, then, you don't want to take the consequences of it! At a certain point you will have to recognize that the only way is to stand by your own inner truth, without making any further concessions. Whoever does so will find himself to be back in the clarity which he is. If you eliminate everything that is *not* real, truth will remain.

Jnana is a path without compromise. So be serious about your business. Drop everything that is false about you, then what you *are* will remain. More often than not the 'dropping' is a painful matter, though to some it may come as a relief. But in either case the false has to fall off.

A big problem to most of you is the fact, that you have been listening to people who claim that Self-realisation is very hard to attain, and that you will have to achieve ever so many things for it. What *I* am saying here is exactly the opposite.

Self-realisation is not difficult, but you tire yourself out by only talking about it. It is trendy to twaddle about Self-realisation. But as soon as you are *really* being confronted by Self-realisation, you take to your heels. Ask yourself what you *really* want, look at it from all angles, and stop making concessions. That is what you lack.

What you lack is this non-concessive approach, and a teacher who won't come up with any nonsense. But most of you believe that the road inwards could actually be bought.

You may be prepared to sniff at it and maybe have a little nibble at it. But that someone would actually come and have the whole meal of this message... that's extremely rare.

(2nd March, 1985)

19

WHAT YOU ARE CANNOT BE LOCATED

Alexander: One of the most startling discoveries of most seekers after truth is the fact that consciousness is not to be located anywhere, absolutely nowhere. This discovery causes many seekers to be unnecessarily anxious, uncertain. For that reason Advaita will never become very popular, for there is little you can 'do' with abstractions. Even at a very high level—if you can speak of levels at all—there will still continue to be a profound need to hold within oneself that which cannot possibly be grasped by words and structures, and to give it a form in some way or another. However, the description or the definition or the understanding will always remain an *object* of consciousness, which cannot be located. Therefore, no description or definition can be considered to be the truth. Thoughts or emotions or the body may be located, but not consciousness itself. Perhaps that is why death, to the majority of us, is the most frightening and uncertain thing you can imagine. Because through death you threaten to fall back into that very 'non-located-ness'.

Your real nature cannot be located and, therefore, it cannot be experienced either. Whatever you experience, it can never be your real nature, however wonderful it may be. Wherever you may look, your real nature cannot be perceived, neither inside nor outside you. It cannot be located anywhere. Nor is consciousness all-penetrating, for in that case it would seem that, apart from consciousness, there would still be something else, different from consciousness, which could then be penetrated. It is similar to the idea, that the universe would be suspended within something else. That which is the absolute condition for all ideas, that which precedes and goes beyond all ideas, cannot be grasped by any idea; it cannot be comprehended. That in which comprehension and non-comprehension become manifest, is what you are, but what you will never be able to see. And the paradox is that, when you see that you can never grasp it, then you are free. But there the matter does not end.

Those among us who are quite familiar with Advaita, are already free from this need to comprehend. Indeed, you come to a point when you know that there isn't anything to comprehend, but at the same time you are not yet free from 'not-comprehending'. You already know what you are *not*, but at the same time you do not know what you *are*. As a result you may actually feel yourself to be even more entangled than when you seemed to comprehend, that there wasn't anything to comprehend! So now the matter has become even more absurd. For that reason during these days we will focus entirely on the need to be free from both comprehending and not-comprehending.

Consciousness cannot be located and, for most of you, that is something scary. To vanish into 'nothingness' seems quite weird, although no one can escape it. Again, this 'nothing' or 'not-anything' is the availability itself.

Visitor: Isn't it the same situation as when the body hadn't come into existence yet?

A: Did you read that somewhere?

V: As a matter of fact, I have been thinking about it. Before the body came into existence, there wasn't any location either.

A: Let us limit ourselves to the present. Is it possible to indicate a location now? That which you are cannot be located, whereas the body can be located. Before you were conceived, and now, and after you will have passed away, consciousness was and is not to be located, not to be made into an object. Yet we try to give it a place—somewhere in the body or in the soul or in the mind—and to project continuity into something that does not know any continuity.

V: I feel that there is a strong need in me to hold on to something or other.

A: Yes, as an object you will have that need. But, as consciousness, can you hold on to something? As a body you can hold on to a tree, but as consciousness? To what? And if such a thing isn't possible, then what are the consequences of that? Or are there no consequences?

V: I have no idea. But, in that case, how can you speak and ask about Self-realisation?

A: All you do is talking *about* Self-realisation, talking *about* gurus, talking *about* enlightenment, talking *about* Advaita and *jnana*.

V: I mean that, in that case, there is actually no need for realisation as such, for what is there to be realized?

A: That realisation *is* the realisation! That which you are *is* already realized; it is the nearest thing possible. But because you are living, you have the experience as if that is *not* the case. It is an unendurable cramp-condition. So automatically you will begin to long for the original state, your real home—consciousness. On top of that you have been made to believe that the natural state is some kind of supernatural, almost unattainable state, something incredibly special.

V: As a matter of fact, I do believe it to be something quite special.

A: It is neither special nor non-special. The only problem with Self-realisation is, that you insist on experiencing that state as an 'I', as a 'person', as an 'experiencer'.

V: But then, that is the one who goes in search after all?

A: Nevertheless it is not that which will find itself as itself. When you go in search, then there is supposed to be a seeker, who is going in search from point A to point B. The seeker is supposed to believe that there is a *here* and a *there*, and above all, that it is to be found *there*. I may point out to you that both 'here' and 'there' are locations which you have constructed out of your particular way of thinking. Whatever you may do, you are always *here*. Yet 'here' *itself* cannot be located.

Everybody is terribly fascinated by what is happening at the level of images and feelings, or—if one isn't all that concerned with oneself—by what is happening 'in the world'. That world, however, is an extension piece of the senses. What should happen is, that once and for all the fact is brought home to you, that *you* are the essence *in* everything. That you are *not* all the little fragments, bits and pieces which you take yourself to be. When you make a seeker of yourself—who is a fragment by definition—you manoeuvre yourself into a most precarious situation. When the seeker is eliminated through a thorough enquiry, the Real reveals itself. The Real cannot be eliminated. Nor is the Real to be located anywhere. That is why Self-realisation is not an experience. Experiences may be there, but, by themselves, they are not the realisation. For everything that is an experience, is a temporary matter, and anything temporary can never be the Ultimate, the Absolute.

V: How do you mean, 'It is not an experience'? Can it not be perceived at all, then?

A: Whatever is made into an experience is, by definition, an object of perception, and therefore temporary. Don't get me wrong: I have no objection against experiences whatsoever—the more beautiful, the better! But what I'm saying is, that no experience can ever be the Ultimate. The only thing which is not temporary, and which, by definition, does not have any form, is the Absolute. With that it labels itself as 'non-experiential'.

V: Are you saying that the 'experience-less' *does* have something to do with enlightenment?

A: In that case enlightenment or Self-realisation, as words, lose their meaning completely. For then you have made the word 'enlightenment', 'liberation', 'freedom', into the thing itself. You have got yourself entangled in words, and in the idea that the word must invariably be linked to an experience. J. Krishnamurti is absolutely right when he says, 'The word is not the thing'. The *word* 'enlightenment' doesn't stand for the enlightenment itself, the *word* 'love' is not love, the *word* 'door' is not the door. At the most words may be references to something else. How would *you*, having disappeared as the *experiencer*, have an experience? It is unbelievably simple to be yourself. But to be yourself as a 'person', or to become enlightened or find freedom as a 'person', is impossible.

Yet you insist on participating in freedom and enlightenment as a 'person'. The entire search consists of your projecting a goal for yourself. However, once you have found 'it', it will no longer be possible to divide yourself up into little pieces and project a goal for yourself. Then you will know: I am everything and everybody and, at the same time, nobody, not-any-body. But I am certainly *not* an 'enlightened person' *nor* a 'not-enlightened person'. In Advaita we call it *'neti-neti'*. If you want to express it in words and images, you can only do so in terms of negation: neither this, nor that. So don't think you are *not* enlightened or that you *are* enlightened: You are neither.

When the whole search for enlightenment and non-enlightenment has disappeared, there is a stillness. Within that stillness you will not be able to locate your true nature—neither as experiential nor as non-experiential. Because then you are *everything*.

V: So, as long as you are seeking, you haven't reached it?

A: As long as you are seeking, you are projecting a goal for yourself. But you are always *already* there! It is out of the question for you *not* to be there already.

V: If you are not seeking any more...

A: If you are not seeking any more, then the mental movements have gone and there will be total silence.

V: Then you are almost there.

A: You are *always* already there! How many times do I have to tell you?! But you as a 'person', as a collection of impressions and data, are *not* always there. For that section there isn't any hope for liberation and enlightenment. On the other hand, the Being as 'I am' is always there.

V: So, as long as you are seeking...

A: As long as you are seeking you are not seeing from the unfathomable, not to be located, homogeneous Presence. As long as you keep on searching outside yourself and inside yourself, you will never discover what your real basis is. In that case you are like a fish in the ocean, who is asking an other fish, 'Do you know where the ocean is?'

This Being is ever present without any effort whatsoever. The guru points this Being out to you, pure and simple.

(2nd March, 1985)

20

WHAT DO YOU *REALLY* WANT?

Visitor: I would like to be established in the knowingness that you are often referring to.

Alexander: See what prevents you from doing so, and do not deny that.

V: Would one be able to speak from a deeper intuition, and could such deep intuition be a path leading to the higher consciousness? What I mean is: Can I be totally open to the other and to myself?

A: All that is New Age babbling, Aquarius conspiracies, wanting to improve the world—That is not what we are referring to here. It is very important first to discover for yourself what direction you want to take. Whether you really don't want to be a secret world-reformer, or a 'connector', or a 'transformer', instead of wanting Self-realisation. That has to be clear first. Do you want Self-realisation, or do you want New Age babbling and bother and change the world? So long as you want to improve the world, you want to improve yourself. And so long as you want to improve yourself, you are living in a delusion, because you just don't *know* what this 'self' is. You do not know what this 'I' *is*. So you are tinkering with something of which you don't have any real idea what it is. If you would handle a car that way, you would get a good scolding. Whereas, if one starts to get busy with this 'I' or, better even, with someone else's 'I', then it is an activity which is appreciated by all. Thus all of our energy, all our intelligence—our whole investment—goes into improving others and in improving ourselves. And, ultimately, what's the result? That you are still doing exactly the same things which you did twenty years ago, only in a more complicated way. You have become more shrewd, more crafty, and you find yourself confronted with even less possibilities than twenty years ago, because you have grown older.

The question is: Can you gather enough clarity to ask yourself what you *really* want? To continue to work on an 'I' of which you haven't the faintest idea what it really is? To continue to work on a world that is merely an idea to you? To start on a 'trip' of self-improvement? Or are you looking for Self-realisation? These two things, however, have got nothing, absolutely nothing to do with each other.

V: So the deeper concern for one's inner life and for one's environment...

A: These are all movements that result from the fact that you're missing your true home. Self-realisation alone will provide that home and is self-sufficient.

V: And this so-called effacing of this 'I'...

A: There is a conscious or unconscious motive behind it. All effacing of oneself as a 'person' is prompted by some motive or other. This so-called effacing and 'de-I-ing' is essentially a false game you play, a crooked game. As a matter of fact, such a strategy for obtaining Self-realisation is an altogether hypocritical strategy.

V: Indeed, I have the feeling that the more I dig, the more I'm hitting double bottoms.

A: We shall see...

(2nd March, 1985)

21

TO LOVE IS TO GIVE — NOT TO LOVE IS TO GRAB

Alexander: The direction which these talks will take is not so much determined by me as by you. Feel free to ask what you want. Ask what your heart is prompting you, and don't imagine that questions may be stupid or of no importance.

Visitor: I have a question regarding the reality. The idea has been formed in my mind, that reality is neither 'inside' or 'outside' of me, but that the reality is a kind of background. In the case of a chair this doesn't give rise to any problems, whereas, when it comes to thoughts and feelings, it seems to do so. I can understand that both thoughts and feelings as well as the chair are objects within the Consciousness you are talking about, but, as far as feelings and thoughts are concerned, what am I to focus on from there? Should I reject everything in order to realize the Ultimate?

A: One of the most important things for you to remember is, that it is not a question of rejecting or discarding anything. Even though a thing may prove to be unreal in relation to the Ultimate, there is no question of rejecting it. It is sufficient to perceive the unreal *as* unreal. An ego or self-consciousness *cannot* be rejected, because, in the very attempt to reject it, reality is being attributed to it! Ultimately only one thing proves to be true, which is that *both* the manifested *and* the unmanifested exist. In fact, they are two sides of the same thing.

V: I can understand that, but your advice is to do an investigation into the *Real*, isn't it?

A: In that case the question that comes up is: With *what* are you going to do the investigation? With which part of the reality will you do your investigation into the reality? In fact, the investigation will be limited to the manifested. Again, that with which you are doing the investigation into so-called reality is *itself* part of that reality. And a *part* of the reality—such as body, mind, or feeling—will never be able to contain the whole. A part can never see the whole, whereas the whole can see the part. For that reason in the investigation you are asked not to identify yourself or to limit yourself to ideas and concepts only.

V: So all you can do is to remove obstacles.

A: Then it will reveal itself. Meditation and this kind of talks can help you to remove the obstacles. And there is no doubt, that a thorough investigation will prove all obstacles to be conclusions, ideas and concepts. Then the whole display of concepts will prove to have nothing to do with the reality you are looking for.

V: Then both the river and the chair will no longer prove to be an obstacle.

A: Indeed, as such they are not a problem. In spite of that we seem to have a very vivid experience of a world 'inside' the body, and an other world 'outside' of us—the inner and the outer.

He who wants to understand things truly, would be well-advised *not* to try to reveal the reality from the standpoint of thinking, feeling, or the body alone. That is why, in Advaita, the emphasis for the investigation is put on the ever-present background. Stop trying to put the Ultimate in such finite forms as body, thinking and feeling. To realize the impossibility of such a thing is a profound insight.

Always remember that there has *got* to be a background, and that it can be realized. In essence everybody *is* that Consciousness, in which everything appears and disappears. As such, you are always effortlessly aware of all of this through the immediate realisation of it. But because you are making a suspect of that which you are aware of, you are unnecessarily creating problems.

The drama is that the identification with the unreal is assuming such proportions, that it appears to turn *against* existence. The fragment, the ego, the self-consciousness, is credited with authority and power. While the 'I'-structure ought to be an auxiliary, it has become a stumbling block instead.

The mind is an auxiliary in order to be able to deal with a world of names, forms and colours, along with all its glorious possibilities. Yet it has become our enemy. Something is fundamentally wrong, and whenever anything is fundamentally wrong, you will have to be at the foundations.

V: How do you tackle that?

A: The drama appears to be that the objective world is making so many demands and is taking so much of one's time, that one doesn't seem to be able to get round to attend to any fundamental matters. The complaint which is heard all around is: I would really like to go deeper into it, I would like to do a more fundamental search, but there is the family... my job... and so forth. This situation, too, is to be appreciated to some extent, for life is so complex, that one is indeed in danger of being swallowed up by it.

We are all being swallowed up by the monster of time. That is the situation as far the limitations are concerned. For that reason certain schools chose not to have a family, and they found other solutions in the form of monasteries or *ashrams,* or by living a secluded life in the forest. But those ways of life, too, have their cares and problems.

He who is really in good earnest about this matter, will surely find time and opportunities. Even if you have clearly seen the issue but once, then the most important work is done. The realisation of that one momentless moment is what is sought for in these meetings. The realisation of that momentless moment is prevented, because almost all our attention is going into personal problems. But personal problems are but the skin of the milk! If you would actually want to do a really deep investigation, you should not search and root into what's 'personal', because then you will in fact but reinforce the strangle-hold of this 'I'.

Ultimately all such personal issues stem from the same root. It may be that in one case things manifest themselves somewhat differently from the other, but basically they come from the same source.

V: I tend to think that *my* problem is shared by a lot of people.

A: That is not an unusual projection.

V: I find that we are so much preoccupied theoretically, that feelings are kept out of it.

A: One of the things you should understand is, that there is no such thing as 'theory' and 'practice'. In fact, it is a strategy of the mind to prevent it from understanding the *real* issue. Apart from that, feeling is a most unreliable signal for doing or not doing things. For many people, in particular for women, it acts as a kind of green light in the sense of, 'It feels good, so I can do it'. Thinking and feeling are conditionings and absolutely unreliable for the kind of research we are dealing with here. Moreover, within the field of conditionings unfair advantage may easily be taken of one's gullibility and ignorance. As far as body, mind and feelings are concerned, we are an altogether chemical phenomenon. You press a button, and it begins to run and to slaver, psychologically as well. All that doesn't impress me so much. I definitely don't consider feeling to be a signal for what is good or what isn't.

V: But on the other hand that's all I've got...

A: What I want to make clear to you is precisely, that there is an area where there is *no* such deception.

V: But as long as I'm not able to *get* at that truth, all I've got is my thinking and feeling.

A: Still you cannot wash away blood with blood.

V: So, what you're saying is: Just let *go* of thinking and feeling...

A: That is not what I'm saying at all—That's what *you* are saying! That is what you've heard and read. That is what all you have collected. And I *do* know that you know all that. But here—and that is going to be your first shock—I am appealing to your *immediate* knowing, to what you *really* know *now*, apart from what you've have heard, read and accumulated. And again, if your search enters the field of the personal, you are lost, because there wrong self-love is playing first fiddle. Actually, we *like* our miseries; somehow we just love them. The situation is probably such that, the moment you wouldn't have any more problems, you wouldn't know what to do. Probably the only thing which is giving you a grip, psychologically speaking, are your problems and your worries. The first shock, therefore, is the recognition, that you actually show great interest in and love for your own problems.

V: I have really only one question to ask: What is true love?

A: Truth, love, God—These are all words for the same thing, looked at from a slightly different angle. There must have been a moment in your life that you were perfectly happy, without the support of any distraction or circumstance. Such happiness comes from a situation that is without any object: Consciousness itself, which, by definition, is without any object. *That* is what everybody knows and seeks. And why should you know it so well, and why should you recognize it as the true thing? Because it is your real nature.

That happiness you are only able to recognize, because a contrast appears wherever that happiness is *not* present. That is why the Self-realized man rarely experiences such intense, deep feeling of happiness, because that is what is constantly known by him anyway. And because in his case it is something constant, and therefore continuously present, it is no longer experienced by him as such. Happiness needs to have an opposite in order to be recognized. In fact, such happiness is an expression of the profound essence—of that serenity and clarity—at the level of body, mind and feelings.

True happiness is always without any object. Deep in your heart you know it. And so long as you have not yet been grounded in the objectless Being, as long as there is identification, there will be bother. Though in reality—and this needs to be said again—it is impossible *not* to be grounded in this objectless Being.

Objectless Being is always that, from which you are living without any effort. Whether you like it or not. To discover the absolute impossibility for body, mind and feelings to come anywhere near that objectless Being, or to touch it even, is the first shock and, at the same time, the releasing of true love. The same shock occurs, whenever an other person develops true love for you. True love is always threatening, because it tends to go straight through your defense mechanisms. So there is no longer any place to fly to, no longer any privacy. In other words, the self-consciousness cannot hide itself any more. All of a sudden you have become *everything*. Everything is known. In love you are prepared to become one with the environment, you are no longer holding back anything. In love, therefore, the tendency is to share and to merge, which is scaring to the ego. Even greedy people become generous, once they have been touched by love. It is love's nature to give—the nature of non-love is to grab.

It is proper to the tradition to which I belong, that the real issue is not being told in bits and pieces, but instead to put the essence of the story in a compact, straightforward and matter-of-fact manner before you. Here we give it all at once. And for most people this needs getting used to. The brain, or the mind, is not going to be satisfied just like that, because the mind is an ordering mechanism. Therefore it is inevitable that you will go and try to fit in what you are hearing here with the ideas and systems that have already been gathered by you.

Experience usually shows that, after people have been coming here for some time, there comes a moment when the ordering mind is chucking it all, because it is being overloaded by a multitude of things. Then arises the possibility to start listening truly. Then you will stop trying to put everything into concepts and strategies, which is altogether preventing you from listening truly.

Such habit will last until, at a certain point, one will no longer be able to bring any kind of 'order' into one's thinking. And with that the thinking mind, with which you had been listening so far, will have lost its authority. This change is not created by thinking, but by a new-born intelligence and, until it has taken place, true listening remains impossible. For then you will have moved from intellect to intelligence.

There comes a stage when the intellect has become so fed up with all those concepts, half-truths, silly notions and defense mechanisms, that it will kill itself, and then the intelligence wakes up, making it clear to you, that truth and life are not to be found at the level of thinking.

V: It certainly makes me panic.

A: It doesn't make *you* panic, but it's the centre of gravity of the thinking mind that gets into a panic. For then the possibility for you to identify with the thinking mind is being undermined in a fundamental way. But, once the intelligence has been awakened, any such panic will disappear completely.

The madness of all visions and viewpoints will then become crystal-clear. The point of gravity is then being shifted from intellect to intelligence. For that reason it will be a good thing, if you would give your whole interest to the subject and follow these meetings intensively. If you come just once or twice a month, it may be that certain things will also become clear to you. On the other hand as long as the intelligence has not been awakened, far too much time will be left for you to build up a seeming order from the identification of the thinking mind.

All this, however, does not mean that the brain would not be functioning any more, or that you would go into some kind of coma or into a state of confusion. As a matter of fact, after the awakening of the intelligence the brain will function even better and clearer, because no longer all the energy is going into the defense mechanisms of an identified mind. Then, for the first time, you will actually be using your brains for the purpose they are meant for.

Whoever takes himself to be the body, mind or feelings only, will not escape the disastrous consequences of it. On the other hand he who realizes at some point *not* to be all the things or objects of the conscious being—which he *is*—will at once experience the blessedness of the natural state. You all know it too well. Death and the world, the environment and the inner life, will no longer be an obstacle then.

The manifested arises totally spontaneously and for no particular reason or meaning from the unmanifested. The one who objects to the manifested, is himself *part* of the manifested. In fact, it is an altogether false situation, unsolvable when viewed from the manifested. Yet a deep recognition may take place, which is the liberation at the same time. To persist in the view that you are a body, mind or feeling, or all three of them, is to call down a disaster for yourself, and to introduce suffering.

V: I can't see what's wrong with them.

A: Nobody is saying that there is anything *wrong* with the manifestation—with body, mind and feeling.

V: But you're saying that they are a disaster.

A: It is a disaster for the one who takes himself to *be* these limitations—if not sooner, then later. If there is the exclusive experience of being the body, mind and feelings only, if one is completely identified with them, then disasters are bound to happen.

Consciousness is unmanifested. When it manifests itself, it does so in animals, plants and human beings—so always in a *form*. Man has the possibility to become aware of his situation. The culmination of this manifestation in a form is man, who is capable of becoming or of being conscious of the conscious being. Manifested and unmanifested Being are one in essence. Man has the possibility to realize it. The animal resigns itself to its fate, while man doesn't. The animal always remains bound by its instincts, man doesn't. A dog is born as a dog, lives as a dog and dies as a dog. A fish manifests itself as a fish, lives as a fish and dies as a fish. Only man is born as a man, he may live as an animal or raise himself, and die as a Buddha. Man's potential is of an immense grandeur. It is altogether unique.

An animal doesn't ask itself any questions, whereas man does. As a phenomenon man is totally unique. The animal, too, is unique, but man has got just that little bit more, so that he may be the culmination of this planet. Indeed, man proves himself capable of extracting the secrets from the manifestation by looking into matter and mind. Man has the power to look inside himself and outside. Man is capable of contemplation, meditation, evaluation, reflection…

V: To me Self-realisation actually means becoming free, and that, as a result, my personality will be functioning better.

A: In our approach there is an agreement that Self-realisation or enlightenment or absolute freedom means, that one is not interwoven with any object whatsoever. If there is no more interwovenness, Self-realisation, which is known by the absence of desire and fear, as well as by a deep inner clarity, is a fact.

Self-realisation has nothing to do with the ideas which we may have about it. If there is one thing which is *not* an idea or the result of your thinking, then it must be Self-realisation. Besides, the question as to what Self-realisation could do for *you*, is completely beside the point. And a 'better functioning personality' has nothing to do with Self-realisation anyway! The belief in such a personality is *itself* the disease. The natural state—the realisation of the fact that you are *Consciousness* and not some personality or other—is the cure. Only then you are dealing with Self-realisation. Before that you are just fumbling. Then each statement about Self-realisation is like a long shot: It doesn't hit anything.

Life only begins when you have lost it.

V: So you are saying that I should lose my life…

A: Yes. Not your biological appearance, but your whole collection of falsities, seeming certainties, masks and strategies of fear which you call 'thinking'. Enlightenment is nothing but to be no longer interwoven, no longer taking yourself to be a body, mind or feelings, or any other imaginable combination. Whatever object is to appear within Consciousness, *I* can never be anything perceived. *That* realisation is enlightenment, nothing more and nothing less. Realizing it twenty-four hours a day. All the rest is a construction, an interpretation, which derives its raw material from Consciousness.

V: That is the definition of it.

A: Yes. What it means is, that such a deep self-recognition is to take place. And, whereas most of us seem to have the idea that this is something very difficult, I claim it to be the simplest thing in the world. After all, what is needed? Nothing, absolutely nothing. There are no conditions for that Consciousness. Such is the case even now. But man is strange indeed...

One day a woman came to see me. She wanted information about Self-realisation. I talked to her for two hours, explaining everything. 'Well', she said, 'I understand what you mean, but where do I find a person who is going to explain it to me?' Patiently I told her the whole story once more. 'I think I am beginning to understand. I shall go to India and look for someone there, who will explain it to me.' While I had been busy for three hours disclosing to her all that's needed!

Questions such as, 'Then how should I...?', and, 'When can I start with Self-realisation?', 'Where should I go?', etc. are only a pretext, an attempt to escape the real story, an evasion from what's actually becoming clear. Everything you need is here in this room. But that crazy mechanism comes from the thinking mind, which is always operating in the future, never in the now.

Even with my teacher enquiries were made as to where one could find a guru.

V: I've got a question at a different level: Here is this body, with its awareness. I also manage to see what identification means, and that all that is the contents of consciousness. But now the question comes to my mind: Should I take consciousness' contents seriously or not?

A: Take *Consciousness* seriously! The contents will take care of itself. What is important is, that you move from the whole world of concepts and ideas to the realisation. Then in practice the manifestation won't be any problem to you. You will go on doing what comes natural to you.

(14th February, 1986)

22

THE EVER-PRESENT

Visitor: The other day you spoke about waking up in the morning, and looking at what is actually waking you up. I think that, at the moment of waking up, the Ever-present makes you alert as to what is happening around you.

Alexander: What exactly do you experience?

V: The Ever-present wakes me up.

A: The Ever-present never wakes you up. The Ever-present *is* the being awake. So what's waking you up are mostly movements. But what are we actually talking about? In spiritual circles 'waking up' means to awaken from a sort of coma, whereas I am simply referring to the fact, that you wake up in the morning. So, what do you mean by 'waking up'? Let us first define the terms, otherwise we are just like two rails that never meet.

V: Two months ago you said: Just pay attention to whom or to what is waking you up in the morning.

A: I only said: When you wake up in the morning, just pay attention to *what* is waking you up. I said: Just *watch* how the 'I'-consciousness jumps into Being. So, when you wake up, there is an unconditioned Being, and three seconds later an 'I'-structure jumps into it. Just pay attention to that.

That's all I said.

V: In my case the 'I' comes in very quickly.

A: All right, that's what you saw. Now, how do you know that it happens?

V: Because I start planning right away.

A: No—How do you *know* that such a thing is happening? Because there is a *background*. Otherwise you *couldn't* know it. There is this background. With or without identification. So this eternal Presence is always there. And within that the 'I'-structure makes its appearance. All that happens now is, that you *identify* yourself with this 'I'-structure in such a way, that it seems to you as if you no longer have the conscious experience of that eternal Presence. Observe it. In fact, you are *already* seeing it. You actually know it *already*. Make that into a deep experience for yourself. Make sure to begin the day that way and, at a certain point, it will not leave you any more. Then you won't identify yourself any longer.

V: I have the impression that, as soon as I come into action, the 'I' is already there .

A: Oh no. I don't need to have an 'I' in order to blink my eyes, do I? How many times have you been blinking your eyes just now? Maybe some twenty, thirty times. Still you don't say all the time, 'I'm blinking my eyes, I have to be conscious of the blinking of my eyes.' It all happens automatically. Similarly thoughts appear of themselves, the liver functions of its own accord, one gets the flu automatically, and death happens of its own accord. It all works perfectly. So all you need to do is do nothing. In fact, the very 'doing' prevents you from seeing the real issue.

V: But I need to identify myself with something, or not?

A: That is not really necessary. It is something you have acquired. There is no need to identify yourself at all. Identification is to invite unnecessary suffering, to create unnecessary problems— That is what I'm saying. Do I need to identify myself so that I can do my shopping? Do I need to identify myself in order to be sitting here? Identification is a trick. It only *appears* to be so. With or without an 'I', the awareness is there all the same. So what I'm saying is: Realize yourself to be the awareness within this 'I'-projection. With or without 'I', that doesn't make any difference. If you realize that position, the Ever-present, it will be all the better for your situation and for the people around you. If you don't realize it, then you will be going from one crisis to the next. But if that is not what you want, then you will have to stop the identification.

You will never hear me say: You shouldn't identify yourself with the 'I'. As a matter of fact, such a thing isn't even possible. What I'm saying is: There is a phenomenon which makes it look, as if this identification with the 'I' is actually taking place; as if you actually go and set up house there. And all the consequences are the result of that identification. In reality, however, nothing is happening at all. It is a question of image-making, a kind of film which you are making for yourself.

Through the power of discrimination you will see how things really work, and then you won't let yourself be terrorized any more by those optical tricks, by the horror house that you are driving through. A horror house of your own making. Indeed, then you will be able to pay attention to nicer things. For, then, there will be energy left, and you will become active.

The depressive, identified person is not active. He says: I'm too tired to light a cigarette. I would love to, but I haven't got the strength even to strike a match. Whereas the non-identified person has plenty of energy. For he is connected to the big power station, the nuclear power station.

V: But all my experiences, all my knowledge, all that I plan to do in the near future, all my undertakings—surely, that's my 'I'?

A: No, it isn't. What you call the 'I' is, in the Advaitic perspective, nothing more than a product of memory. The 'I' and memory are one and the same thing. If there wouldn't be any memory, the 'I' wouldn't be there either.

I cannot be troubled by things that I do not know. I am only troubled by things that I know. My attachment, too, is a form of memory. An agenda, or memory, tells you what you are to do on such and such a day; or rather, what you *could* do, for there is no 'must' for anything of course. Your memory tells you what you are, and then you identify yourself with that. At the same time a gap in your memory does not mean a gap in your existence. Memory is responsible for what you *think* yourself to be. All what you can possibly know about yourself—that you are a nasty fellow or a nice guy—is all memory. It is all accumulated, retained knowledge.

So your existence can function quite well without any such memory. The world—that which you consider to be 'the world'—is held together by memory. So this 'I' is nothing but a memory structure. And, for the matter of that, not even reliable. For if there is anything unreliable, then surely it is memory.

Everything which you presume to know about yourself is, looking at it technically, most unreliable. Whenever you start telling stories about past events that were shared by other people, then those people will always correct you. For in your fantasy you have been very creative, and what *really* happened at the time often turns out to be quite a different story. Therefore, what you call 'your past' isn't all that real after all. It is all a product of your own making. Looking at it from this perspective, the 'I' can never stand its ground before Being. And, somewhere, somehow, you know it only too well. So in the morning, when such an 'I' threatens to jump into Being, then that is being perceived by something, that is *different* from memory. Similarly, whenever your memory fails you, then too, you *know* it, that you don't know something.

The knowing that is associated with memory is completely different from the knowing that comes from Being. That is why in Sanskrit there are two terms for it, *'vijnana'* and *'jnana'*. *Vijnana* is knowledge through memory, whereas *jnana* is *real* knowledge, Knowing *itself*. When you wake up in the morning, then all that can possibly appear there, are things that are tied up with memory. For the world is a construction of memory. The 'I' is a construction of memory. But it is perceived by something *other* than memory, and that is the *real* knowing. And these phenomena are taking place at the same time.

V: I understand what you're saying, but I don't experience it that way. It is just as if I'm simply sitting in my 'I', planning all kinds of different things. But what you are saying is: That is not what you really *are*.

A: No, you can never be that. I can never be a product of memory alone. I am more than the sum total of the parts. If I add together all the things that people think of me, plus what I think myself to be, then the picture will still not be complete.

V: That may be, but in my experience it *isn't* like that. All I experience is this so-called 'I' of mine.

A: If you experience it in the sense of experiencing *being* that knowledge, then you are right. But if you experience it in the sense of *having* that knowledge, then you are wrong. Just write down what you think yourself to be.

That is why psycho-analysis is a never-ending story. Self-realisation, too, is an endless situation, but then in the sense that it is without beginning and without end.

V: Is it possible to lose your memory, while the senses continue to function?

A: As a matter of fact, memory goes quite deep. Memory is also in the body. You only need to sniff up a particular scent and, all of a sudden, you are a boy or a girl of eight. In that respect smell acts quite strongly, and so does sound.

V: So do feelings, such as fear.

A: Yes, but in the case of fear it first needs to be preceded by images. There is no fear without thinking. There is no fear without images. So, if we'll just stick to the senses, smell can be very spiritual. You are walking in the woods or you smell a particular fragrance, and at once there is an association. The same applies to taste etc. Memory is responsible for the production of images.

This 'I'-consciousness and memory are one and the same thing. Therefore, there is no 'I'-consciousness, no identity, without memory. The problem, however, is not this 'I'-consciousness, but the *identification* with the 'I'-consciousness. And in practice that is what's causing the confusion. Memory ought to be an aid, but often it is an obstructionist. Memory ought to be an aid, so that we are able to function properly in the objective world. Memory is responsible for what we consider to be 'the world'. Memory ought to be an aid, whereas now it threatens to turn against us. We do not have the proper insight in this matter. And again, insight has nothing to do with memory.

V: I feel that I am attached to memory.

A: No, you are not attached to memory: Memory *is* attachment. So, in order to overcome attachment, you only need to understand memory. The whole mechanism of memory is attachment. No attachment without memory.

If I don't know that this thing here belongs to me, then I also cannot be attached to it. How can I be attached to something I don't remember, something which is not stored in my memory? Therefore, the *jnani* lives free from the ballast of memory, free from any psychic memory.

V: Suppose I lose my memory?

A: Then you are in trouble. With or without memory, you're always in trouble...

V: In that case there is something, which your memory wants to retrieve.

A: Yes, your identity. For 'memory' also stands for 'identity'. You can see it on television sometimes, for example, in the programme called 'Crime Watch'. A person doesn't know his identity any more. He is able to remember just a couple of things. He doesn't have a passport on him, nothing. Maybe he was robbed. Who is he? What is his identity? That he *is*, he knows. But *what* he is, he doesn't know. Identity is memory. If there is no memory, the 'I' cannot exist. And if there is no identity, then there cannot be any memory. They are interlinked. They exist as an optical illusion. As a product of memory I, too, have got an 'I'. But not in reality.

V: Whenever you experience something, it is being stored in one's memory. But often, when you want to repeat that experience, it turns out to be a mere semblance of what was once there.

A: Yes, Patanjali defines memory as 'not allowing something which has been experienced, to disappear'.

V: But even when you aren't doing anything special, you need your memory, as for example, when you want to recall certain things, don't you?

A: The English word for recalling things is 'to remember', 'to impart again'. Through our memory we are seemingly able to experience things again. But, as a matter of fact, we are then looking with our memory: I see that you have been to the hair-dresser. I see that you don't have that car any more—How can you see something that isn't there? That way our memory is a means for keeping things in mind that are of the past, though as such each memory is something conceptual. They are pictures which are practical for keeping the world together. Nothing more.

V: Is there any memory in the case of a little baby?

A: Yes, there is. A baby has already got impressions when it is born. We call it the mental blue-print. At the same time the baby begins to construct a world, even though it doesn't perceive all that much yet. Nor should you think that a baby actually smiles. A baby imitates, it makes grimaces. Sitting in a tram or bus, a small child may be staring at you quite unashamedly. Now, if you just look back at the child with a straight face, it will also keep on looking that way. Next, if you pull a face just for a moment, then, again, the child will imitate that nine times out of ten. I always do it. So I look back at them equally unashamedly. Next I'll do something with my eyes, and then they, too, will do something with their eyes. We have a secret code. And then you have those queer goings-on above the cradle! We think that the baby is actually smiling back at us, but it is only trying to imitate our grimaces. So in the case of a little child it is both a question of imitation and of the inner life of the child itself.

V: What can you give me?

A: I cannot give you anything which you haven't got already. I can only make clear to you, how my path has been. My story is your story. As simple as that. Because there *are* no other people. My advice to you is to do a thorough investigation. See how things are put together.

One thing, however, you have to understand clearly. There are *two* things that you may be working on in your life: objective, concrete matters, such as a car that has broken down, and which you are going to repair. That is something concrete. Or you are going to cook *nasi goreng*, or do consciousness-raising exercises. All that is concrete. You can establish schools for it. You can take courses in it.

But there is another form of learning, and that is the one we are dealing with here. With the things I am putting before you, you cannot do anything. With what is being said here, you cannot do anything. It won't give you any profit, nor any loss. So you could as well not have started it. It won't make you any richer and it won't make you any wiser. For 'wiser' also is something objective. The only thing that is possible is, that you will become free from the burden of self-consciousness, that you will know how things are put together. That's all. Nothing else.

V: But isn't that everything?

A: Yes, it is. But what I keep on saying is, that there are but very few people who are really interested in this. It is rare to find somebody who is interested in this. Such a person no longer feels the need to have small groups here and there. Those are the mature students. But these you come across only once in a decade. Such a person does not come in order to become 'happy' or to reinforce his or her self-consciousness; or to become healthy or to learn to read auras. For all such things he has left behind. The only thing such a person wants is Self-realisation.

V: I find that the reason for my coming here is, that there is some sort of greediness in me. I want to be realized *before* my death rather than at the moment of passing away, therefore I want to *have* that realisation. So my question is: What can I do?

A: Do you want me to be perfectly honest with you?

V: Yes, of course.

A: You cannot do anything. Absolutely nothing. There is nothing you can do about it. You can't do anything to speed up the process. You can't think out any technique. The only way-of-doing known to me is *not*-doing. In Chinese it is called '*wei wu wei*': doing by *not*-doing. So we will have to face that dilemma. On the one hand there is absolutely nothing to be done, and on the other hand an intensive form of *seeing* is to be done. But such *seeing* is not 'doing'. Such seeing is your *in*-ground in things. And you should *see* without projecting a 'doer' in it. Then you will have the synchronicity that we are more or less aiming at.

What comes nearest to it is the total acceptance of what *is*. Acceptance, however, supposes two levels. You have the level where you accept with the personality, with your 'I'-structure. For example, you experience a certain situation as being difficult, and because you have no other option, you have come to accept it, for things just can't continue that way. That is what we usually mean by 'acceptance'. Somebody has died. It asks for acceptance.

Or somebody that you love is being unfaithful to you, and you'd rather not have it. Then out of self-protection you say: 'I will just have to accept it.' You accept it, because you don't have any other alternative. That is the involuntary acceptance. But that is not what concerns us here.

What we are saying here is: Total acceptance means total synchronicity with the *now*, because that is all you know. All the capital that you have is this eternal *now*. There is nothing apart from what is *now*. If not it wouldn't be there. You can't show me anything which isn't *now*. Even what you call 'the past' is happening *now*. When you are being troubled by the past, it is happening *now*. When you are glad about or troubled by the future, then that is happening *now*. And if you want to change anything, then it will also have to take place *now*. Therefore, *now* is the only thing you know. Or to put it better: All that you know is *now*. If you are going to attain Self-realisation, then it will be *now*. And not later on. And not yesterday, and not next year. So it is a matter of total acceptance in the sense that there is actually no more person standing in between to accept it. That is true acceptance. It is a different word for real synchronicity with yourself. That is the beginning of Self-realisation.

V: As for me, I don't expect to be able to get realized right now.

A: It is all due to thinking. You could ask yourself: Is it possible for me to create a situation, where the *total* acceptance of existence—*exactly* as it is, and *not* as you have thought it out, not as you would *like* to have it—can take place? Is that possible or is that not possible? If it isn't, then there is an 'I' jibbing at it. It must be an accepting *without* the figure of an 'I' who is accepting it. There is an accepting at a far deeper level, and that level has got nothing to do with your 'I'.

V: Can you see whether someone is ready for it?

A: I don't see anything at all. I'm not interested in your case. Really not interested. I am not at all interested in your Self-realisation. For to me all of you *are* Self-realized. So why should it be of interest to me? Everyone that is sitting here *is* the absolute Consciousness. Whether you like it or not, whether you realize it or not, it doesn't make any difference. There are only gradations of *ignorance*, gradations of *interwovenness*. What matters is *your* interest, not mine.

V: That's why you actually don't like it.

A: What is there to like or dislike for *me*? I don't want to be dead, and I don't want to live, for I *have* nothing to want. Long ago I stopped wanting or not wanting things. I am a cork on the ocean, just like you. But *you* have an outboard motor attached to it, and I haven't. So if the sea wants me to go into a certain direction, should I then say: I want to go the other way? I join in the little dance, just like Shiva. I dance the dance of existence.

V: So I shouldn't do anything?

A: You *cannot* do anything. 'You shouldn't do anything', is the same thing again. Acceptance means that there *isn't* anything to be changed. Wanting to change comes from the 'I'-structure and is a preservative *against* acceptance.

V: So to be in the *here-and-now* basically means not doing anything?

A: No, it doesn't! You *are* the *here-and-now*, therefore you can't get *out* of the *here-and-now*. And the problem is that you want to get out of it. Because you are not content with the here-and-now, you go in search of fulfilment. You go in search of something else than what *is*. But there *is* nothing else. Something else than what *is*, is simply not there! And to want something else than what *is*, is just being childish.

V: If there is a beginning of acceptance, then there is synchronicity with Being. My experience is that, at that moment, everything disappears.

A: Yes, and since you *don't* want everything to disappear because of your interwovenness with everything, then in a sense you are even preventing it.

V: You prevent it, but it dissolves automatically.

A: Yes, that is *the* solution. For something that dissolves, disappears.

V: Yes, that is what I experienced. But when that happens, there is a lurking danger of wanting to translate it all. Some sort of emotionality, a sort of fear crops up, and then you want to put that into words. Where does that fear come from?

A: We want to exchange experiences. As soon as you stop investing in a number of things, then other matters will get the opportunity to manifest themselves. For example, if you haven't had your sleep one night, then you will tend to be more emotional, for in that case the defense which you would normally have, will have diminished. As the defense decreases, other things that had never come to the surface up to now, will be able to manifest themselves. So also as you get older, when you're getting on for sixty-five, your resistance, including your physical resistance, will have become less. Things that you hadn't looked at so far, will then begin to surface in all intensity. In the case of people who have been in a concentration camp, quite often you can notice that, when they are around sixty-five, nasty things are coming to the surface. For these things, too, want to be seen. So, as the defense decreases, other layers become visible. Until all is empty.

The fact that you want to share those experiences is a different matter. But if there is anything that cannot be shared, then surely it is the emptiness.

(4th April, 1987, morning)

23

FEAR OF THE UNKNOWN DOES NOT EXIST

Visitor: Is thinking different from memory?

Alexander: No, thinking is also memory.

V: You also said that thinking is fear. In that case would it be possible for fear to exist without memory?

A: No, that is out of the question. You can only be afraid, if you know what is going to happen. Our memory is responsible for a great many things, and fear without memory is impossible.

Fear can never exist without memory. You cannot be afraid of something you don't know. That's the reason why you cannot be afraid of death. What you might be afraid of though, is the disappearing of things you're familiar with, but not of the unknown. Fear of the unknown is out of the question. A thing that is unknown to you, cannot strike you with fear. And everything that you do know is based on memory.

V: This morning the subject of identification, interwovenness, came up for discussion. The sense-organs are found to be taking in impressions. As these somehow find their way in the body, it looks as if they are bumping up against something, against an 'I', a 'person' who is storing away the impressions. But when I look carefully, I find that that is not what happens, because everything somehow just disappears; there is nothing to check anything there. On the other hand the discussion on identification and interwovenness would suggest, that something is interweaving itself with something else.

A: As a matter of fact, there is no such thing. It is an optical illusion. It only *appears* to be so.

V: Indeed. And if it were to have any reality value at all, then nobody could go to sleep peacefully, for in that case the whole manifestation would be against our letting go of anything. Instead, it is every man's experience that his going into a state of deep, dreamless sleep is actually doing a lot of good to him.

A: Which is a state of total detachment as well. If we would be attached to things in any *real* sense, which, as a matter of fact, we are assuming here, then it would indeed be impossible for us to go to sleep. Besides, it would be impossible to do anything at all. And because this 'I' doesn't have any reality value, you are quite right in saying that it doesn't bump up against anything. The whole idea of things bumping up against something or other is maintained by the belief in it. And if you would actually learn to see and to look truly—which I'm inviting everybody to do—then you will find that no bumping is taking place anywhere. With the exception of an *imaginary* ego or 'I'-consciousness, which is without any truth content. It is a complete delusion. It isn't *my* invention though, so you can't put the blame on *me*!

V: It is a delusion, but it is there all the same.

A: As a delusion, it is. Now, if we can just perceive the delusion *as* delusion, and truth *as* truth, then what could you possibly be attached to? If I'm able to see what delusion *is*, then delusion cannot bind me. If I can discern the Real from the unreal, then I'm free. And if I cannot, then I'm bound. So what matters is the discrimination between what is true and what isn't. *That* possibility you have. Whether you make use of it is up to you.

V: Does this house exist?

A: Yes, at a certain level it does.

V: I, too, exist like that.

A: Yes, you do at a certain level. I'm not denying the fact that you exist, but what you *identify* with, what you are attributing continuity and eternal value to—of that I say: It is not prudent to invest in such a bankrupt 'I'-condition.

Your 'I' is bankrupt by definition, and you just have to take a closer look as to how the situation stands, which is what we are doing here. Your bankruptcy has been petitioned already. You still think you've got a million in the bank, and in the mean time your house has already been sold. And here we are not dealing with a house, but with your inner bankruptcy.

V: Still one has to go on living all the same...

A: All that happens in a perfectly natural way. Some people think they are going to land in some form of non-activity. Not at all. In fact, you will be getting a million possibilities more, because before you were just a small fragment, focussed on one or two little things, and now the whole world is open to you. What am I saying? The whole cosmos! What? Far bigger even! That is freedom indeed.

V: I find it difficult to see it that way, because I don't experience it like that...

A: No. But it is not a question of anybody *demanding* you to experience it that way. At least not the way *I* experience it. Seeing is believing, but not believing in the sense of accepting a form of belief. Seeing is *knowing.*

V: How do you know that this isn't just another thought structure, some sort of idea again?

A: If it is, then it is so. But why such a vote of no-confidence with respect to yourself? What did you experience as an idea?

V: I suddenly had all these thought flashes, and then it occurred to me: All that there is *now*, is all there really *is.*

A: Such ideas are fleeting thoughts. They come up from somewhere, are perceived, and then they disappear again into the same thing.

V: And what about that which stays permanently?

A: That will never leave you. On the other hand everything that *may* leave you—sorrow, pain, joy, your dog, your husband, your wife (today you're happy, because she is looking at you with those beautiful, brown eyes of hers, but tomorrow she may be making a wry face, and then your happiness is gone...)—is apparently *not* this ultimate reality.

V: So, if you are looking properly, then whatever you see, *you* are always present there. But because you are *seeing* it, you can never *be* that.

A: You have to make a difference between a *mental* world—all the things that are made into an idea—and a *sensory* world. When I'm conjuring up a whole world before you, then that is a world of ideas. On the other hand the fact that we are sitting here in this room, constitutes the sensory world. In the initial phase you must learn to see what a mental projection is, what *ideas* are. In the second phase you are going to see *facts*. And in the third phase you will learn to see that facts are ideas as well. What is called 'a fact' by you, is again being seen by something else. That is all right for Self-realisation, but in daily life you are just dealing with the difference between ideas and facts.

V: If you have that perspective, then it no longer makes any real difference *where* you are or *what* you are.

A: Exactly. Even if I would be in China.

V: It doesn't make any difference. You may even be dead.

A: Well, 'dead' is another story again. In any case, it doesn't make any difference as long as you're living. Whether this room is filled with thirty people or with sixty people or with three people, to the availability it doesn't make any difference. It doesn't make any difference to the awareness as to *what* it is aware of. Just as it doesn't make any difference to the white cinema screen, whether a porno film, a crime film or a most wonderful movie is projected onto it, for the screen is the availability, nothing more. Only afterwards you can say: I have a preference for this or for that, and then you can start a discussion or an argument about that. But the fact remains that, as Consciousness, we all are that availability, the 'love-ground' of things.

V: And you can use your memory to observe this properly?

A: No, not memory. Memory is only an aid for knowing how to get home. In fact, nothing more. It *ought* to be a help, but at present our memory is at the service of that illusory figure. It is a sort of slave to this illusory figure, for upholding the illusory figure, whereas in reality it is simply a help for our regular, daily affairs. And because all our energy is actually going into upholding this illusory figure, memory is functioning so poorly at the other level.

V: Then what is it, when you realize that you should have made a more accurate assessment of a certain situation? Then you're looking back on it, thinking in retrospect: 'I should have done things differently.' But that you realize only afterwards.

A: That is comparing, for which you also need memory. You will have to see though, whether the data which you are getting through memory, are reliable, whether they actually correspond with your experience. And the touchstone is your experience in the world. If something doesn't fit in, it will show itself. Through the discriminative faculty you will find out. Our imaginative thinking is making things look quite different. But then, thinking is not the reality. Thinking is an aid. Thinking and memory are at your service, whereas now you are living under their terror. You will have to set your house in order. And in a way *jnana* means setting your house in order. Seeing things as they really are. Because of our intelligence we have the ability to trace things to their cause, and we have that ability to a high degree. We do have that wonderful possibility. And I think it is such a waste not to use it. This applies as much to objective things, as it does to subjective matters. Thinking can be a help, but also a great disturber. An idea carries two possibilities within itself: Either it is an aid, or it is a deluder.

V: Does memory disappear, once you have seen through the projections of the thinking mind?

A: The *psychic* memory disappears. It means that, if you happen to meet somebody who, at some point in the past, had been mean to you, the whole projection mechanism is not just going to become operative again. You no longer associate things to that extent. It dissolves then and there.

V: And if you allow something to tell its story? Then it is the projection mechanism, isn't it?

A: These things are taking place in time and space. For example, you think that you know that you are not the body. However, you shudder the moment you have to undergo an operation. So, apparently, there is something which doesn't quite fit in with your reasoning. And it doesn't, for in your case it is a question of *mental* realisation, not a *real* realisation. In such a case the matter has not really been seen. Had it *really* been seen, then it would have dissolved. Or, for example, your mind has kept very quiet and serene for some time, and then you think: 'Now I'm enlightened—It's happened!' But then, all of a sudden, terrible emotions are coming up, and you are at a loss how to deal with them. What is the matter? So then you will have to take a proper look at the situation. What does it mean? That somehow you were under the impression that, once a person has become enlightened, no feelings are going to be released any more. Again a concept. Somewhere you read it, but it had not been tested by truth.

V: Therefore one always has to keep a close watch as to whether things are still an *object* to you—in whatever way that might be.

A: Every object is *automatically* known. At a certain stage life in this knowingness will become such a natural condition with you, there will be such a perfect synchronicity with everything there is, that there is no longer any tension, no longer any conflict, whatever happens.

V: I'm a puppet on the waves.

A: A cork even.

V: I'm drifting about aimlessly...

A: Well... aimlessly. You never know where such a wave is going to go. That is left to the sea. The sea and the wind will see to it.

V: On the other hand you are also saying, that we should get our priorities right. That we will need to make a choice. In my thinking that is somewhat at odds with each other.

A: It means that the cork is either beginning to invest in an outboard motor, or it will surrender itself to the oceanic movement called life. It is a choice you make. And, looking at it from that analogy which, of course, doesn't fit as far as the details are concerned (as no analogy does), it is wiser—as no direction can be indicated anyway—not to invest in the outboard motor, and to let life live itself.

If there is surrender, then there is the acceptance of whatever happens to come up. And 'acceptance' does not mean a sort of 'let-it-drift' situation. *Because* I accept the situation, I am able to react adequately. It is a very dynamic accepting. And there the 'cork' theory doesn't stand up.

And if it is a case of total acceptance, then, as a consequence, it also implies the total acceptance of things that are possibly not to your liking.

V: Does interfering in the situation mean, that one is putting up resistance?

A: Interfering *is* resisting. And why do we interfere? Because we are not living in accordance with the basics of natural law. In the jungle life follows the broader laws of nature: The choice is fixed upon the animal that is most senior; one asks forgiveness from the spirits; the oldest and most ailing crocodile is shot, so that the species may be preserved. But what does western man do? He kills everything, cuts down entire virgin forests. No insight into natural law.

V: So a counterforce must be found.

A: It is there already: Aids is a counterforce. Only after a couple of million have been cleared away we will begin to think. We shall have to learn how to handle matter. The handling of matter is, looking at it from a wider perspective, the exam which humanity is sitting for.

V: You once said that between the unmanifested and the manifested there is the field of perception. But I can't see anything in between.

A: The field of perception is absolutely necessary in order to experience the two at one and the same time. But that is not a problem. There is not some 'block' that you are running up against, there is no obstacle for you to be who you are. The obstacle which is put up is an imaginary one, not a real one. An illusory quality of one hundred per cent! That ought to make you enlightened by now...

V: If I put up resistance, then it basically means that I'm not accepting the situation.

A: Sometimes you may accept through resistance. Watch it though, that you don't make it into a formula—the 'let-it-drift' formula. Sometimes the acceptance of a resistance which you may feel coming up within you, can be quite essential.

V: So to actually feel that resistance within you is the acceptance?

A: You need not *identify* yourself with it, but it certainly may be made manifest. Everything has the freedom to come up within you. Whether you give in to it, is a different matter.

V: So by not accepting something, I'm creating a new situation. But that situation, again, is looking for a solution as well.

A: Everything is looking for a solution. And if *you* dissolve, everything will be solved.

V: Does a thing dissolve, if you pay it the right attention?

A: If it is truly seen, in its totality, it will dissolve and disappear, and you won't know any more what it was. That is the beauty of dissolving: It doesn't leave any traces.

There are two possibilities: Either you see immediately what you *are* and, as a result, you will know what you are not. Or you are going to see what you are *not*, and in that case that which you really are, will remain.

If you can see what you really *are*, then that excludes the second possibility. In practice the second possibility proves to be more suitable for the majority of people. But if you can find the intelligence and the sensitivity and the alertness and the power and the fortunate conditions to see immediately what you really *are*, then that excludes all that you are *not*. These are the only two possibilities. Still I would maintain, that the first way is much easier and much more intelligent. But in practice it normally takes you some twelve years of looking.

V: Could that be due to our western attitude?

A: It may well be. The oriental often has a clearer view of things, because he doesn't have so much of mental ballast: To him the ego never *was* that important in the first place.

V: Do we delay the process, because we are overloaded by ballast?

A: We are *fascinated* by the ballast.

V: I would like to ask one more question about the personality. Do we project the personality onto the illusory figure from memory, from what we were taught as a child? And do we next imagine ourselves to *be* that personality, because we are not looking properly?

A: It is all acquired. This phenomenon which in India is called 'ahamkara', the personality—the 'I-am-ness' with its contents—is in itself not all such a disaster. But if it is going to turn against you and terrorize you, then maybe it is about time to subject it to a thorough enquiry. That enquiry is self-enquiry.

V: But shouldn't one investigate it, even if it is quite acceptable?

A: If it is acceptable to you, then you won't investigate it. You start to investigate it only, when it begins to hurt. As long as it is acceptable, there won't be any problem.

A great number of people find refuge in a certain way of thinking, in some form of religion, which is good enough. But there is another category of people who are vaguely anxious, and who discover that, for them, it's not the right thing. Those are the people who find themselves in circles such as these, and there is a growing number of them. In any case, don't be persuaded to accept things just like that…

V: That's not what I mean. By examining what you are *not*, you are at the same time running up against certain behaviour, certain thought patterns of yours. And in each case I can see clearly, that it concerns a projection onto an object, and the object may be me.

A: True. But as far as I'm concerned, it seems more sensible to see directly what you *are*, for that will exclude what you are *not*. If that is not successful, then you will have to see what you are *not*. Again and again meditation and alertness will teach you and will make you see what you really *are*. And in case it is being overlooked, that which you are *not* will be brought home to you: through conflicts and experiences. It is always 'both—and', not 'either—or'. For all is happening at one and the same time. Look upon life as a possibility, and not as a silly 'must'.

V: There ought to be openness though.

A: Availability and love are openness by definition. Freedom is a birthright. You cannot *give* freedom to the other, because freedom is what the other *is*.

V: But a relationship often means *not* giving freedom.

A: Quite true. In that case you are not giving freedom, but you are taking away someone's freedom instead. Then you are making the other prisoner. Therefore, if you are giving freedom back to a person, you shouldn't consider yourself to be that noble, for you are only giving back what had been his legitimate property all along, before he even knew you.

What I call love is the perfect acceptance of the other, when the other is able to manifest himself completely in the way he wants to, deep in his soul. And that *you* provide the facilities and material to let that garden grow. But *giving* freedom to the other seems somewhat similar to having a dog on a chain, and then getting yourself a longer chain, so as to enable him to have a pee at the tree further down.

V: Then again, I think one should be able to exchange the experiences, which you gain in freedom, with others.

A: I don't think you should ever do that. It's a disease among seekers. You should never exchange experiences, for in doing so you belittle the experience. Experiences are strictly private.

V: Still you may be so full of it, that you want to talk about it.

A: No, you must know how to keep a secret. People chatter too much about their inner life. You get that kind of partners, who are discussing everything with each other. It's pure masochism. True love doesn't need to talk over anything. Everything is clear. If you love each other very deeply, then you won't need to tell anything to the other. Then it is only quiet. If you have a lot to discuss with each other, then you are practising a sort of psychiatry in your relationship. And that, of course, has nothing to do with love.

(4th April, 1987, afternoon)

24

PRACTICE MAKES THE LIVING

Visitor: What I notice when emotions are coming up is, that there is always a tendency to name them. That is obviously not 'letting it tell its story', as you call it.

Alexander: The very fact that you are noticing it means, that you are letting it tell its story. You are able to *see* that you are rationalizing, that you want to gloss over something. That is all perfectly perceived. As if it was a game. Just as long as you do not interfere. It grows bigger and bigger... and then it's gone. And it does not leave any traces then. What's important is to look carefully. And then each situation is of course wonderful, because each situation has got its own, unique story. From a practical standpoint that is what can be said about this question.

For example, you notice that you are getting red in the face, or that your heart is beginning to beat faster. Then, apparently, there is some interwovenness somewhere or other. All that doesn't matter. If you just pay attention now, then you will transcend the situation without even noticing it. It is possible to look at such a phenomenon totally fresh, free from memory, free from everything you've learnt. And if you do it, you will transcend the whole issue. For then it is just telling its story. Then there is the acceptance of the fact.

Of course, you won't succeed at the first go. The habit of starting to rationalize things is persistent. The habit of dragging in the past is strong. But you can let all those reactions do their work without going into it. You *can* let issues such as jealousy or wanting to be in the right tell their story. *That's* what's important. It's all right to have judgements, to have rationalisations come up, to have ideas come up. Everything is allowed to tell its story as long as you, as an unmoved spectator, are seeing in all clarity and intensity what *actually* is going on there. Then what I'm saying is, that it will dissolve then and there.

V: If something is troubling me, then I have the choice either to interfere or to accept it.

A: Wisdom is to step in at the right moment and to keep off when necessary. Of course, everything is at the service of surviving.

V: Yes, surviving—except for the survival of the 'I'-consciousness.

A: As far as I am concerned, the 'I'-consciousness, too, may survive. I have no problems with it. *You* are having problems with the 'I'-consciousness, not me. Always to step in at the right moment is something unique. That is why no rules can be laid down for it. Some directions, some references, some indicators, but no rules can be given as to how you should live your life. You learn the living through practice, and practice makes the living.

V: There is memory, and there are thoughts. Thoughts come and go. But real thinking doesn't seem to take place, until you actually communicate with a thought.

A: What you call 'thinking' is no more than a current of thoughts. Then, at a certain point, you also think that there is a 'thinker'. There are only thoughts that are being perceived, strictly speaking.

V: When you are in meditation, you can observe the thoughts.

A: Even now you can, can't you?

V: Yes, but now there is more of interwovenness.

A: Thoughts are always objects. That is why I always ask people: What *are* you thinking right now? Because then you are making the thought into an object, and next you go and look at it. And in order to look at what you are thinking, in order to be conscious of what you are thinking, there has to be a distance. What are you thinking right now?

V: I try to look at my thoughts, which I find difficult.

A: It isn't difficult. They just appear. The thinking process itself is a thought. Each idea, each naming, each interpretation is a thought and, therefore, an object. It cannot be otherwise. And an object is always at a distance, otherwise it cannot be perceived.

V: A feeling can never be there on its own. A feeling comes up through a thought.

A: First the thought comes and then the feeling. Feeling goes deeper than thought. That you *think* yourself to be crazy—fair enough. But that you behave accordingly, that you *feel* that way, that's worse. If you *think* that you are a giraffe, I will manage to talk you out of it. But if you actually *feel* yourself to be one, then the case becomes more difficult. Because a feeling is far more real to you. It goes much deeper. Thus a feeling often acts as a green light for doing or not doing something. But first this is preceded by quite a few thoughts. Feelings always come in second, for they are always running behind the thoughts. We call it 'thinking-feeling', because they are always interrelated. They are inseparable—body-thinking-feeling. Thinking and feeling form a kind of two-in-one, a symbiosis. If there are no thoughts, then there aren't any feelings either. Feelings that are coming up, are thoughts become corporeal, frozen thoughts that have become defrosted at a certain point. In contrast to feelings, thoughts do not go deep. A thought may *seem* to go deep, but it is basically linked to a deeper feeling. Thoughts are all at the surface.

V: Actually, thoughts don't do anything to you. If you are *thinking* of fear, then that won't affect you in any way. But if you're actually *having* fear, then you will certainly be affected by it.

A: Fear is always linked to a thought, and the thought is linked to an identification. Again, that identification is associated with the sense of fear. It all happens quite quickly. If no identification takes place, then you cannot have a sense of fear, because in that case there is no identification with a thought pattern. For example: Your girlfriend tells you that she is going to leave you. Now, the picture of the relationship that was there in your mind is suddenly being changed by an other picture. You thought everything was just going fine between the two of you, and that things were going to continue like that for another hundred years. That's what you had counted on. You had invested in it. And now, all of a sudden, things have taken a different turn, and all at once you are faced with a situation to which you haven't yet adapted yourself. First you are thrown out of a certain mental picture, and now you are looking at an altogether different picture: I'm going to lose her, I will feel alone again. And in the process all sorts of feelings are being stimulated, going as far as the feeling of your mother or father leaving you. Fear. You react out of proportion. Now, if you only can take the right distance, so that you can actually *see* how it works, then it will tell its story and it's over. And if you can *stay* in that alertness, the possibility of identifying oneself is precluded in the long run.

V: And in that case there is no further cause for anxiety in the future, for then you can always rely on that one point to fall back upon. If only you can stay in contact with that, nothing untoward can happen to you. That is to say, you may still have a setback, but you can always come back to that one point.

A: You can always have a setback. For if you couldn't, then you just wouldn't have any further opportunity for growth. Just like a little child that is learning to walk. The child also falls, but the walking is such fun! He may fall ten or thirty times, yet each time he is back on his feet. Even if a regiment of Russian tanks were to trundle over you, you will yet stand up again. That is how you should live. That is true spirituality. And that is the nice thing about Self-realisation. Never mind the troubles you are letting yourself in for—They only help. Whereas the majority of you would simply collapse instead: 'Oh no! Now I've just managed to identify myself yet again. How stupid of me! But no, I shouldn't condemn myself!' In times of panic men always think they are going to die, while women think that they are going to go mad. You can set the clock by it.

V: I can understand that I can never *be* any of the things I perceive. I can reason it out, and I can find out for myself. For example, I can see my hand, therefore I cannot *be* the hand. But the next moment all that has vanished completely from my mind.

A: How do you know? How do you *know* that it has vanished?

V: Apparently that's what I perceive. But that perception only takes place afterwards. The moment you're asking me, 'How do you *know* that?', then I think, 'Of course!' But that is not perceiving it consciously then and there.

A: But how do you *know* all that? You know it, because you just *know* it. It is an *unconditioned* knowing.

V: So what?

A: Exactly—so what? This is something which is of the utmost importance. Because it means that there is an unchanging background, which knows everything all the time. It means that there is a 'knowingness' there, which indeed *knows* that there is knowledge and views about things, and that, at the same time, it doesn't change matters in any way.

How do you know that you are asleep? How do you know that you are happy? How do you know that you are unhappy? There is a *knowing* it. You, however, insist on understanding it *as a person*, which is perfectly impossible. Things can only be perceived, because you are seeing them through something that is *different* from what you, as a person, all think to know or not to know. And because one day all those 'concrete' matters will leave you, you can never consider them to be your *real* 'I'. You can never call them 'yourself'. So then why invest in them needlessly? Why attach so much value to it?

There is an unconditioned knowing, which knows exactly how things are put together. But *you* prefer to have your own show. This ego is like the clown who takes a bow for the acrobats who actually did the job. That is how this 'I'-consciousness operates. Suppose you have made a nice painting. Creating the painting as such was something that came about quite naturally, in fact even without your noticing it. After you've finished painting you say, '*I* made this painting'. So even though, by itself, painting the picture had been a completely spontaneous process, you have now made it a part of your identity. That way we always want to put our signature on actions which are really taking place quite spontaneously, and which we then claim as being 'mine'.

V: Is discrimination also something which is being known?

A: Discrimination is a kind of sword which enables you to cut open a new world. Each time you have a discriminative insight, a whole new world suddenly opens up before you. And it doesn't stop there, for there is no end to it. It is the sword which enables you to discriminate between what is true and what isn't. It is an incredible miracle, which is only given to human beings. You can even sharpen the sword. Then it will cut through all darkness. By the power of discrimination things will be exposed. The monsters of fear are killed by the sword of discrimination. Therefore in each case I attach great importance to the development of a person's power of discrimination.

Whenever I listen to the stories of people who found themselves in a crisis during World War II, I notice how sharp their discrimination must have been at the time. Now, by this I don't mean to say that all of us have got to go through a similar situation. On the other hand things can also go too far in the opposite direction, when everything is just going too easy. In which case you may have a generation which, although taking an interest in things, is basically making a mess of it, because the discriminative faculty has not been sharpened. If the power of discrimination is not adequate enough, then it will lead to a crisis; and a crisis in turn will again lead to the sharpening of the discriminative faculty. As with everything, it's a circle. Everything goes in circles: day and night, seasons, years, an entire life-time, planets, water...

After I've had my tea, the tea finally ends up in the toilet. Next it disappears into the sewage, and from there it flows into the sea. Then it changes into clouds, from where it falls down on the land again, down on the mountains in Austria. Comes into the river again, comes back into my teapot, and I drink it again. The gold that we are wearing now, the Pharaohs had it already. The leaves that were falling millions of years ago, are being burnt by us even today. These are primary data. Attraction, repulsion—These are natural laws. Everything is ordered. And why is that? Because that's the way it has been ordained. That is the order of things. The order exists on a smaller scale, as in micro-organisms, as well as on a larger scale. And although we, too, are part of that order, somehow we are under the impression that we can live *outside* that order. But that is *not* so. Perhaps in our thoughts we can, but in reality that is not possible. In reality we are part of a bigger order, which in turn is part of an even bigger order, and again that order is part of an even bigger order still. Man has got the discriminative power to be aware of this.

V: The animal has got awareness as well.

A: Yes, awareness, but no *self*-awareness. For, once an animal has been caught by a lion, then, all of a sudden, it becomes totally calm, even in the paws of the lion. It doesn't know the pang of death.

V: I once saw a movie in which a lion was shown catching a zebra. You could see the eyes of the lion and the eyes of the zebra, and in both cases the eyes radiated a total calm, both of them surrendering.

A: The difference with man is, that we have got *self*-consciousness, and then we mix up this self-consciousness with that which we really *are*. So our position is somewhere between the beasts and the gods. There is an animal part as well as a divine part in us. And the battle between the two still continues.

V: So in that sense there has hardly been any evolution since. After all, these things were observed even a thousand years ago.

A: At the same time even a thousand years isn't all that much. We tend to measure everything by the standard of the one hundred years that we are living here. Then a thousand years is ten times hundred, which, to us, may seem a lot. We are capable of launching ourselves onto the moon, but the man on the moon may still have to contend with his own jealousy, fearing that his neighbour below may be up to some tricks with respect to his wife. Deep within, man is still a cave-dweller. Despite all our knowledge we are still toddlers inside.

V: Could it be caused by the fact, that we have too much knowledge?

A: It could be. We have eaten from the tree of knowledge, and as a consequence we have fallen from the earthly paradise. In spite of all our knowledge, despite everything that we know, in spite of a brilliant intellect, we often prove ourselves to be incapable of solving the most elementary problems.

V: Yesterday I happened to run into this man who appeared to be fully drunk and full of hatred as well, and I started shouting at him. So then he came up to me, and all I could feel for him was just loads and loads of hatred. Inside me there wasn't a single noble feeling I was aware of.

A: It is very important not to deny anything. Don't deny your basic emotions. Never say to yourself: 'I don't *have* that. I have already transcended that.' It is better not to say that you are like this or like that, but to pay full attention instead. Each situation is completely new and stands on its own. No guarantee can be given as to how you are going to react to a certain situation.

(4th April, 1987, evening)

25

SEEING IS BEING

Visitor: I would like to know something about how to create the conditions for Self-realisation. As far as I can see, sleep is very important, as well as sticking to one's routine. I need about five, six hours of sleep. Often, when it is dark and cold, I don't feel like getting up, and so I stay in bed. Then I begin to dream and, subsequently, I wake up exhausted. I try to train myself to get the energy to jump out of bed as soon as I wake up.

Alexander: Consciousness knows three states: the waking state, the dream state, and deep, dreamless sleep. Somehow these three phases should be in balance, so that things are kept in their proper order. And that order is different for each of us. One person can do with four hours of sleep, while other people may need as much as eight or nine hours of sleep, otherwise they cannot function properly. In any case, in a 24 hours' day you certainly need to have at least one or two hours of deep, dreamless sleep, in which there is a total absence of *self*-consciousness. And there needs to be, for such total absence of self-consciousness is indispensable for us. On the other hand the less you invest in self-consciousness during the waking state, the less you need of dreamless sleep, because in that case you are actually *already* in a deep, dreamless sleep while awake. However, because of our identification during the waking state and, of course, on account of the biological clock, sleep is very essential. It is also said that, if man couldn't dream, he would go crazy.

Now, in the case of Self-realisation, what do we see? There we find that the amount of dreaming has become less, that in fact it has almost disappeared completely. This is somewhat difficult to prove, because any brain tests will show that at least some activity remains. In any case, the sleep of a Self-realized man is generally peaceful. And if his sleep is disturbed, or if he just happens to be a bad sleeper, then that is not a problem to him, because there is always the calm background. In his case, therefore, there won't be any identification with the condition of bad sleep. So, as insight deepens, sleep too will gradually be transformed, as will the dream state.

You may also be aware of the phenomenon where, while you are dreaming, you find yourself to be the observer of the dream at the same time. Maybe as a child you were more familiar with this. At that time you may even have had the feeling, that you could give a certain direction to your dreams. For at that age identification has not grown all that strong yet, and dreaming is then still a kind of movie. Then you can still go to sleep, hoping to have wonderful dreams. You could say that, in the case of a child, the position of the observer is far more innocent. Whereas later on, when we have learnt to identify ourselves with anything and everything, we get carried away by all sorts of dreams.

It is of vital importance to understand that the states of deep sleep, dreaming, and waking are *changing* conditions, and that these three states are perceived by something *else* which is Consciousness itself. The aim—if you can speak of an 'aim' at all—is learning to see just that. Herein lies the whole discovery of Self-realisation. In the process your identification with all the various movements will be reduced so that, at a certain stage, situations will no longer disturb you. As the whole issue becomes clearer to you, you will grow to be less dependent on any given situation, and you will be less inclined to identify yourself with all sorts of things. This process may be called *'sadhana'*. *Sadhana* is the path you are treading, where you are making one discovery after the other. It is just like an onion: You peel off one layer after the other, but at the core it is empty.

Deep, dreamless sleep is most essential. It is best to get up as soon as you realize that you are awake. Such deep, dreamless sleep is absolutely necessary, and the surprising thing is, that a similar condition may be attained during deep meditation. But then it takes place in the waking state, where, as you are meditating, you will notice that you have actually come to the same state.

What deep sleep really is, nobody actually knows. It is a riddle. All we know is, that there are these three alternating states of waking, dreaming, and deep, dreamless sleep. And again, they can only be known because of something else which is there, ever awake. If not, you would never be able to know whether you had had a good or a bad sleep, whether you had been dreaming, or what's been happening in the waking state. These three states are perceived by something which is always *immediately* present. If you would only constantly realize that for yourself—and that *in*-ground you always have, you always do *have* that immediate realisation—then mystery after mystery will be revealed to you. It cannot be otherwise. That is the basic doctrine. For the rest it is each individual telling his own story. And because each path, each revelation, is strictly personal, each one of them belonging to one particular manifestation, therefore these things can never really be shared with others. As far as I am concerned, experiences cannot really be shared.

V: Isn't it amazing, that we should thus surrender ourselves to sleep? We cling to our self-consciousness and yet, all of a sudden, we surrender ourselves.

A: It proves that, by itself, self-consciousness doesn't have any power. It is subordinate to the 'fourth' state, called '*turiyatita*'. One who realizes that this 'fourth' state is not really a state at all, but *the in-ground in the other three states*, will for the rest have few problems with those states.

Indeed, such surrendering to deep sleep is an incredible mystery, because, while you are asleep, anything may go wrong with the body. During the night you may get a cerebral haemorrhage, you may suddenly have a cardiac arrest, and still you do surrender yourself perfectly to that state. There are people who will start to reflect on such matters and, as a result, dare not go to sleep any more. But they are overcome by sleep all the same. You should not think, however, that deep, dreamless sleep is the same as Self-realisation, because ignorance is still present there.

On the other hand the 'fourth' state never sleeps. *Turiyatita* is ever awake. In any case, there has to be some form of basic trust in existence as such, if not you wouldn't even *dare* to go to sleep. Then, if you were to go to sleep, you would be in a state of great panic. And in greater panic even while in the waking state.

V: Something similar may happen to you, for example, when you wake up in an environment that is completely alien to you, or if you happen to spend the night in a forest all by yourself.

A: I think everybody should do it once. In India various means are adopted in order to overcome fear. One of them is to spend the night all alone in the jungle. I once did it. It is quite something. Your sense of orientation has disappeared completely. It is really quite a scary situation. After all, you may be eaten up. So all sorts of fears come to the surface.

V: When I first started practising meditation, I was completely ignorant of such things. Then I locked myself up in a room which was pitch-dark. At first I was terribly afraid, because I thought there were ghosts there. It took me some time before I was able to observe things properly, and then I discovered that there was nothing at all.

A: One should know about these things. In ancient texts about meditation you will find an exact description of all the things that you may expect. In that way they prepare you for it. And when you are actually being initiated into meditation, you are given an exact description of the colours which you are going to see, and of the manifestations that may present themselves to you. Though we may look upon these things as part of our own inner projections of fear, there is a regular pattern to it. If you are prepared for it, then you will know what these phenomena mean, and then, as long as you are well-centred, they cannot do you any harm. Then all sorts of fears may be overcome that way. And there is quite a number of them. Most people do not get to that point, but apparently you invited these phenomena yourself, which is something brave to have done.

V: According to Freud, fear is always connected with the fear of death.

A: Yes, but then his daughter didn't agree with that. She said it is not the fear of death, but the fear of losing love. And I would rather agree with that.

Every human being is love itself. But because we keep on forgetting that, we look for love in other beings. In matters of attention and love we tend to be rather demanding and insistent. We want to *get* love, to *have* love. Once you've forgotten that, at the bottom of your existence, you *are* love, then you go in search of love in your environment. That is also the way you were taught. As soon as you come to realize that you *are* love, then you will recognize that love in others as well. Then you realize that love is the *re*-cognition of the essence of the other; you perceive that the other, too, is love. But first you must have recognized it within your own being.

V: Is there no more fear, once you have realized?

A: Ultimately you will be free from fear.

V: How do you handle pain?

A: I prefer not to. I just handle it. I don't *think* about it. I do notice a sense of relief though, for example, when the dentist phones to cancel my appointment. As a matter of fact, my day looks somewhat brighter then. So I let it tell its story. I don't pretend to be free from fear, for that would be lying. Nor can I say I have fear, for I don't know it. It's just that I haven't been in a situation yet, where fear might manifest itself. For example, I don't know what I would do, if I would be tortured. So far it has never happened, so I don't know.

V: Is fear also a kind of urge to survive?

A: It certainly is as far as the body is concerned. But what I have seen for myself is that, whenever there is fear, there is identification. And if there is no identification, then there cannot be any fear. So in that case it cannot seize you. Fear of death is the fear to disappear. Identification with the body. But if I know that I am *not* the body, but the Consciousness in which this body appears, and in which it will disappear one day, then where is the fear of death?

V: I have always had the idea that a Self-realized man, or an enlightened man, didn't smoke, didn't drink, etc. Yet Nisargadatta Maharaj used to smoke *bidis* non-stop. So, is a certain form of self-discipline not really necessary then? Or is there no longer any need for it, once you are enlightened?

A: Even now there is no need for it. But something will force you to follow various disciplines, until you know again how things are put together. Then there won't be any more forcing. Then there won't be any more 'must', but there will be 'may' instead.

There are infants that do not live very long. A little bit of night-frost and it is over. On the other hand there are people that may be put in the freezer, and they come out all right. One person can eat a lot and nothing happens, while the other has eaten one small croquette, and he is sick like a dog, or he may even have a heart-attack. Each has his own responsibility in this matter, because everyone knows what is bad and what is good for himself. I'm not going to tell you not to drink or smoke. That is your business. It isn't *my* body. And if you want to drive your car after you've had too much to drink, then that's your business too. If you *don't* want to do all those things, then that's fine too. But the interesting thing about Nisargadatta Maharaj was, that he stopped smoking the moment the doctor advised him against it. And I can't see most people doing that.

I take the view that everything is perfect as long as you can touch a thing, and also can let go of it again. But if it has got hold of you, then you are on the wrong path. If you can't keep off the drink, then there is a problem. The 'Foundation For Ideal Advertising' has a beautiful slogan: 'Do you have problems because you're drinking, or do you drink because you've got problems?' Where is the borderline? It applies to drinking, to smoking, to drugs, to sex. If it gets hold of you and it is keeping you in its grip, then I disapprove of it—that is, if I'm asked about it. But if you can touch a thing and also can let go of it again, then that's perfect. Why not? If sex becomes an addiction, things become a mess. If drinking becomes an addiction, things become a mess. Is smoking becoming an addiction? Then there will be problems.

But if you can do both doing *and* not-doing, then there won't be any problem. Everything is a possibility. Everything is available. But can you let go of it again? That is what matters. So be aware of what you get hold of.

V: Is it any use to live a healthy life?

A: Not as far as I am concerned. Nor to live a long life.

V: I mean it more in the sense of an integrated life. A healthy body without spirituality isn't of much use either.

A: Ashtavakra was one of the greatest men of enlightenment that ever lived. He was called by that name, because he had eight defects, '*ashta vakra*'. He was hunch-backed, his mucous membranes didn't function well, and so on. Eight defects, yet he was perfectly enlightened. Enlightenment has got nothing to do with health. Absolutely nothing. If you have a healthy body—well, that's fine for you, but it has nothing to do with enlightenment. There are always people who will ask you, 'Why did Nisargadatta and Ramakrishna die from cancer of the throat?', and, 'Why did Ramana Maharshi have cancer?' For such people ought to have died in perfect health—That's what those people would have preferred. Healthy and athletic. Supple and athletic. To die perfectly healthy like a true yogi—What madness!

V: All right, we are not the body. Still the body is an instrument. I often take better care of my car than I do of my own body.

A: I know all that, but it has nothing to do with Self-realisation. The majority of those healthy people have but very little intelligence and are not spiritually-minded in any way. Nine out of ten people are healthier than all of you put together, yet they have never heard of spirituality.

V: My deepest desire is truth. Is it the same as realisation?

A: Yes, it is.

V: But if truth is one's very self, then what is there to seek anyway?

A: The search is the running *away* from Self-realisation. All seeking is a *not*-accepting. Seeking is a movement *away* from acceptance. That is why the spiritual seeker is the most pitiable figure you can imagine. These things are told to you out of compassion.

V: Now and then I feel the need to sum up things. For, after a whole day's discussion, I tend to become confused.

A: You can observe that. Why do you want to sum up things? Because you want to squeeze them into concepts and ideas. Just observe what you are doing: You feel like wanting to sum up things. Now, we just saw that things are definitely not to be summed up. Instead, they are only to be *seen*. Total acceptance is not some *doing*, not a form of summing up things. But because the thinking mind is realizing that its position is being threatened, it has a tendency to start summing up everything. And after you have summed it all up in a number of ideas, then you will be able to say to yourself, 'Now I understand it'. While, as a matter of fact, you just missed the whole point. The invitation is to *see*. A summing-up is not *seeing*. A summing-up is to organize anew the confusion, which should be seen and transcended instead.

V: My summing-up would be: Letting go by seeing.

A: But that isn't going to be of any use to you! It is something like macaroni with potatoes—It just doesn't make any sense! The very *seeing* transcends. Each summing-up is to start up a religion, to set up a creed. The seeing *is* the setting free. Seeing is Being.

(5th April, 1987, morning)

26

CONSCIOUSNESS IS NOWHERE NOT

Visitor: What exactly is Self-realisation?

Alexander: No longer to be interwoven with body, mind and feelings. Knowing who you *are*. But you are interested in a perfect formula. You would prefer to become a catholic, if it wasn't for the bother of it—As long as it is convenient.

V: I find it hard to report at home about the issues that are being discussed here.

A: Because there *is* no issue. And you cannot report about nothing. What I try to make clear, doesn't exist. Nor can it be reproduced. If you could reproduce it, you would have made it into a concept. If I am asked right after the lecture what I've been talking about, then I don't recall it. For that reason we have recording equipment to help us. That will recall it. Something which has been transcended, is dissolved. That is why you can't remember it, retain it. What you can remember about yourself, is memory. But what you *are*, you can't remember. Memory is a different word for attachment. But you cannot be attached to nothing. You cannot be attached to the 'I-am-ness', to what you *are*. But you can certainly have an idea about everything that may be taken away from you, about everything that you are attached to, even when life is showing you, that all those things may just disappear before your very eyes. Everything that you want to hold on to, will be beaten out of your hands. On the other hand what I *really* am, cannot be beaten out of my hands, nor can I remember it. Because I *am* that. What I am *not*, I can remember. That is why memory is responsible for the personality. But I am not the personality.

Your interest lies in a continuation of the false, in the continuation of the *contents* of consciousness. That is what you have invested in. Your investment lies in being a good boy or a good girl, or in daring to do something. All of which is kindergarten work. It's all right when you're still a fourteen year old, but not when you are forty. Your only interest lies in the improvement of your miserable condition. As soon as it improves you say, 'I'm doing fine'. Until things take an opposite turn again. We are not dealing with the personality here.

V: Is there one single question to be asked from the reality?

A: A million questions even.

V: Do all words concern the manifested by definition?

A: Yes, they do, unless you can see a word as a reference.

V: Are there still any problems in the *un*manifested Being?

A: Of course not. But even now there aren't. A problem is something manifest. What *is* a problem basically? You don't investigate. There is just no end to asking questions for the sake of satisfying the intellect or the thinking mind. And the solution never lies there. Try to ask questions that have nothing to do with body, thinking and feeling.

V: That is not possible.

A: Did you investigate that?

V: Well, before any question may arise, there has got to be a thought first.

A: First there is a non-comprehending, and from that a question is formed. Try to ask questions that are *not* meant to make a system of thought fit together. The whole phenomenon of asking such questions is an absurd phenomenon. First understand the *process* of asking questions, and then ask questions freely. We are so used to making problems about all that is produced by body and mind, about all that is produced by the *manifestation*. Somehow or other man is not capable of living simply in the reality he experiences, from second to second, of seeing and accepting, and of *being*. Still that is all the capital you've got. The Ever-present never leaves you, for that is what you *are*. All your yoga, all your sex ideas, all your anti-sex ideas, all your little health cures—they do not lead anywhere. For the Ever-present is always there, with or without cure. Consciousness does not ask you whether you like it. You either join in the cadence of life, or you go against it. That's all.

V: So in that case there is nothing further to ask.

A: That is a conclusion. But *are* you in that position? Is that *really* your experience? It is either a question of total acceptance or of fiddling. And fiddling is not the truth.

V: You're saying that fiddling is not the truth. But truth *is* the Totality. So if I say that I'm basically the truth, then even if I would be telling a hundred lies, then that is not going to make any difference. For nobody can change anything about *the* truth. It simply *is*.

A: In that case you are talking about *two* forms of truth: *absolute* Truth—which every man *is*—and *relative* truth. Now, if you are looking at things from *absolute* Truth, then you won't feel the *need* to tell a hundred lies. On the other hand if there *is* such a need, then, somewhere, something is not quite right. As long as truth has not been completely integrated by you, things will turn against you. In which case you will feel that, somewhere, something is not fitting in. Truth is to be perfectly integrated in the reality you are living. If that is not the case, it will have its revenge. If you say, 'If everything is just an illusion, then I can get away with anything', then you are forgetting one thing: That you are seeing everything as an illusion, except your *own* hocus-pocus. Then you look upon everything as an illusion, except yourself. And if there is any illusion at all, then surely it must be *that*.

V: That from which everything originates cannot be experienced. But can it be known?

A: Certainly. Because knowing and experiencing are two different things. In fact, knowing *precedes* experience, whereas experience is already something objectified. Experience is *objectified* knowing. But knowing as such is not objectified.

V: Is it possible for the Self to know where it comes from?

A: The moment the Self knows where it comes from, it is made into an object. Then it has already become thinking. It is very important in the end to see that the Whole contains all the parts, whereas a fragment such as body, thinking or feeling, can never contain the Whole. Knowing *is* the Whole, the Totality. And this knowing is simply *there*, whether you like it or not. Absolute Knowing includes all the fragments. But a fragment like thinking, a fragment like feeling, a fragment like a body, or even a combination of all three of them, cannot possibly ever include the Whole. A fragment is always a kind of Baron von Münchhausen who is trying to pull himself out of the morass. Such a thing is impossible.

The Knowing is the *unconditioned* knowing, which includes all *conditioned* knowing. But, as both of them are simultaneously there, the possibility of identification with a fragment is there all along. And whenever that takes place, it *appears* as if a fragment would know something. Now, what you are seeking is satisfaction for this fragment which, however, can never be satisfied. Therefore see the Totality, and then the fragment will no longer be a problem. But if you see only the fragment, then even the Totality becomes a problem to you. The only thing you can reflect on is the fact, that the Whole includes all the fragments, and that a fragment can never include the Whole. Realize that you are the *Totality* of things. Each time when you identify yourself with a fragment, you are bound to get stuck somewhere or other. *Because* you are not a fragment. You are even more than the sum of all the parts. If you add up all that you can possibly know, even then you are still more than that.

V: But you can't be the Totality, unless you are in the here-and-now...

A: You *are* the Totality *in* the here-and-now. It *has* never been otherwise, and it *will* never be otherwise. But you prefer to put yourself forward as an idiot in a fragment, in a personality, in an ego or in a non-ego, in an emptiness, or in whatever you want to call it.

V: Is this total Being unlimited?

A: There are absolutely no limits to it. Which is why we are limitless. Which is why happiness is limitless too. This is the only thing which needs to be realized.

V: So body, mind and feeling can never realize it?

A: Exactly. Strictly speaking you cannot say, 'I am Self-realized'. Nor can you say, 'I am not Self-realized'. It is better not to say anything.

V: When exactly will body-mind-feeling stop seeking?

A: At death. And not even then, for by that time you will have learnt to identify yourself to such a degree, that you want your miserable concern to continue. In that case you will have to be incarnated again. You can also jump off the roof, which some people believe to be a solution. But all such things are not going to be of any help. Accept what *is*.

V: So the Knowing has nothing to do with the individual person?

A: I bow before your wisdom.

V: Hence the expression, 'If I understand myself, then I will also understand the other'.

A: If you understand yourself, then you're having certain *ideas* about yourself. Then you may happen to come across other people that have the same ideas. And in that case you 'understand' each other. But nothing worse than to 'understand' an other person. For in doing so you belittle the other. In doing so you reduce the other to an *idea*. Man is more than an idea.

V: The notion that consciousness is flowing everywhere, still sticks to my mind.

A: Consciousness *doesn't* flow. In fact, it is absolutely still. A brooklet flows. Consciousness is everywhere, it is nowhere not. Therefore, it cannot flow.

V: Then how do I get rid of that concept?

A: Who wants to get rid of a concept? A concept is a concept is a concept. A tree is a tree is a tree. It cannot be said enough. There is an old Chinese poem:

> *When I was a child,*
> *trees were trees,*
> *men men,*
> *and horses were horses.*
> *The air was the air,*
> *and the sun was the sun.*
> *Then I went in search,*
> *and I became spiritual.*
> *Then trees were men,*
> *men were the sun,*
> *the sun was clouds,*
> *and clouds were water.*
> *Now that I have found myself again,*
> *trees are trees again,*
> *and the sun is the sun,*
> *men are men again,*
> *a cloud a cloud again.*

V: So the Totality is basically a source from which everything originates.

A: If you really could see the point we are dealing with here, then you cannot say anything meaningful about it any more. You might say something poetic like, 'It is the Source', but even that is not altogether true. No fragment is capable of voicing the Totality. Whatever you may say about it, it can never be That. And if you want to say anything about it at all, then it will become a Zen poem, or a *Tao Te Ching*, or a *Upanishad*. Besides, everything *has* already been said, so it isn't new even. Of all the things silence comes nearest to it, because silence is the absence of things. Silence is the possibility within which sounds may appear. Emptiness comes close to it, but that also doesn't quite cover it. That is why it is said in the ancient *Upanishads*, 'Though It is knowable, yet It cannot be known. Though immediately visible, yet It cannot be seen. His is an unnameable name'...

Once you see it, then you can no longer be occupied with it.

V: Is the ego the cause of the fragmentation?

A: Ego *is* the fragmentation. Egotism is the belief in an 'I'-structure. And then, on closer investigation, it turns out that there *isn't* any structure, or it will have to be a fabricated structure. This ego is a fabrication. And this fabrication is perceived by something which is *bigger* than that fabrication, by That which is ever present. Besides, such an ego appears *and* disappears at times. So, naturally, such a thing can never bind me. It cannot free me nor can it bind me.

V: Is the Self-realized man always in the here-and-now?

A: Yes, just like you.

V: But I'm not conscious of it.

A: That doesn't make it any different—You are in it all the same. The here-and-now is a fact. Whether you are aware of it or not. Even now you are enlightened, but you are not aware of it.

V: What actually is the difference between being asleep and waking up?

A: The difference is the difference. A difference is being perceived there, where there *isn't* any difference. The difference is perceived by something else, which *itself* doesn't know any difference, which is perfectly *in*-different. And with *that* you are seeing the difference. There has *got* to be this background, and that background is what you *are*. While the difference is there to enable you to see how things are put together, to enable you to experience things, to enable you to be conscious of things. As a matter of fact, differences are absolutely necessary. For, if you wouldn't know any differences, then you wouldn't be conscious of things.

Consciousness wants to become conscious of itself. In order to do so, it creates discord. Meanwhile everything is perceived by 'uni-cord'. You may find it expressed in dreaming, and you may find it expressed in waking. There is a story to everything: 'The Adventure of Consciousness'.

V: While listening to our questions, it would seem that people are more interested in duality, whereas that very duality seems to stand in the way of the Absolute...

A: Duality makes the realisation of Consciousness possible. By too much of digging into duality, however, by all our efforts to look at just *one* side of the matter, you are precisely inviting that side to come forward. That is a never-ending story, which doesn't get you one millimetre nearer to Self-realisation.

V: Consciousness is manifesting itself in order to become conscious of itself. Is that what is called 'creation'?

A: Before creation the only thing that was there in the universe, in the cosmos, was the *absence* of things. Absence within a Presence. Nothing was there. Not-a-thing, not any object. It was the total implosion of the universe. Then followed the *ex*plosion. Within that space, within that availability, creation started going. At this point in time, however, we have come to stress the material aspect of things to such a degree, that we take that aspect to be the only reality. But that is not the case. So the manifested will just continue its quest for itself, for its own origin. And then, in the long run, the expansion of the universe will be ready again for an implosion. It is inevitable. We call it the 'breathing of the universe'. And one such explosion is called 'one day of Brahma'.

V: How do we know all that?

A: We know it through something which is *bigger* than all that. That is Consciousness. And That is nowhere not.

(5th April, 1987, afternoon)

27

THERE IS NO PRECONDITION FOR BEING CONSCIOUS

Alexander: You will have noticed without any doubt, that you are hardly left with any other alternative, than to make all your experiences, all that you call 'I', into an image, into an idea. Irrespective of whether this idea relates to an outer world-perspective or to an inner world-view, you have got an idea about yourself, a 'self-image'. At the same time there is the feeling deep within you, that this image may not be what you *really* are. And, indeed, it isn't, for if you would actually come down to that which you really *are*, then you wouldn't find any place there to call 'yourself'. And this is basically what is scary about it. At the same time this very fear is the inspiration, the motor which is causing you to create such a self-image.

What you basically experience about yourself is that in reality there is a 'nobody', a 'not-any-body' there. If I start looking for 'Alexander', I cannot find one, although I may have certain ideas *about* Alexander. Similarly, Rajneesh cannot find a 'Rajneesh'. You, too, won't find any 'John', nor will Krishnamurti find a 'Krishnamurti'. All that you could possibly come up with are *images* about something, images which have been created by you for fear of the reality. And, conversely, someone who no longer fears what he really *is*—namely the emptiness, or to put it quite differently, the availability or presence—will not feel the need to create any further images about himself. And the life of such a person will then be free from the pressure or stress of the self-consciousness, and even from the effects of a 'de-pressurized' self-consciousness.

Now, in practice, what does it mean? It means that, if you identify yourself with an idea, with an image, or with a fragment—despite the fact that you *know* from your own inner experience that you are basically *not* that—then you cannot but miss the whole point about yourself. For you will then be creating a self-consciousness, an 'I'-consciousness with all sorts of ideas, none of which applies to your *true* being. Such identification also accounts for the feeling you tend to have, that somehow, somewhere, things are always just falling short of perfection, that the picture is never quite complete. Everybody has that experience.

In whatever way you are going to express the truth about yourself, even if you were to remain totally silent, without saying a word, even that will not make the picture complete. Then you would say, 'It isn't total emptiness either'. And then you will just stop saying anything about it. For nothing applies. Deep down there is a *knowing* that you are *not* an idea, that you are *not* the body, that you are *not* the mind, that you are *not* the intellect, and that you are *not* any feeling. Such a situation may seem insecure to you, but in reality it isn't. The reality about yourself is totally without any location, is so much spatial, that at present you have no other alternative than to pour it into some form or other. That's also the way you were trained, that's the way you were educated, that's the way you were drilled.

So long as you haven't invited that emptiness, so long as you haven't actually realized that availability, all you can do is to squeeze yourself in a self-consciousness and live from that position, in quest of that which you have been all along. And whatever you may want to say about it, it is wrong. If we want to speak about it at all, then we try to speak as little untruth about it as possible. But whatever you may come up with, it can only serve as a reference. Just as the *sign* 'Amsterdam' can of course never be Amsterdam itself. In practice, therefore, all those who are treading the path of self-discovery, are to be constantly alert, constantly aware, constantly present, as a result of which all things will automatically become clear.

The right *sadhana* is an effortless *sadhana*. In fact, all effort is a cramp already. The only thing which is always without any effort whatsoever, is the awareness in everything. And that isn't *my* discovery, nor is it *your* discovery: That is the simple truth. Not because *I* say so, but because you can directly see it for yourself. Looking at it from the outside, you could say that there is a lot to be done. But, as you get a closer look from the inside, then it will become clear that nothing *can* be done. Though this might seem contradictory, in reality that is certainly not the case. As far as I am concerned there is absolutely nothing that can be done in order to be aware, in order to be present. It is absolutely ruled out that you could possibly do anything in order to be aware. For awareness is your primary datum. The thing is, we are all living by our *secondary* datum. And that is how we get carried away by the caravan of thoughts and feelings which, in the majority of cases, leads to a distorted situation.

Then what is the way back? The way back is to see that there *is* no way back. What is the way? Seeing that there *is* no way.

Visitor: But in order to be aware, you have to do something?

A: No, you are already aware.

V: But don't you have to throw all the ballast overboard?

A: That is what you have heard, what you have learnt, what you were told. You have it from hearsay, it is second-hand information. You've heard it whisper. And since you are too lazy to find out for yourself whether that is actually true, you just swallow it. For that is the way you were trained. But this question requires investigation. It requires *self*-investigation. In this matter you cannot depend on any authority. Not even on the authority of the teacher, or rather, *not* on the authority of the teacher. Here you are asked to do *self*-enquiry. Just see for yourself, whether it is actually *true* that nothing can stand in the way of awareness. Nothing is standing in the way of your presence. There is no precondition for being conscious. On the other hand conditions are certainly necessary in order for you to exist in any 'particular' way. Conditions may be made regarding the *contents* of Consciousness, in order to give it a certain direction or change its environment, or in order to change yourself, meaning, of course, the *image* of yourself. Any ambition, however, to change such a self-image is the very outcome of *non*-Self-realisation. So this is really a question of 'all or nothing': It is either 'seeing' or 'not-seeing'.

V: And if you *do* see it, then would you call that 'being in your centre'?

A: What we are just trying to explain is that, quite strictly speaking, there *is* no centre to be found. Because you *are* everything. When I look up to the sun, then my attention stretches from the earth to the sun. When I look into the universe, then my attention, my consciousness, is embracing the universe. Obviously the whole universe does not fit into my eyes. That is impossible. And when I look inwards, I see the same space. Just go and lie down on the grass and look up: infinite space. There is no end to it. Then close your eyes: infinite space as well. And then it would seem as if some 'person' is standing in between, but that is definitely not the case. You are a spatial being. If not, how could you be *conscious* of space?

Consciousness is bigger than space, for space is perceived by Consciousness as an object. Space is therefore appearing within something even *more* spacious. It applies to both outer space—that is to say, what is *called* 'outer' space—and to inner space. Thus you *are* everybody and everything. Such is unlimited Consciousness. The fact that you taught yourself to limit that Consciousness to body, mind and feelings is too bad, but the Self-remembrance will nevertheless just continue to knock at your door. And that is the reason, too, why at some stage a person may start getting interested in this kind of questions. And why? Because you actually *know* it already. It's just that you need to be reminded once more. And in some cases reminding will take place over a long period of time, while in others it only takes a very short period. This *seeing* is Self-realisation—nothing else.

V: At the same time this 'I'-consciousness appears to be the active party, constantly creating ideas and taking the way back.

A: It is the active pole within the *non*-active pole. By itself Consciousness is without any activity, so the activity of the 'I'-consciousness is manifesting itself within something *non*-active. When I'm looking to see what time it is, then at that moment, too, I am measuring time *within* timelessness. So when an 'I'-consciousness appears, then it is perceived within something far bigger. It's just that I happen to know that I'm that far bigger thing and not the smaller thing. For that is what I was told, and subsequently I found it to be true. But you are making it all far too complicated. You first want to make the 'I'-consciousness turn somersaults and have it do all kinds of interesting tricks, and then you just hope to have reached 'that other thing'. That is impossible.

V: But don't you need the 'I'-consciousness for making the link then?

A: You don't need anything. You *don't* need to have the 'I'-consciousness, for it is there *already*. But you have divided yourself into fragments, and then you have come to believe that you are nothing *but* the fragments. The fact that you think it to be so, isn't so bad, but you have even come to *feel* that way. And a feeling goes even deeper than a thought. The 'I'-consciousness can never be the problem. Never. The 'I' is not a problem. It takes its place in the whole history of existence.

V: It isn't a problem, provided I stay aware of the greater awareness?

A: No, it doesn't work like that. The greater awareness is *itself* aware of a possible 'I'-consciousness which, of course, has to be smaller than that in which it is seen. By definition this hand has got to be smaller than that in which it appears. How could it be otherwise?

V: So basically it is exactly the other way round?

A: Yes, it is.

V: It's *me* looking at the 'I'-consciousness.

A: Quite. If not, you wouldn't even know that you *had* such a thing in the first place. That's why I tell sometimes: I have got a house, but I *am not* the house. I have a bed, but I *am not* the bed. I have a body, but I *am not* the body. I have a mind, but I *am not* the mind. I *am* consciousness, but I do not *have* consciousness.

The only thing which you *are*, is Consciousness. The rest you *have*. So this is basically all that you need to remember.

V: What I have difficulty with is not the fact that we are one with the Emptiness, but all the things that are standing in the way towards it.

A: That you are the Emptiness, that you probably got from somewhere else. You are the Emptiness and the Fullness at the same time. You are not just a fragment. Properly speaking you are *everything*.

V: Yes, but my experience is that my thoughts set off a chain of activities.

A: There is no question of *your* activities. Yesterday it briefly came up for discussion. Someone asked, 'In that case, is there anything *you*'re doing?', and I said, 'I don't do anything.' As a child I was taken along to the zoo without my wanting to. And now I am taken along to this place without my wanting to. Because in some brochure it says that I have to be here. Now, what is the difference between my being taken to the zoo or my being taken to this place? There is no real difference. At that time I was just taken along, it wasn't my decision, it just happened. And now this is happening in exactly the same way. There are all sorts of reasons that are perfectly unclear to me, in combination with a billion of causes for certain effects, which are causing these things to happen, including the meeting with my grand-parents at the Central Station in Rotterdam. So to say now that there is a free will... I think that's putting it strongly.

Without my wish I was taken to hospital as a child, because I was ill. Without my wish I had fallen ill. Without my wish I ran a temperature, which subsequently dropped again. Without having any say in it I was put into hospital, apparently because other people considered my manifestation to be of importance. But, as far as *I* was concerned, I hardly had anything to do with it, and even now I haven't. Whenever anything is happening in connection with my person, then everybody is just starting to get himself concerned with it, even without my asking anything. And when I have arrived at some place, then at once everybody will start off asking me: 'Have you had your tea?' So then I'm obliged to have something to drink and have my meal there, and then they will start treating me affectionately in all kinds of ways, and so on. All of which happens perfectly naturally. I don't need to do anything.

When you go and stand at a bus stop, then at a certain moment a bus will arrive there. It is all unbelievable! It is all taking perfectly care of itself. Billions of causes and effects. And to me even my speaking here is happening for no obvious reason. It is the collective pressure of billions of causes and effects, with which *I* haven't got anything to do. Really nothing at all. Nor am I responsible for it. For it isn't *me* who is doing it.

V: This self-consciousness harbours suspicion with respect to the Consciousness. It needs courage to break through that. What exactly is that courage?

A: Just realize that that presence is right here, that the availability is right here, that the conscious being is right here—and stay in that. Then, as you unwind within that very Consciousness, all things will automatically become clear to you, including such questions as courage etc. Don't focus on the past any longer. Don't focus any more on what happened then. This whole fascination for the past is a disease. It is an excavator. Even when there is nothing left to dig, you still go on digging from sheer force of habit. Your thinking, and more particularly your *comparative* thinking, your *analytical* mind, has become one big excavator. Because you think that a solution might well be forthcoming by knowing the past. And that may be the case, if you have been through some horrid things in the past, but for the average person with his average little problems it is absolutely unnecessary.

And I'm taking it one step further even by saying that, the more you realize that you *are* the availability and that presence, the more everything will become just that much easier, and then you will automatically see it. Just watch it, that you don't start looking for a solution through an analysis of the past. The past is dead, a remembrance, a product of memory. Life *itself* is providing its moments. Life is providing for its own manifestation. Constantly. So you needn't do anything in the sense of getting yourself actively concerned with questions like yours. Such questions only come up in the beginning.

Stay in 'I am', and then, within this 'I-am-ness', everything will automatically become clear.

V: You once said that the behaviour of someone who has reached enlightenment, doesn't necessarily have to change for the better. I don't get that.

A: You have to make a big difference between a Self-realized man or an enlightened man, and a saint. The Self-realized man is someone who knows what he *is*. So he knows that he is not a 'good' man, but he also knows that he is not a 'bad' man. And that, basically, it doesn't really matter. The real truth is, that it doesn't really matter at all. Nothing is unacceptable. On the other hand in the case of a saint, it's a different story altogether. The saint lives in conformity with the codes of his environment, as the environment prefers to see things. By contrast, the Self-realized man doesn't *have* any code. How is one to behave as an enlightened being? What *is* enlightened behaviour for that matter? It just doesn't exist! Then you could say, 'Yes, but if it is a question of enlightenment, then you will have stopped doing "bad" things anyway, won't you?' Well, it all depends... I have witnessed some very odd examples.

We remain obsessed by behaviour. Good and bad, morality—that kind of things. But Consciousness is far beyond morality. It may be that a man who is Self-realized is indeed showing decent behaviour. In that case he will have more clients than someone who *isn't* behaving so decently. That will be the only difference. After all, any person showing indecent behaviour will usually be considered a bit of a threat. Such a person does not set an example.

V: Then aren't there any rules to go by?

A: Good and bad are ideas. As Shakespeare, also a man of very great enlightenment, once wrote, 'There is no good or bad, but thinking makes it so.' Good and bad are notions. There is no such thing as 'good' or 'bad'. They are always related to something else. Just look at the things you hate most, and you will know where to find your own fears. Therefore you will go along with the teacher as far as your own fear will take you. Then you will say, 'Up to this point I can accept things, but now he is taking it a bit too far.' And at *that* moment you will have touched upon your own fear.

We all represent the most filthy as well as the most sublime. Everything is inside us. It is this silly *self-*consciousness which is restricting itself to a greyish midway by identifying itself, saying: 'And *this* is me'. Until it becomes clear that you are *everything*. And if ever it will become clear, then it will be with Self-realisation. You are everything. Including a Hitler, including a whore, including a saint. Everything is *in* you. Which is not to say that everything must be made *manifest*. That's a different story altogether. But everything is within you. Nothing is impossible, otherwise the possibility wouldn't be there in the first place. All that has ever become manifest, is possible. But we first invent a reality for ourselves, and then we are asking ourselves how all those things are possible. Apparently they *are* possible. To send six million Jews to the gas-chambers is, apparently, possible. All the ideas which you have built up for yourself, have nothing to do with the reality. Absolutely nothing.

V: Personally I would be quite afraid to do anything very bad.

A: Man—and all manifestation for that matter—is an extremely vulnerable phenomenon, subject to billions of influences. It is unbelievable that all is going as well as it does.

V: I actually feel bad, whenever somebody is being mean.

A: Yes, madam, but that's all part of the game, because we happen to live in a world, in which there are always *two* possibilities. If there is 'fun', then there is also 'trouble'. That is what duality is about. If there is 'pleasant', then there is also 'unpleasant'. The same hand that is caressing someone, may also torture. Now, is that a matter of being conscious? No, it is a matter of being *realistic*: These two possibilities are just *there*.

The only thing that is really important is, that you sweep before your own door. Instead of covering the whole world with leather, it is better to wear your own shoes!

V: Is consciousness also a fragment of the Whole?

A: Time is measured within timelessness. Space—the fact that I can perceive space—means that there has to be something bigger for space to appear in. Even though space is the most spatial thing you can imagine, its appearance must be within something which is even bigger than space. For that reason space is not the ultimate. So what is that, within which you are able to perceive space? That is Consciousness, which is even bigger than space. And Consciousness is what you *are*. But because we have learnt to identify ourselves with body, mind and feeling, we imagine Consciousness to be limited to a particular place.

Even in love you will find that that is not the case. As you grow in love, you become more spatial. As soon as your love diminishes, you become smaller, you become cramped. But as soon as there is love, everything becomes more spatial. Where there is no more love, everything will become stifling, for in that case the self-consciousness will make everything 'watertight' for itself. But as soon as love appears, the self-consciousness opens up, and almost automatically it becomes one with the Supreme.

V: And this openness is the so-called Nothingness?

A: 'Nothing' is a combination of 'not-a-thing'. No-thing, not-any-thing. It is something wonderful to realize, that you are the space in which everything appears and disappears. That is the *in-*ground, that is your primary datum. There are no troubles to be found there. Maybe just an odd little problem or so, but that will solve itself of its own accord. Just as *all* things solve themselves of their own accord.

V: In order to be able to experience timelessness, we have to use definitions, concepts, senses. Otherwise we wouldn't be able to experience it.

A: Is that so?

V: I don't know.

A: You are putting it as a proposition—That's why I'm asking.

V: To me it just doesn't seem possible to experience time-less-ness without using any concepts, so without using any words, any definitions.

A: Why limit yourself like that? Why should you have to say to yourself, 'I'm *only* the Emptiness'? Or why should you have to say, 'I'm *only* the body'? You are *both* the Emptiness *and* the body at one and the same time.

V: Yes, but as far as I am concerned, it is far more easy for me to understand the body, the manifested...

A: Oh no! You don't understand anything about the body. The fact that you can *perceive* the body doesn't necessarily mean, that there is anything to *understand* about it. Besides, *you* are not doing anything at all there! Suppose you have a small injury somewhere. Then that will just heal of itself. Regardless whether you do something about it or not. In the same way you also become ill without your consent. And one day you will also die without your consent, without your wish. Similarly, there are people who just go on living year after year without wanting to, while others, who would prefer an early death, live up to the age of hundred. Again, there are people who would like to become a hundred years, yet they die when they are twenty-one. A mother who is looking after six children, is snatched away from life, while some madman in an asylum goes on living to become a hundred and ten. It all seems totally unreasonable...

Realize what you *are*. You are always everything at one and the same time. So *both* this *and* that. For Consciousness doesn't exclude anything. *You* are excluding things. For example, when you are saying to yourself, 'I'm only the Emptiness!' Then you're heading for trouble, because you will get filled up anyway. Or you'll say, 'I'm the Fullness!' And then you suddenly find yourself in a phase of Emptiness. You are *both* empty *and* full, at one and the same time. In fact, you can only *be* full, *because* you are empty as well. Simultaneously. A cup can only be used, can only be full, *because* of the possibility of its being empty.

V: And the realisation of both these possibilities is there at one and the same time?

A: Yes, the realisation of it is simultaneous. Whereas now the *self*-consciousness is creating *conditions* for Self-realisation. It is something like the water telling: 'I don't *want* to be wet', or, 'I must *first* be dry, and *then* I will realize that I'm the wet water. So before that I'm first going to lie nicely in the sun in order to become dry, for that is the condition for realizing that I'm really wet.' But that is of course crazy. That is the gibberish of the seeker.

Why do we have problems? Why do we have troubles? Because we are seeking happiness for *ourselves*. Ninety-nine percent of our actions is aimed at seeking happiness for ourselves. Yet 'ourselves' does not exist…

V: So there is 'something' and 'nothing' at the same time? Is that duality?

A: That is duality. But duality is borne within something bigger than duality. There is one thing which knows *no* duality, and that is Consciousness itself.

V: But how do you realize 'something' and 'nothing' at the same time?

A: Just look at the clock. What time is it?

V: Twelve past twelve.

A: How do you know what time it is? How do you actually *know* that?

V: Because I can see it.

A: So just now you realized time *within* timelessness—*at one and the same time*.

V: But where is the timelessness?

A: Why is it that you need to look at the clock at all? Because right now you already *are* living in timelessness. For you *are* a timeless being—Awareness, Consciousness. At the same time you want to know what time it is. Ah! Now it's twelve hours thirteen. Again you are measuring time within timelessness at one and the same time.

V: How can I use this beautiful example in other cases?

A: Suppose there is a feeling coming up… Let's just take some wonderful feeling: You are all of a sudden overcome by feelings of love or so. Now, how do you *know* that?

V: Because I can feel it.

A: Right! Suppose there is an other feeling besides. Then could you feel it simultaneously? No, because you can only have one feeling at the same time. On the other hand the *opposite* of feeling has to be there, which is *non*-feeling. Yet only *one* thing may be felt by you. Therefore this *non*-feeling or *absence* of feeling cannot be but the *background,* against which the very appearance of feeling becomes possible.

An other example: You are entering a dark room. You want to switch on the light, but the bulb happens to be defective. What will your reaction be? You would probably say something like: 'All I can see is darkness'. Now, with what light were you able to see the darkness?

One more example: As you are getting on, your hearing diminishes. Then, at a certain moment, you notice that you aren't hearing any more. Now, how did you register the absence of any hearing?

V: Through the knowledge of the potential hearing.

A: Yes, but how do you actually *know* it, that your hearing has diminished?

V: By comparing it.

A: Sure, in the end you may call it comparing. But how did you actually *know* it? Suddenly you are deaf. How do you actually *know* that you are deaf? How do you *know* that you are seeing a dark room? By what light are you seeing the dark room? By what light do you hear or do you register the absence of hearing?

There is not one place to be found in your existence, not one place to be found in your body, no place whatsoever about which you could say, 'This is what I call "myself"'. For all of you are reaching outward to the very widest horizons, as well as inward to the very widest horizons, and that is what we have in common. Nothing else. For the rest we don't have anything in common. When you are looking outward: infinite space, without end. And when you're looking inward: infinite space as well. So why should you constantly identify yourself as a *finite* being, when you are always having the immediate realisation of *not* being finite? And as for this manifestation which is capable of thinking, which is capable of feeling, which is capable of eating and drinking and tasting besides—it is but a gift on top of it!

V: So is there an entity perceiving it?

A: There is no entity perceiving it. Wherever you may look, you won't find any entity or identity. For you are *without* identity. And each time when you *do* assume an identity, you will get into a crisis. The identity crisis. People with identity problems have *thinking* problems. The ideas which they have built up about themselves don't tally with the so-called reality. So they will find themselves in a crisis. And even if they try to make the reality fit in with the help of all sorts of images, the truth remains that you do not have any identity. There really isn't any place to be found inside of you, which you could possibly call 'John' or any other name. Now, if it's just for the sake of putting some name on a piece of manifestation—fair enough! But there is absolutely no way that you could possibly point to a place and say, 'And *this* is me'.

And this realisation is what unites all of humanity, for Consciousness is unlimited. Consciousness doesn't have any limits. And why? Because everything that can possibly come into existence is appearing in Consciousness, stays in Consciousness for a while, and will disappear again in Consciousness. So the fact that identities are bound to disappear, as at death for example, does not mean that *you* will have disappeared. Of course, as an illusory figure you will have disappeared. Self-realisation means that you have disappeared *already*, so even now, before your death.

V: That's why it doesn't make sense, when you're being told that you have been unconscious. For you can never *be* 'unconscious'.

A: No, unconsciousness doesn't exist, strictly speaking. On the other hand one may lose the control over certain channels which connected you to what is called 'the world', the whole mental production.

V: But one cannot 'lose consciousness'?

A: Certainly not.

V: Then how did the expression come up in the first place?

A: Obviously it is a manner of speaking. About someone who has become unconscious you could just as well say that he is 'in a coma', or that he has 'fainted'.

The nice thing about all this is, that you can verify it immediately for yourself. There must have been a moment in your life, when you began to experience yourself as 'yourself'. At some point you must have turned a huge somersault, when you began to assume an identity. There must have been a first beginning, when you became conscious of yourself. That is the case even now, but now it has become completely interwoven with all sorts of things.

And Self-realisation means that the interwovenness has become loose, that you are swimming through the nets in which you thought yourself imprisoned. Because the reality is full of holes. Then you will realize anew what you really *are*. And that is what you have been all along, but at present you are not aware of it. It's nothing bad, though I think that to persist in that situation would be somewhat unwise. In that case you would not be doing yourself a service.

(2nd May, 1987, morning)

28

ABOUT 'SPIRITUAL AUTISM'

Visitor: Sometimes I am able to observe the things that are taking place, and then I realize that I am *not* those things. I watch myself moving or talking, but to do so I really need to take quite a big distance. Is that what you mean by 'perceiving' things?

Alexander: It is what it is, but in the beginning you can hardly avoid such a pitfall. Because in almost all cases the motive which is causing you take a distance is, that you are not willing to connect with that which is presenting itself to you. So as such it may well be a way of keeping oneself out of things, though in the long run that will have its revenge.

Now, in order to perceive something, there has to be a distance. That does *not* mean, however, that you are going to *take* a distance. What we mean by 'perceiving' is a reference to the fact, that there is a distance *already*. If not, you just wouldn't be able to perceive a thing in the first place! However, many people draw the conclusion that, as *self*-consciousness, they should take a distance from things. And that is not what is meant here. So what you have to understand clearly is, that you have the ability to perceive everything—thoughts, body, pleasant or less pleasant feelings—*because* of the fact that there is a distance already.

The whole search, this whole spiritual journey which many people are making, is more likely to be an escape from reality, from what *is*, than a truly connecting anew with what *is*. So it is not so strange, that you would fall into that kind of trap. But if you do make it into an escape, then that is not going to make you any happier—That much will be brought home to you. Once you are really connecting with things, you will find that things are usually not all that bad. However, spiritual autism is something which quite a lot of people will have to deal with.

V: What do you actually mean by 'spiritual autism'?

A: Any form of taking a distance in the wrong manner. Autism is nothing but being unwilling to join in. Life is inviting you, is giving you an opportunity, but you say 'no'. You could also say 'yes' all the time, but of course that would amount to the same thing, only the reverse of it. Existence is an inescapable fact, and therefore it is not a question of 'yes' or 'no'. Existence exists. You can't get round it. He who sees that there is really no escaping it, will see the acceptance at the same time. And if you think you *can* escape it, then there is no acceptance of life. However, as you learn to accept the ugly, then along with it the beautiful will automatically come back. Then the whole scale of feelings will become possible again.

Obviously, such an ego is pure poverty. Spiritual autism is a form of narrowed consciousness. It is nothing but the unwillingness to connect with things under the cloak of spirituality. A form of withdrawing oneself in a more or less secure little inner world. Some people even use their meditation for it. In a sense philosophy, too, is nothing but spiritual autism, because it tends to exclude several possibilities. To identify yourself completely with any fragment whatsoever means, that you are basically excluding possibilities. For example, if you say, 'My guru is the only true one', or, 'My way is the only way', then you are being spiritually autistic. Then you have enclosed and curtailed yourself.

All that needs to be seen is right here—pleasant or unpleasant, dark or light, clarity or confusion. Just *see* what is there.

About 'Spiritual Autism'

Then there won't be any need to *take* a distance, nor will there be the need to let go of anything. For whoever has got the idea that there is something to let go of, is also living under the impression that he is attached to something.

V: Then the same holds good for involvement.

A: Absolutely. If the clarity is there, then the involvement will also be there. Involvement means 'not excluding anything'. In that case you are simply identified with the availability, with that which you truly *are*. And once you have come to identify yourself with that availability, with the presence, then you are also giving the opportunity for everything to become manifest. And from that loving awareness the whole thing relaxes. Then you are part of humanity again.

That presence, that conscious being, that seeing, is never absent, for that is the Ever-present. With realisation the illusion disappears that there would be 'other' states, that there would be 'higher' states of consciousness, or that there would be people who are 'higher' or 'lower' than you. We also call it 'the Union with the Teacher'. Of course, union in essence, not in manifestation. Then you are being raised as it were to the level at which the teacher wants to make the whole thing clear to you. An other word for it is '*satsang*': 'meeting the Essence'. At that moment you also realize, that you need somebody to show you that you *don't* need anybody. And that, in fact, you have nothing to do with the guru. He is the obstetrician, and then the baby is born. It may be that a friendship develops after that, but that is an exception rather than the rule.

V: Is that also a trap?

A: Ninety percent of the disciples gets stuck in the sphere of the teacher, unable to let go of him. It *is* a trap. The last thing for you to be attached to is always the teacher. So we don't encourage any friendship between teacher and disciple. It always gives rise to problems. And the teacher will behave unsympathetically on purpose, lest the least attachment should develop. The biggest trap is the personal relationship with the teacher. You cannot have a personal relationship with the teacher. It is quite impossible. Nor does he have any preferences, for no one. Because he perceives everybody as the one Consciousness. One of the worst things you can do to a teacher is to make something of him which he isn't. For in doing so you isolate him at a social level. Thousands of teachers have been caught that way. Rajneesh had been isolated completely, Krishnamurti was completely isolated. Don't think it's fun!

In the tradition of Advaita Vedanta there is no place for it. No room is allowed for worship, for the personality cult, for the guru cult and other such things. I find that quite healthy, for otherwise it may give rise to awkward situations. Not only for the teacher, but for the disciple as well. For instance, people say that one ought to have respect for the teacher. No. Either there *is* respect or there isn't. But you cannot say that there *should* be respect. That would be somewhat like saying, that you *should* love somebody. You can't force such things. If there is respect—fine. If there isn't—fine too. But enforced respect *is* no respect. That is terror.

The only thing that matters—at least here—is to create a situation in which the transmittance of that clarity becomes possible. And then the greatest gift you can give to the teacher is your Self-realisation. After all, that was your objective in the first place. His reward is the fact that you live in that clarity, the fact that you are seeing it. For the rest nothing.

V: The first time when I came here, it seemed as if I had understood everything that you were saying. And now I don't understand anything at all. Still I want to realize it before I die.

A: What is happening to you, happens to a lot of people. It is a phase in which not a single concept, not a single idea which you have about things, is giving you any more hold. You could call it a kind of dawn, a kind of birth of the real Self. You can hardly avoid becoming emotional then. You can hardly avoid thinking that you are going to go mad. You can hardly avoid thinking that you are going to die. Because, as a matter of fact, that is what is happening to some extent.

V: Then what *is* it to die?

A: To die means, that you are no longer in control of anything. That there is no longer anyone there to hold your hand. And that, when all the concepts have fallen off, you cannot live in them any more. Then you will have to go and live in something else, which means that you are going to live in your *natural* state. At that point many people take to their heels, whereas right then it is of the utmost importance to stay in the Being as alert as possible. Then, at a certain point, things will dissolve. And then you will no longer need to have any concepts whatsoever. One day you will discover that your ideas are totally crazy, and that there is absolutely no further need for those silly ideas.

V: I have the impression that there *are* moments when I actually see it. But then I slip back into an idea or some such thing. Now, if I am in the natural state...

A: But you are in it *now*! There is no one here that *isn't* in his natural state. It is perfectly impossible. And the fact that you believe your *self*-consciousness rather than seeing things directly, *that* is your *sadhana*. That is your path. And if you have seen it once really clearly, then it will never leave you any more.

V: An awful lot of courage is needed in order to be what you are.

A: Let's put it this way: An incredible lot of courage is needed in order to be what you are *not*. An incredible amount of energy is needed in order *not* to become enlightened. Everything is referring to Self-realisation. So you need to be incredibly dedicated in order *not* to become enlightened. *That* is what's incredible. In a way you are busy all day long preventing yourself from becoming enlightened. And that is the reason why we invite you to start doing 'nothing'. Not in the sense of no longer developing any further activities, but in the sense of no longer claiming any *doership* for yourself. Learn to see the true perspective. And once you see it, then you will experience the blessings of it. For that will give you immediate happiness, immediate strength, immediate courage. *Im-*mediate: That is the Source.

V: Is there a difference between men and women as far as the pitfalls of the seeker are concerned?

A: The big difference is that a woman is basically not interested in talks such as these. The discussion doesn't concern her. The whole issue doesn't really interest her. Because intuitively she *knows* that it cannot be solved through thinking and analysis. A woman knows it in her *heart*, but she just doesn't mind being told about it once more. As something to follow the main course. Also, most women don't have any questions to ask. Mostly they will tell about their experiences, but a real question actually never comes out.

On the other hand a man will have done his homework, which he will then put before you. But a woman will always come up with a story: At that time I used to feel like this, and at that time I was feeling like that. And she simply puts it down as a gift. As a small bouquet. Progress is being reported. As a matter of fact, a woman just wants to be present. Like a dog near the open fire. Nothing else. The very *desire* to understand it isn't there, because she basically knows it already. It's just that she likes to hear it once more. Whereas a man may want to discuss it for months, because it keeps him occupied.

A woman's pitfall is the heart. The pitfall of a man is the head. A man tends to rationalize too much, or he may simply get stuck into logic. While a woman will often get stuck in emotion and in all sorts of attachments like husbands and children and gurus. But I'm convinced that a woman may actually attain to Self-realisation while listening. She only needs to identify herself with the position from which she actually knows it already. In her case it is basically a question of constantly *recognizing* it. And then, at a certain point, she will naturally recognize herself. And nobody who will notice it. She doesn't even notice herself that she is enlightened. But in the case of a man it is quite a happening, a big celebration often. Because now he *understands* it. He is part of humanity again!

V: Are there many women who are enlightened?

A: Just as many as there are men. Every time a man becomes enlightened, there is also a woman who becomes enlightened.

V: Then why are they not known?

A: Because men tend to make a lot more noise about it. As soon as a man becomes enlightened, the first thing he will do—he can't wait for five minutes—is to gather at once disciples around him and start explaining things. Whereas a woman will simply sit down and enjoy it, that's all. Such an idea just doesn't occur to her. Also a man is more gifted verbally. If a woman begins to talk about it, it soon becomes nonsense. That is why there are no female gurus. What I'm telling you now is a traditional truth.

Although there are many women who are Self-realized, they cannot say anything sensible about it. They just sit there and radiate. That's all. It is proper to a man to start making a noise about it and propagate it, to be creative about it. Men and women have absolutely equal opportunities for Self-realisation. Only what they do with it in practice is very different.

V: What is the secret of Self-realisation?

A: The secret is the *availability*. The secret is being *present*. Not wishing to become, not wishing to change, not wishing to interfere, but letting things tell their story. For everything is happening in one and the same space, it is happening in one and the same Consciousness. He who has seen that, has seen all there is to be seen here on earth as far as I am concerned.

V: Is surrender to the teacher a spontaneous happening?

A: In our tradition you do not surrender to the teacher, but instead you are willing to learn. All that we ask is a readiness, a receptivity to reason: to be a *disciple*. And to be a disciple means to be prepared to learn something, to be prepared to look. What it basically means is, that the self-consciousness has matured in such a way, that it is no longer looking for a solution *within* that self-consciousness. So in a sense it means, that you have realized to have reached the limits of your possibilities as far as your own insights are concerned, as far as your own efforts go. It means that you are now willing to give over things. You only do it, if you have reached the limit, the very end.

However, such disciples are a rarity. After all, everybody prefers to sort things out for himself, within his own self-consciousness. Still learning will only become possible, seeing will only be possible, insight may only come, and Self-realisation is only possible, if you have reached the very limit. When nothing else

About 'Spiritual Autism'

is no longer of any real interest to you. A disciple is someone who really doesn't see any further possibilities for himself within the self-consciousness, and therefore he will seek advice from somebody else.

V: I find this very difficult. After all, in daily life one also has got things to do.

A: Nobody objects to your doing anything in daily life. We are dealing here with a quality which is immediately recognizable, a quality of listening, a quality of attitude, a quality in the way you meet one another. If that quality is there, then I will stake everything. I stake proportionally, you could say. So what others are staking, that I will stake as well. Whenever anybody is saying that he has not found it, or that he is not getting enough, then it means that his stake had not been high enough.

V: I would like to know something more about attachment. When my father was quite seriously ill, I could actually see that there was something there, which I found very difficult to part with.

A: At death and birth you are naturally being confronted by the change of form. As a matter of fact, that always is quite a confrontation. At birth, when for the first time a mother is looking at her child, then that is of course something incredible. Consciousness looking at Consciousness. And what's more, that has come out of *you*! Again, when that same Consciousness disappears from the eyes, because a person is passing away... well, then you actually have the possibility to prick through a dimension... That is why I find the situation here in the West so deplorable. We hardly get the chance to see anything die, nor do we hardly see anything being born. That is what I like about India. There all those things may be witnessed quite openly.

Remember that whatever you see, whatever you feel, whatever you think, whatever you know, there has got to be a distance *already*. You need not *take* a distance. By the very realisation that in everything you perceive there is a distance *already*, you will always be able to connect with things in a new way. Sometimes something similar is being demonstrated to you, when you are trying to hold on to something, and then that is suddenly being beaten out of your hands. Then, as soon as you let go of it, all sorts of things become possible again.

Once the illusory figure has relaxed completely, and you are seeing through insight, through Self-realisation, that there is no longer any need for you to hold on to anything whatsoever, then everything will be possible.

(2nd May, 1987, afternoon)

29

LET THINGS TELL THEIR STORY

Visitor: What is the difference between 'working on oneself' in a psychological way, and watching out for pitfalls while engaged in spiritual matters?

Alexander: The one thing has nothing to do with the other. All so-called spiritual paths are focussed on one thing only, which is the liberation from the self-consciousness. And not the maintaining or sorting out of the self-consciousness. In practice it means, that we are not dealing here with anything associated with the psyche. It is all right to discuss it at some point, but here we are in no way bent on developing the psyche. We do not occupy ourselves with psychological matters or mental movements or feelings, nor with physical problems. Here we are engaged in learning to discover anew what you *really* are. And then it is an extra gift to discover, that the psyche is falling into its natural order, that the whole range of feelings becomes possible again, and that, in some cases, the body is feeling somewhat less tired, becoming a bit healthier perhaps, although there are certain limits with respect to one's health. But all that is an extra gift, whereas in quite a few instances these things are put on the market as being the goal. The goal of Advaita is the liberation from the self-consciousness.

So you do not use Advaita for solving all sorts of problems, which is only saying that the motive for using Advaita to that end is not correct. The gift of Self-realisation is, that there are no more problems left. But that is not a goal in itself. Still these things have that kind of air hanging around them, as they are freely being suggested everywhere. Now, practice shows that quite a lot of energy lies stored in those mental and emotional problems, and that these require a lot of attention. Then you will have to make a choice: Either you are first going to solve these problems in some way or another, or you take the risk and move on to the essence.

V: I notice of late how addicted I have become to deal with myself and with others in a psychologizing way. That tendency has gone deep into me...

A: Yes, quite deep.

V: And I actually find that to be a huge obstacle.

A: To what?

V: To liberation.

A: No, no, no. What you are beginning to see is, that *that* is where your investment lies. You are now becoming aware of it, and so half the work is done already. It is telling its story.

V: Is that why you were telling Herman, 'Just let it roll'?

A: Exactly. Once you *see* it, half the work is already done. And not seeing with a grim alertness, but with a relaxed alertness. You will be astonished to see, how deep that tendency has gone. It has gone into your very bones.

V: And to try and stop it would only serve to reinforce it in a way?

A: Yes, in a sense it will reinforce it. Once again, if you give it the space by identifying *yourself* with space, then it will tell its own story. Don't expect any support from the environment in this. But the very relaxing is its own reward, you could say. As long as you do not *want* anything. What you should want is *not* to want anything. Yet another such paradox!

V: Is it true that the teacher sees everything?

A: No, the teacher doesn't see anything. If there is *one* person who doesn't see anything, then it is the teacher. This is yet another such belief that has cropped up at a certain stage. The teacher doesn't see anything of you, absolutely nothing.

V: He only sees one's true Self?

A: Not even that. He just knows *himself*—that's all. And by knowing himself, he knows you too, but not all of your antics. He is just amazed about them. Most of the time he doesn't even want to hear about them. The teacher knows *himself*, and because of that he knows *you*, but at a totally different level than the level at which you wish to be known. For you wish to be known from your problematical side, you want to be known through your problems, you want to be known by your fads. You wish to be appreciated at a mental level or at an emotional level, or at the level of the body. And that is precisely what the teacher is *not* interested in. He may nod politely and smile for a moment, but he won't even hear you.

On the other hand it is true, that the teacher's manifested consciousness has opened up to such an extent, that he will notice everything. And at times it may be that the light is let in in such a way, that he is totally synchronous with the things in which the disciple is engaged. The teacher knows himself, and through that he will know *you*—as you are *in essence*. But he will hardly take an interest in you as a form of manifestation. That manifestation may be fine, and maybe things *are* running synchronously—you may even have common interests—perfect! But apart from that he is not interested. At least not in that context. So don't imagine that the teacher is acutely aware of your problems or so. Such matters are rather to be left to a psychiatrist. The teacher doesn't sense any problems at all, because he doesn't *see* any problems. He doesn't even *see* them! For he is looking straight *through* the problems—at the Self.

V: I would like to know something more about the states of waking, dreaming, and of deep, dreamless sleep. When I look, or try to look, at these three states, I can record at the most that I had a good sleep, for example. At the same time I'm left with the feeling of having missed something.

A: Don't worry about that. You may start off by trying to see the availability in the waking state. Then you will notice that the attention is automatically being shifted to the dream state. And next you will notice that the availability is also becoming manifest in deep, dreamless sleep. At that point the 'fourth' state, what is called '*turiyatita*', will automatically become available. Don't give it too much thought. Just investigate. The only one who is constantly present—present at all that you see—is *yourself*. Therefore, the solution is to be looked for within one's *own* field of vision. Again, you may take a horse to the water, but you cannot make him drink. For that is something he has to do himself. So this, too, is something which you will have to do yourself.

First you broaden the availability in the waking state. Then the availability will move into the dream state, and next it will automatically reach the deep, dreamless sleep. And once all the three states have become one integrated, self-evident whole, then you will automatically find yourself in the 'fourth' state. But the drinking you will have to do yourself. We shall see how thirsty you are. Of course, in a sense the teacher's work also ends there.

V: There is only one Consciousness, and yet all that I experience is this here... *(pointing to his body)*

A: Now, are you actually *hearing* from those two shells of yours? Are you actually *seeing* from those two meatballs of yours?

V: No, the sound is there.

A: Exactly. It is manifesting itself within a space that is covering 360 degrees. That space is the availability. The same applies to vision and touch. It all takes place within the availability, which is unlimited. And the sense-organs are the gates of that availability, which is perfectly unlimited. Let's just discuss vision for the moment. You are looking outwards: no limits there. You are looking inwards: no limits either. Now, do you actually find yourself to be standing in between the two? No, the seeing extends to all directions. So my consciousness, or rather *the* Consciousness, stretches as far as consciousness can go. That's why you are *everything*. The fact that you are continually identifying yourself with a limited phenomenon, is a question of conditioning, a silly idea which you've picked up.

The body is an *idea*. Consciousness is in no way limited. And certainly not to this particular location. That is why you are an extension of me. You are that part of me, which I call Pauline. You are that part of me, which I call John. You are that part of me, which I call Susan. Your name is the name of a particular location.

Now, how is it possible for me to experience you? Because you are part of the one Consciousness which we both *are*. And why should you end *there*, or why should I end *here*, where my foot ends? Suppose I wouldn't be able to project any depth. Then I just wouldn't see any difference at all. And why should I end at my foot? You are simply that part of me, which I call Pauline. But That in which it appears, does not have any name.

V: I can see what you mean, but I just don't *feel* it that way! I feel the pain in *my* toe, not in *yours*...

A: Then what about the healers?

V: Well, yes, they do...

A: Because they identify themselves with the availability. We don't feel anything, because we don't *want* to feel anything. We don't *want* to identify ourselves with the availability. As a matter of fact, there have been gurus who had become so much sensitive, that they could feel the pain of the whole world. You can direct your attention: It may be directed outwards, and it may be directed inwards. You may also screen yourself off. It is all one big playground. Consciousness is unlimited. That profound recognition is there, when you are looking outwards: infinity. So also when you are looking inwards: infinity. And what's standing in between is a piece of manifestation.

V: When something happens and I want to let it tell its story, should I do so at all three levels? At the level of the body, of thinking, and of feeling? Or should I just let it happen?

A: It will happen of itself. Rule one is: *You* are not letting *anything* happen. It is the same as when you are eating something. The whole process takes perfectly care of itself. In a way thinking also works like that. So just let it do its work. Don't interfere. Observe. And then it will tell its story. But we have become so used to go and join in with all the movements! Just leave your situation alone and then it will tell its story. And the effects of such 'leaving alone' will go way beyond your imagination. For it is not just a matter of allowing oneself to have feelings, allowing oneself to observe one's thoughts—No, it is far more grand and far more beautiful than that. Just practise a little. When you are having a walk, then just observe with great intensity. Connect with everything. Open up all your senses. When you look, make sure you *are* looking. And then, at a certain point, the synchronicity will emerge of itself.

The thing is, you people always tend to relapse into the psychological sphere. Which is fine as an area of interest, but it is definitely not going to lead you to that clarity. I don't see any solution within psychology. So you will have to look deeper. What is deeper than psychology? What is deeper than the mind? What is deeper than feeling? What is deeper than the body? It is That which makes all those things possible.

V: So it is sufficient to observe the self-consciousness?

A: The self-consciousness *is* being observed! And what we are advising here is: Let that self-consciousness tell its story as much as possible, and learn to look at that self-consciousness with love. Not from a distance, as if you would have nothing to do with it, but by letting it quietly have its say, in great detail. At a certain point you will get the knack of it, and it will be a blessing to you. Because then, as a result of that, you will stop accumulating any new troubles. You will no longer embrace any new problematical situations.

If you are angry, then just *look* at how it is manifesting itself. If you are jealous, then let the story come up, and just *look* at it as you would look at others. And for others you know it only too well. Why? Because then you are at a distance, then you are not *really* involved. But you are terribly involved in yourself, and that is why you don't see things as they are.

(2nd may, 1987, evening)

YOU ARE CONSCIOUSNESS

Visitor: I still don't understand what you meant yesterday by 'spiritual autism'. Does it mean believing oneself to be engaged in spirituality, while actually withdrawing from certain people and groups. Or feeling oneself to be 'chosen', once you have become part of a spiritual group?

Alexander: Yes, these are all cramps of such autism. But the main thing is, that you are not really involved, while in fact you believe yourself to be very much involved. This may take on all kinds of forms. In my dictionary you are spiritually autistic the moment you are no longer the availability.

Whenever you are seeing through the self-consciousness, then you are excluding other things. And then at once you will think, 'Oh, I shouldn't exclude anything! I should embrace everything!' But it doesn't work like that.

V: So I take it that, as soon as you start thinking, you aren't available any more?

A: As soon as *you* start thinking you aren't. But if it is just a question of a thought appearing in your mind, then that is not going to bother you. If a cloud appears in the sky, then that also isn't going to bother the sky. Within the availability everything is possible. But once I am identified with a fragment, making myself smaller than I really am, then I'm excluding things, and I'm being autistic. As such even that isn't a catastrophe, but it can take on a cramped form, so that it may sometimes look as if you are very spiritually engaged, while practice shows things to be just the opposite. Whatever the situation may be, one thing is definite, and that is that, under all circumstances, *you* are the perceivingness, that presence. The story is being told, and *you* are the spectator of the story.

Do you see that this presence doesn't *want* anything, that in a sense it cannot *avoid* anything, go out of the way of anything? Even though in practice this is not going to be easy for you, I don't think that's an argument. As long as you bear in mind that the presence, that being, that conscious being, doesn't *want* anything nor *exclude* anything. That which you really are, doesn't exclude anything. On the other hand the *self*-consciousness *can* exclude things, which, in certain situations, may even be a necessary thing to do. But that you will have to learn for yourself, because each situation is perfectly unique. Not one situation is the same.

V: What actually *is* Consciousness?

A: Advaita knows three ways: the negative approach, the positive approach, and both the negative *and* the positive approach. In the negative approach you go looking for that which you are *not*, hoping in the end to arrive at that which you really *are*. That is the '*neti neti*' approach, meaning, 'I am *not* this, I am *not* that.' I cannot *be* this, nor can I *be* that, because all those things are without any everlasting value. Then ultimately something must remain: That which I truly *am*. That cannot be negated any further.

Then there is the positive way. Why should I actually go and discover what I'm *not*? If I can discover straight away what I truly *am*, then that will automatically exclude all that I'm *not*. Once I know that I am really an elephant, then, as a consequence, I can never be a giraffe. Nor will I need to go and take a closer look at a giraffe to see whether I might be a giraffe after all. There is a certain type of people that has recourse to the positive approach.

And then there is the 'combination' type, who is using both the positive and the negative way: 'I'm both this *and* that.' Negating means that you have actually *seen* that this or that thing is not the ultimate reality. But that does *not* mean that all those things have got to go. In fact, things just stay, for nothing *can* go. We tend to think that anything placed outside our field of vision would actually have vanished. So all sorts of poisonous stuff is thrown into the sea, and then we *think* that all that has disappeared. Only now we are beginning to realize this to some extent. So you should never think that things can just go like that. No, things have really got to be *seen*, so that they can be negated truly in the sense of: I am *not* these things. And at the same time it does *not* mean that, as a result, they will actually have disappeared. It only means: I now *know* that I'm not all those things. Then what remains is what I really *am*.

Consciousness can never be objectified. Consciousness can never be known the way in which you cognize other things. Yet of all the things known to you it is the most well-known thing. Because of the Consciousness objects are possible, but Consciousness *itself* can never be made into an object.

V: Could you say something more about the positive approach?

A: 'You are absolute Consciousness'—That is the positive approach. You just *know* it. Because that is your immediate experience. If not, how do you know you exist? Therefore, you are absolute Consciousness. Finished.

V: I knew there was no answer to it, but at the same time it keeps me occupied.

A: No, this is the answer. You are consciousness. '*Aham brahma asmi*', 'I am absolute Consciousness.' 'I Am Who I Am.' Do you want to hear more?

V: I don't want to *hear* more. I want to know what it *is*!

A: You *are* that! You now *talk* as if you want the positive way, but you actually want the negative way. You basically want to hear what you are *not*. For what you really *are*, I just told you. It is very rare to have someone who can just accept it. So I happen to be of that type. All I did was to trust the words of Nisargadatta, when he said, 'You are absolute Consciousness.' And that is where I put my trust. That's all. And trust is a great thing in this matter. 'If *he* says so, well, then it must be true.' I'm a bit of a child that way... You all have grown complicated, therefore a whole story has to go with it. Just try the negative way!

V: I don't know.

A: How do you *know* that you don't know something? You just *know* it. That knowing is something *im*-mediate. And *that* is Consciousness. You are absolute Consciousness. Suppose you enter a dark room. Then it strikes you, 'Oh, it's dark in here.' Now, with what light do you see that it's dark in there? With the light of Consciousness. Everything refers directly, *im*-mediately, to Consciousness. That is the only thing you need to remember. And just forget everything else about negative and positive, for all that is nonsense. Have you got that?

V: Well, to some extent I have...

A: What then?

V: I realize that I *know* or *don't* know.

A: But how do you *know* that you know or don't know?

V: I just *know* it.

A: There you stop!

V: If one is not identified with anything, then is it actually possible to have any feelings at all?

A: Only then. For only *then* you are able to connect with *true* feeling. Whereas now feeling is like a big tub that has been covered up. *Because* you are identified, you don't feel anything. Your feeling has been blocked by that silly self-consciousness. You have made yourself altogether small. You have made yourself into something which you are *not*. That is why I'm sometimes telling you: Listen to your *gut* feeling. Do not live against your own better judgement. Pay the price for it. If you *do* prize it, then you should also pay the price for it. It's as simple as that. For there is nothing *wrong* with feelings, there is nothing *wrong* with thoughts. That anything would be wrong with them, is all spiritual bother. You have made your feelings into an enemy. You have made your thinking into an enemy. You have made your body into an enemy. And now you manage to make even Consciousness into an enemy!

In the tradition of Advaita feelings have the freedom to come up. What you *do* with them, is quite a different story. But they should have the freedom to come up. For a life of suppression is not *jnana*.

V: Is every identification a fabrication?

A: If it is a fabrication, then it is a fabrication. And if it is, then that, too, is being perceived by you. Through the power of discrimination you will find out. But a feeling is a feeling is a feeling.

A feeling comes up, appears for a moment to tell you something about a certain situation, and then it disappears again. There has never been a feeling that hung on. No more than a cloud, which also never hung on. Did you ever see a cloud hanging on in the sky for a hundred years? Definitely not! The blue sky is the Consciousness, and within it the clouds appear. And the power of discrimination is the aeroplane which takes you to the blue sky.

V: Is identification basically standing in the way of the availability?

A: Nothing is standing in the way of the availability! Nothing. Absolutely nothing!

V: What does it mean to die 'consciously'?

A: As a matter of fact, *everybody* is dying consciously, because the knowingness is always there. Even if you happen to be very faint at that moment, still you will be perfectly clear and conscious of your faintness. Even if you are in a coma.

V: It is said sometimes, that having children will stand in the way of one's Self-realisation.

A: If that would be true, I would close the shop immediately! The two have got nothing to do with each other. A child may consume you—There I agree. But it doesn't disturb anything. And certainly not your Self-realisation.

(3rd May, 1987, morning)

31

LIFE IS A DIVINE PLAY

Visitor: How can identification actually arise?

Alexander: It cannot. It is an optical illusion. It is ignorance.

V: But the illusion, too, has come from the one conscious being, hasn't it?

A: Yes, it is a play. That is why we call it '*lila*', the divine play. It is God's little joke. And what God is, you don't know. 'I know myself in a cloud of un-knowing', a Buddhist once said in 1610. It's not that you don't know anything. You know all sorts of things, but at the same time you don't know anything. You are everything and you are nothing—at the same time. You are the body and, at the same time, you are not. Life is an absolute paradox. And the tension of that apparent opposition causes you to be conscious of things. If there was no opposition, you wouldn't be conscious of anything. This whole play of Consciousness—conscious / un-conscious, light / darkness—is only there in order to make you conscious of things. You only have to see those things in their proper perspective.

Vedanta means 'the end of knowing'. Whoever realizes that in reality no interweaving or identification is possible, will relax within conscious being. Finished. And such a one is always himself.

V: I want to know why there should be attachment. You don't need to be attached in order to live, do you?

A: Prove it to me that you are attached, *then* I will detach you.

V: I am attached to my child. If my child would die, then that would create a gap which I won't be able to bridge.

A: I appreciate that. However, if your child actually *were* to die, then you still wouldn't be able to prevent it from happening. If you would die yourself, you wouldn't be able to prevent that either. You can't just *stop* the process. Attachment is a mental attitude.

V: When I look into this question of attachment, then I *do* in fact see, that it is just thoughts, and not the phenomenon itself. For suppose that such a thing would *really* take place, then I just wouldn't be able to do anything about it.

A: That is why I say: *Prove* it to me that you are attached, *then* I will detach you. The fact is, that you *won't* be able to prove that you are attached to anything.

V: But I *can* prove that I'm attached to the thought.

A: No, you can't, because that thought will disappear again. Your mind is not all the time occupied by that thought. The thought itself only exists for a few seconds, and then it's gone. So how could that thought be attached to anything?

V: May I ask, then, why I'm so afraid to lose my child?

A: Because the moment a child is born, the opposite, too, is being introduced, as is the case with everything else. The moment you fall in love with a person...

V: ... then you are afraid to lose that person.

A: And that is actually why we don't really fall in love any more. As soon as you are very deeply in love with somebody, and that feeling of happiness is springing up, you are immediately afraid that that person may be taken away from you. So you immediately begin to organize all sorts of things in order to keep that love within reach by signing contracts and getting married, and so on. But, of course, it doesn't work like that.

V: So, along with the child being born, or with the falling in love with a person, the fear of losing them arises at the same time?

A: Yes, that is the dualism of it.

V: And I will just have to accept that?

A: You have to accept *both*. If there is life, then there will also be death. The two always go absolutely together. Whoever accepts death, can live. But he who *doesn't* accept death, doesn't live either. More people actually die from the *fear* of death than from death itself. Accept the one as well as the other, then the fear, too, will disappear. Whereas if you take only one side of the matter, then you are thereby introducing fear. Perfect acceptance, from moment to moment, and the absence of fear are the key to happiness. Then the whole thing relaxes, and there will be synchronicity with existence.

V: Is fear the same as resistance?

A: Yes, it is a different word for resistance, defense. And thinking is entirely at the service of that defense. Someone who doesn't know fear, hardly thinks. Someone who is happy, doesn't *need* to think. On the other hand one who is confused, puzzles his head off. Someone who is sad, puzzles his head off. Thinking is defense, defense, defense. The happier you are, the less you will need to think.

V: If I'm not attached to the body, then why should I live in it?

A: When you come up with a question like that, I smell a rat somewhere, because it could be a form of autism. The reason why you find yourself in a body is, that you want to have experiences. But if you happen to have gone through so many traumatic or shocking experiences, that you don't *want* to have any more experiences, and next you seek refuge in spirituality, then you will have become spiritually autistic. For the purpose of life is to *live* it. And that is also what you want. You want to experience, experience and experience over and over again...

Everything you do is aimed at having experiences. From playing at marbles to playing with your car or wanting to have children or wanting to have spiritual experiences. Why do men take a second wife? Why do women take a second child? For the experience of it. Why do we mix with many people instead of associating with just one person? Because we want experiences. Why do you put on the TV? Why are you inquisitive? Why do you eat? What makes you taste new dishes? Why do you need to read a book? Why do you read the newspaper? For the experience of it, sir! Just try and stop having experiences. You won't be able to stand it for thirty minutes! You can't sit quiet for *ten* minutes even. If you have to sit quiet for ten minutes, then already you are in trouble. All existence is dancing towards experience. Did you ever observe a child? It makes a grown-up dead-tired, for it just goes on and on and on. Experience, experience, experience...

The fact that we have become so dull, so totally in a coma, doesn't detract anything from the meaning of life. The meaning of life is to love it! And you only need to fall in love or to begin to love somebody truly, and everything starts to bubble and to live. Because love intensifies. Sexuality intensifies. Food intensifies. Then you are making life come *alive*. That is what it means 'to *in*carnate'. Otherwise it will be 'to *ex*carnate'. There isn't a crystal to be found that is going to develop itself in any other way than according to the natural pattern that it is carrying within itself. And why should *you*, who are *part* of nature, be an exception to that? You *are* no exception. You just have got that bit more in you, which is the fact that you are able to be *conscious* of it. There lies your strength and, if we aren't careful, at the same time your destruction.

V: I can't understand why it is so important to have experiences.

A: I'm not saying it is important. What I'm saying is that existence is showing you, that the motive for all your actions is to have experiences. Whether you want it or not, whether you like it or not, it makes no difference. To go through experiences is a most compelling motive in life. As a matter of fact, that *is* life. And we just do as if we have something else to do. And we just do as if it is to be found elsewhere. We just do as if things are going to be solved *later*. But that is not so.

V: I suppose what really counts is what you're focussing on? If you keep focussing on the Consciousness, then it doesn't really matter what else you're doing—not?

A: But it *isn't* a question of your focussing on anything! We passed that phase long ago, I hope. You must have seen by now, that the 'I-am-ness', the conscious being, is *already* present *everywhere*, that it is nowhere *not*. So what remains? The manifestation. And he who has realized himself to *be* that Consciousness, will thus feel perfectly natural in that manifestation. And if you are *not* feeling all that comfortable in the manifestation, then you will just have to look a little bit deeper. There is no other way.

V: I've always tended to look upon the urge to have experiences as something that's being forced upon me.

A: No, just the opposite! Quite the opposite! The urge to have experiences *cannot* be stopped. That urge is the very purpose of life!

(3rd May, 1987, afternoon)

32

ALL KNOWLEDGE IS IGNORANCE

Alexander: Many people who have had a nodding acquaintance with Advaita, and even people who are thoroughly acquainted with it, very often make the mistake of thinking that all knowledge is nonsense, that it is not important. In Sanskrit there are terms for it which are more differentiated, *'jnana'* and *'vijnana'*. *Vijnana* means knowledge in the sense of 'having knowledge of', to know something about something, while *jnana* denotes the real Knowing, which has nothing to do with objective knowledge. In Advaita 'ignorance' is meant to convey, that all knowing in an objective sense can never constitute the real Knowing. All the knowledge that you have *about* things can never be the real Knowing. And here we are dealing with the real Knowing. So this Knowing and the objective knowledge have nothing to do with each other. In the expression, 'All knowledge is ignorance', the knowledge referred to is the knowledge that may be gathered in by the mind or by feeling. These will never enable you to know the Knowing, because only the Knowing can know itself.

Visitor: What is knowing through feeling?

A: Feeling is known by this Knowing. But, on its own, feeling doesn't know anything. In spirituality it is common-place to say that the real Knowing cannot be comprehended by the head. So then one moves on to the heart, saying that, by contrast, the heart is capable of comprehending it. But the heart, too, doesn't comprehend anything. What can the heart comprehend? Nothing.

V: It can feel.

A: I have no objection against feeling, but, by itself, it doesn't know anything. Feeling *is* being known. And the Knowing which actually knows any feeling is called 'real Knowledge' in Advaita. All the knowledge which you have about things will do for the world. It is good enough for moving in an objective world, the world of name and form. But that knowledge is not sufficient, is quite insufficient even, in order to understand what Advaita is all about, what Self-realisation is all about. Each feeling *is* being known. Each thought *is* being known. Each sensation *is* being known. Therefore this Knowing has got to be there already, before even the slightest bit may be known.

For example, you know that you are listening, that you have the sense of hearing, that there is therefore 'light' in your ear. At a certain age you may start noticing that your hearing is diminishing, or that your eyesight is diminishing. But *that* by which you actually perceive that you are not seeing well, is that Knowing in the eyesight. And this applies to all the respective senses, to all thoughts, and to whatever you can think of. Thus it is perfectly clear, that there is an independent, perfectly innocent, virginal Knowing present within you, which is never really involved in anything whatsoever. In Advaita it is called '*Atman*', the Self. And it is the best known thing on this planet. But at the same time it is the least known thing, because you prefer knowledge in an *objective* sense.

V: So you cannot really *talk* about the Knowledge of Advaita, at least not directly?

A: That has always been the problem of Krishnamurti. All his life Krishnamurti tried to speak in terms of thinking and feeling about That, which is *beyond* thinking and feeling. In this respect I found Nisargadatta to be clearer. He said, 'Words are references'. They are references, and so you should never take the word literally. For that reason it remains an absolute dilemma to speak about That, which cannot be spoken about. But that isn't *your* problem. That is the problem of those who are speaking about it. *Your* problem is to decode the language used, the references, and to learn to see and appreciate its true value.

It is rare to find people who are capable of speaking about that fundamental Seeing. That is why in India those who *do* have that capacity, are considered to be superior to the gods. The whole tradition of the teachers, the gurus, is based on this phenomenon. There are actually thousands of people in Europe and in India, who have completely integrated this fundamental Seeing, but they are just not capable of saying anything sensible about it. Just like someone who is good at playing the violin, and nobody actually knows why. So language is used as a vehicle in order to go *beyond* language. As when you remove a thorn from your foot with an other thorn, and then both are thrown away.

At some point you will find yourself in a situation, where there are no more words. It is something unavoidable, because your true home *is* beyond language, beyond words, beyond feeling, beyond thought. For thought, too, is language. Feeling also is a form of language, more subtle and deeper, but nevertheless a form of language. Music too is a form of language. When it comes to the real Understanding the word 'understanding' is no longer applicable. In fact, not a single word is applicable then, yet the clarity is all there. That is why the ultimate *satsang*, the ultimate meeting with the Essence, is Silence. That is not to say that mere silence—the absence of sound—would necessarily have to result in *real* Silence. Just as it doesn't follow that, if there is sound somewhere, that any *real* Silence wouldn't be there. Real

Silence is of an altogether different order. Real Silence is true understanding, true insight, true knowing.

You could almost say that the teachers of *jnana*, i.e. Advaita, are inviting you to get 'evaporated' into That, to 'sail' unawares into That (to use a Dutch expression), to get 'drowned' in That, to get 'lost' in That.

V: To me it seems absolutely impossible without a teacher to...

A: Impossible. Absolutely impossible. Without a teacher you can forget it. Even if Krishnamurti tells you *not* to take a guru. Even a bad guru can still be a good one. To say that realisation is possible without a teacher is somewhat like saying, that you can be born without a mother. Can you attain to Self-realisation without a teacher? Impossible.

V: Nor can you die without leaving the body.

A: When you die, it isn't *you* who is leaving the body, but the body will be leaving *you*. Don't think you are inhabiting a body; it is just the other way round. During the night you have lost the body, and next morning it re-appears in the Consciousness, in conscious being, in knowingness. In That it will also disappear again. You will witness your own birth and your own death. And by that I don't mean this apparent, physical death. Mind you! What is meant here is a truly dying of all that is false, of all that is *not* the essence.

This is not to say that henceforth things are no longer important, that you won't be having a washing-machine, or that you'll only have one meal a day. For that has nothing to do with it. Let's please get this right, for it has led to most crazy, masochistic techniques. A life of suppression has nothing to do with Self-realisation. Instead, from the knowingness, from that presence, will follow a perfect synchronicity with existence. There will be neither negation nor embracement. So there is neither a desire to stay alive, nor a desire to die.

V: Is there no purpose then?

A: Again, each word that is said about it should be seen as a reference, not as an absolute truth. A word can never be absolute. Only the Absolute is absolute. There are no words for it.

V: Then are words going to be of any use to you as a disciple? Or do things happen naturally? Is it a process which you cannot influence at all?

A: Of course, if there is a deep interest in the subject, it will be of great help. If you are focussed on men, then men will come into your life. Are you focussed on money, then money will come. If you're focussed on furniture, then you will see furniture everywhere. Are you looking for a car, then you will see cars everywhere. If your focus is on God, then God you will get. And if you focus on Self-realisation, then you will get Self-realisation. So at a certain stage the right focus has to be there, which is what is actually lacking quite often. And the right focus means: the right approach. It is like a small fire: There is only a sparkle left, and that has almost gone out. Such is the condition of most people. And the teacher will blow and stir up the fire to a total blaze. 'Holy fire', as it is called. Indeed, whoever digs deep, will hit upon fundamental matters.

However, we remain basically interested in the *self*-consciousness. We are interested in all that moves. We are terribly fascinated by thoughts, we are terribly fascinated by feelings, and we just keep on looking into that direction. But for Self-realisation that is not enough. We pay the wrong sort of attention to the wrong sort of things. Pay the right attention to the right thing, and the Self cannot but begin to blossom like a begonia that is getting its fertilizer. It cannot be otherwise. But your attention is fixed on that other knowledge. Real Knowledge has nothing to do with the intellect, or with knowing a lot of things. On the contrary. 'Blessed are the poor in spirit.' So for most of you there is hope...

V: Does 'right attention' mean not paying attention to the *contents* of one's thoughts?

A: Attention is said to be *drawn*. It is an involuntary movement. Attention is drawn towards something that is moving. When the TV-set is switched on during mealtimes, you watch it, even if you don't want to. Formerly the family would constitute a circle, and the attention was kept within that circle. But since television has been introduced, it has become *half* a circle. You can observe this phenomenon everywhere. Attention is directed towards anything that moves. At the same time there is a Knowing in you, which is able to perceive all this. And when the attention is directed towards that Knowing, then you are at the base of the matter. That is what is being imparted here.

So all we basically need to see is, that the attention is moving. This is perceived by something which is *not* moving. So focus on the very fact, that attention is moving. That everybody can realize. Again, the Knowing *never* moves. The Knowing is motionless, perfectly still, perfectly homogeneous. There is no movement in it. Being without any movement, it is firm like a rock. Impossible to get it to move. It is the *in*-ground of all movement. Whoever realizes himself to be that Knowing, will be drawn out of the self-consciousness, out of the identification, out of the trick of attention. He will have stepped out of the trick of interwovenness.

V: And is the attention itself also being known?

A: Of course! If not, how would you actually *know* that your attention is relaxing? Or that you are able to focus your attention so well on anything? It *is* known. Here we are dealing with that fundamental Knowing.

V: Is it possible to *un*learn this constant, wrong focussing of the attention?

A: No, because any new form of learning is the same malady. As a child, why do you learn so terribly quickly? And why does it become increasingly difficult as you grow older? Because when you are a child, you are still looking freely. Innocently. Whereas as you grow older, you are looking with knowledge. And so, because you have been trained to look from conditionings and to look from objective knowledge, you have become harnessed. Now, how to get out of that? By realizing what you *are*. Then that knowledge will still be there, but it will no longer be a problem to you. The fact that I learnt that two plus two makes four, will not bind me, nor will it make me free.

V: Is attention, which is constantly moving from one thing to the other, the binding factor?

A: What is binding me is the fact, that I believe two plus two to be four, or that I believe myself to be Alexander Smit. And that you think yourself to be so and so who, at one time, used to stay in Africa. Or that you are a potter. The idea as such doesn't bind you, but the *identification* with the idea does. So, if someone were to tell you, that you're actually quite a bad potter, then you will get mad at him and you'll start throwing your pots at him. Such is the terror of that knowledge. And until you have recognized that identification in yourself, you won't recognize it in the other. Until then each word from an other person about yourself will be of great importance, because you too are living in the same illusion which you are holding up before yourself. Then you, too, will believe what the other is saying, thereby allowing yourself to get carried away or to be fooled in some other way. Thus you will have entered the sphere of belief, preparing to follow a banner or, if necessary, even to cut an other's throat in the name of God, in the name of religion or of the devil, or in your own name. So that can never be a real solution for your existential dilemma, which is really what we are dealing with here. At least, if you *are* interested in a real solution, and not in something fragmentary. Fragmentary solutions are everywhere.

V: Actually, I think it's not possible at all to talk about this attaining to clarity.

A: You may talk about it, but at a certain point the words will have lost much of their meaning. At a certain stage that clarity will simply be there, and then it just cannot be disturbed any more, not even by a thought, because that thought will then be seen exactly as it is. Just as this house is not going to bind me nor free me, so also not a single thought can bind me nor make me free. For I *am* essentially free. You *are* essentially free. Not the talking *about* that realisation or that actualization, but the realisation *itself* is of an unprecedented beauty. And if that is true for me, so it is for you, nobody excepted. The consequence of that is the *im*-mediate recovery of the earthly paradise, that is to say, a recovering *without* a medium, *without* anything or anybody mediating. For it was always available already.

The story of the earthly paradise is not so odd after all. People were naked there, naked in the sense of not being clothed with knowledge. For, once the emphasis is put on objective knowledge alone, then immediately you are out of the earthly paradise. Then your nakedness will have gone. Nudists are quite familiar with this. Just go and have a swim in the sea completely naked, and at once you will feel free from bonds—and that's only a foretaste. So that nakedness is quite close. But out of fear we have put on 'clothing', we have got ourselves a personality. By itself even that isn't such a terrible disaster, but now it is beginning to turn itself against us. This personality is now acting in such a destructive manner, that it seems to threaten our existence as a whole, including the world, the objective world. It is not only finding expression in relationships, but also in pollution, in greed. There is food in abundance in the world, but out of sheer greed and fear it is not being shared in the right manner. It is an attitude, a *mental* issue. All these things are lying at a much more fundamental level, but nobody is looking there.

V: Of late something has come over me of, 'I'm dead already': I am already that, which I will be when I'm dead.

A: True indeed! Jesus is saying somewhere, 'You must lose your life in order to regain it'. And it is absolutely true. You have to *lose* your life. Then, when all the false has gone, truth will remain. Absolutely. That has always been the case, and it *will* be for all time to come. But it is not a physical death. Nor is it a mental death in the sense of no longer taking any interest in things. And it certainly doesn't mean the death of one's feelings. On the contrary, you are suffering the death of your feelings and are killing your potential, *because* of all those silly defense mechanisms of the personality, of this so-called ego.

In various circles where there is no knowledge whatsoever about these matters, you are always being told, 'Oh, these things are ever so dangerous, for you will lose all interest in the community.' Nothing can be farther from the truth. And this so-called interest in social issues is nothing but an escape. You only have to look at all those silly characters appearing on television. The Amsterdam TV-channel, for example, is just nothing as compared to your own potential with its billions of channels. *That* potential is really open to everything. Some time ago somebody came here and told me, 'I have come here with an open mind'. But you cannot come with an 'open mind', for the mind is closed by definition. However much open it may be, it remains a tunnel vision. On the other hand Consciousness is all-encompassing. Consciousness—that which you truly *are*, the Presence—is the very availability and openness to everything. And *That* you are!—'Tat tvam asi'. Nothing less. As for me, I wouldn't be content with anything less!

V: Why are we content with less?

A: No idea. Maybe you were taught to be a good boy. I'm not familiar with the phenomenon. I've never been content with less. I think you have to be a little bit greedy, spiritually. Sometimes Nisargadatta, too, would put me to the test, when he just started talking some rubbish. Then I would tell him, 'But that is absolutely impossible. What you are saying now is crazy'. And then he would really start going. You people are content with toys.

V: Does the Knowing also distinguish between 'toys' and what aren't?

A: Looking at it from that angle, anything objective will be 'toys'. So also all the bodily phenomena, which are equally known by that Knowing. Did you ever observe a baby? I always find it one of the most amazing phenomena, whenever that tiny little hand knows to find the exact spot, where it is itching. How is it possible? Because it is *known*.

So the Knowing is present from the very first to the very last moment. It is That which never leaves you. Therefore depend on That which never leaves you. And whoever abides in that Knowing is Self-realized. Such is the case even now, only you are not aware of it. To become aware of that fact is the true awareness-raising. If you want a fundamental, real solution, then stop giving your attention to the toys of the awareness-raising industry. If you want the Real, if you want to understand truly, if you really want to see who you *are*, then ultimately you will have to come to a teacher of Advaita. There is no escaping it. Even the *kundalini*-man or *kundalini*-woman with great *siddhis* or whatever you like, will eventually come to a guru of Advaita. In the end they will come to a *jnani*. In any case, they will have to hear the story at least once. Ramakrishna, too, had to get acquainted with Advaita, before he really understood. And that applies to everybody. In this tradition I have yet to hear of someone, who had seen it all without the guidance of a teacher.

V: Why is it that, although you *know* to have seen it, you nevertheless relapse into your former condition?

A: Because you have to hear it a couple of times. You have to see it a couple of times, until it has become so clear to you, that it is not going to leave you any more. By the very fact that it doesn't leave you any more, you will know whether Self-realisation has actually taken place. The only one who will know whether you have really seen it, is you.

(5th May, 1987)

33

CONSCIOUSNESS: YOUR TRUE POTENTIAL

Visitor: Is real knowledge actually only the perceiving of what appears and disappears in the Consciousness?

Alexander: That which is always there, which never leaves me, which is invariably present, is entitled to the name of 'I'. All the rest—I walk, I stand, I feel, I think, I did this yesterday, I did that yesterday, I am so-and-so, my name is this and that—is changeable. But that which *knows* all this is the unchanging Knowing in the changeable knowledge.

V: But in that case there is basically no 'I', nor a 'you', nor whatever?

A: I'm glad you are saying it yourself. Of course there isn't! And deep in your heart you *know* there isn't. The ego or the self-consciousness is like a billiard-ball, and the various 'I's are like billiard-balls that collide with one another, and then go their way again. But through the real Knowing you may merge with one another. For that real Knowing is *love*, a different word for love. That Knowing cannot be located anywhere. That is why I say: Consciousness cannot be located anywhere. As soon as you locate something, you have made it into an object. Even to say that Consciousness is all-penetrating is not correct, because that would be assuming that there is still something to be penetrated *outside* of Consciousness. Sometimes I say: It is nowhere not. It is not limited in any way. In front of me is infinite space, behind me is infinite space, inside me is infinite space—infinite. Consciousness knows no limits. Why? Because it is the availability *itself*. That is *Brahman*, the greatest potential of all. From That everything is born, within That everything manifests itself, and within That everything passes away.

A different word for it is God. But obviously we have made God into a concept, a Mister or a Missis. God is neither feminine nor masculine, but That in which man or woman and all the phenomena may manifest themselves. So there is no question of your being able to locate it. The location 'John' is an indication of the location for a phenomenon. But what John actually *is*, John will never know, nor will I ever know it. At the same time something *is* being known. And *that* Knowing is the only thing which is entitled to the name of 'I'. *That* you may call 'I', because That will never leave you. So you, and everybody that is sitting here, including the speaker, all have come from that Consciousness, are all being perceived by that Consciousness, and will disappear again in that Consciousness. For a thing which has originated from that Consciousness, cannot be any different from That from which it has originated. To realize this in every action and in every non-action is Self-realisation.

V: Is that 'Being'?

A: That is Being.

V: So instead of an 'I' there is 'Being'. And no concept is attached to it?

A: If a concept is attached to it, then that concept is not going to make me *more* free, nor is it going to bind me. When I see an elephant pass by, then I have learnt to make that into a concept, so that I'm able to say that it is a phenomenon with a trunk. But the concept as such doesn't bind me, nor does it make me free. At the same time the concept may actually be quite useful to me—as a concept. But I should not get the idea that, because of the concept, I am able to see and understand the elephant in any more real or better sense. God's presence may be seen in everything: in the elephant, in the tree and, of course, also in human beings. Because there *is* nothing but that Presence.

The word 'Vedanta' means 'the end of knowing': There is nothing more to be objectified. And if there is nothing more to be objectified, then you will fall into yourself.

V: There is this 'Knowing', yet at the same time this separateness persists. What is it? Habit? Memory?

A: It is imaginable that the personality, the illusory figure, is actually never going to surrender its position as a matter of course. The self-consciousness will continue to embrace to the last anything that will give it an apparent certainty. What may actually be quite helpful, is to pursue the references you may get, or anything that gives you inspiration, and to persevere in that direction until things have become clear.

I once saw a movie by Walt Disney, in which a little angel came passing by, holding a magic wand which radiated lots of little stars, and this made everybody feel wonderful. I wish I also had something like a magic wand, but it doesn't work like that. So it has really got to be seen by the location called 'Charles', or the location called 'Bertrand', or the location called 'Ina'. And the realisation of the one has nothing to do with the realisation of the other. My realisation bears no relation to what *you* need to see. Naturally to be able to share that clarity—the effort that is put in on both sides—is the most wonderful thing you can experience in life. For this is the *Essence*—All the rest is a hobby.

If you miss *That*, then you've missed it all. Then you are actually missing the whole point of your existence. That is how I see it. That is how dramatically I put it. For the greatest joy and the most wonderful holiday and the greatest worldly pleasure are a dark night in comparison with the clarity referred to here. Why? Because *That* is your true home. That is where you come from, That is what you are in, and That is where you are going to.

It is all-important that that realisation takes place as soon as possible. And fear or other things are no reason not to get on with it. You have to go for it. Instead of running away from fear, you should approach it and just investigate it. But, of course, you have learnt to run away from fear, even though you've sometimes heard it said, that you shouldn't. You shouldn't run away from it, you shouldn't stop for it, but instead you should go straight at it! You have to confront it. Is there any fear? You just go and find out how it works. And no bother about your trembling with fear—That's of no importance whatsoever. Just be a little brave! If there is a dog growling at you, then don't run away. Instead run up to *him*; then it's *he* who will run away. But if you go off running fast, the dog will think that you want to play with him. And so does fear. Are you on the run for fear? Then it will follow you, thinking that you want to play.

V: The most painful fear is to be separated from my own love.

A: It is an *apparent* separation. You once learnt that, somewhere, there is an electric fence. But that fence has been cleared long ago. Still you are afraid to get a shock. The biggest shock will be, when you realize what a wasted life you have lived. If, one day, you will get to see how things are *really* put together, then almost everybody will say: What have I been doing with my life, for goodness' sake? Now, if you discover it when you are thirty, then naturally it won't be all that terrible. But there are also people who discover it only at the very end, which is a bit of a pity.

Go to the essence. Don't bother about the separation. See the knowingness in everything, then the separation will automatically disappear. It cannot be otherwise.

V: I want to ask something about the space, the 'not-any-thing' which we were discussing once. How can you see the difference between the consciousness and that space, because I see consciousness also as a kind of space.

A: Yes, a space within which things may appear. Sometimes consciousness is associated with *'akasha',* which is a different word for space. But compared to consciousness space is still too limited. The concept of space is still narrow and cramped as compared to consciousness.

V: Can that space both be light and dark?

A: Yes, of course it can. It doesn't make any difference. If you enter a dark room, and you don't see anything there, then there has to be a certain light, because of which you are actually able to *see* that it is dark in there. Then you'll say, 'I can't see anything'. But *who* doesn't see anything? So there has to be a certain light which is not a physical light. We call it the light in the Consciousness: That which sees that you are the light in that darkness. The light in darkness as well as in daylight. So Consciousness is altogether detached from anything whatsoever. It is the very knowingness in things. The knowingness of darkness, of light, of good, of evil and, therefore, the *pre-*condition or the *in-*ground in things. Christ says somewhere—and this is a very mystic statement—'I am the Light of the world.' Not that he was the *only* light—that we *all* are—but he had realized it himself deeply.

V: How am I to picture that light to myself?

A: Why should that be a problem? Just look at what *is*. This light is not perceivable. Why not? Because it is the perceiving *itself*.

The closer you get to the essence, the sillier the words become, and the less the contents is answering to the description. But the contents isn't going to answer to *any* description, for consciousness is *without* description. He who goes for the essence, will see the essence. Keep yourself exclusively occupied with essential matters. It doesn't matter *how* you live your life. Even if you live like a villain, it doesn't matter. That has got nothing to do with it. If you are living like a saint, if that is your hobby, then that's fine too. All that has nothing to do with Self-realisation. We still think that Self-realisation means leading a kind of good life, or a rebellious life, or a vigilant life. All that has got nothing to do with it.

V: If it is true that all of us are essentially Consciousness, then why the effort on our part?

A: Yes, it is complete madness. And that is why I strongly advise you to stop it. That's all the effort on my part. Once you've seen through the illusion of the self-consciousness, you will be connected to the big Light. Even now you are, only the illusion of the self-consciousness is so big, that it appears *not* to be so.

V: What I find so fascinating about it is, that there is actually no such thing as a private little consciousness.

A: In a certain sense you *do* have it, namely in the form of a private *self*-consciousness. And that is quite all right for crossing the street, good enough for all the things in the world. But at the same time we should realize what we *really* are. Then your life will run its natural course. As nature ordained it.

V: Are experiences important?

A: In Advaita you are advised not to claim any experience to be 'the Ultimate'. And never to act as if *you* had that experience. And that is quite a sensible tip, for there are thousands of people who get stranded on the most wonderful experiences, or instead have been stopped by somewhat less wonderful, unpleasant experiences. Advaita does not stop until the One is perceived 'which knows no second'.

V: Is the Essence all-knowing?

A: Yes, but not in the wrong sense of the term. There are certain people who will have a peak experience, and then they think they know it all. Such all-knowingness is a kind of foretaste of the Self-realisation, but still associated with *self*-consciousness. Then the self-consciousness will go and claim the experience, and you will have megalomania. Next the self-consciousness will imagine: I can do everything, I know everything, etc.

V: But the experience could well be authentic?

A: Absolutely. You *do* know things of which you think: How do I actually *know* this? It is there, very deep within you. It may well be, that everything is lying stored in the genes. It is quite possible that the whole of science and everything that is happening on this earth, is being transmitted genetically. As a manifestation. And that it is thus able to manifest itself in the mirror of Consciousness.

It is possible that our potential is not able to come out fully, because we are so much hampered by all the silly notions that we have. It is quite imaginable that all the information is lying there already, stored genetically as in an enormous computer, but that we just can't get at it. For the unheard-of intelligence that we basically possess, is being curtailed, since we are completely blocked inside the organisation of the brains. And this process is starting at a very early stage. So I can well imagine that someone who *isn't* hampered that way, may actually develop into a huge pearl. And this is the nice thing about human beings. When a dog is born, it dies as a dog. When a monkey is born, it dies as a monkey. But man is born as a man, and he may die as a Buddha *or* as a Mussolini—which is also possible. But the potential is there. It has produced a Mozart, a Bach. If you just have a look at where things have gone wrong, then you will find that the potential has not been able to come out, because emotionally or psychologically you have been blocked. So it is of vital importance to have things flow freely. Still, as I see it, you have to be at the Essence.

V: Is there a connection between solving the blocks and Self-realisation?

A: It is a gift on top of it! When Self-realisation has taken place, a flowing through takes place. Even energetically.

V: What do you mean by 'energetically'?

A: A free flow of energy to the subtler areas, the subtler bodies. Clairvoyants are able to detect, whether someone is actually Self-realized or not. But now the emphasis is so much on the mental blocks, that one actually believes them to be an impediment to Self-realisation. That way you are obviously never going to get out of it. As when a physician were to tell an alcoholic, 'You can come and see me for a cure, but first you must stop drinking'. But that was the problem in the first place! Or he is telling someone who is suffering from bad sleep, 'I'm not going to start doing any work on you, before you are sleeping really well'. That is madness.

V: This profound Knowing or *jnana*, is it a form of knowledge which is only there in the time of a moment?

A: No, for time itself is also being cognized. And time, too, is an optical illusion. That fundamental Knowing, *jnana*, is outside of time. Therefore that Knowing is never born nor can it die. Birth and death are time-bound phenomena. That which is known can also die. The body can die, but *jnana* cannot die. That Knowing is never born, because it is outside of time and space. And something which is outside of time and space cannot die, cannot be born.

V: I'm not able to make a connection with the word 'Knowing' and...

A: You shouldn't make a connection with the *word*, you should make a connection with the *Knowing*. Am I making myself clear? The Knowing is outside of time and space, because time and space are being cognized by something which is *outside* of time and space. I would not be able to perceive time and space, unless I stand *outside* of time and space. How do I know time? Because there must be something time-*less* as opposed to it. The real Knowing is timeless, it is *outside* of time and space. This is something quite essential, for you can't really speak of Self-realisation, unless you have clearly seen through the whole issue of time and space. Memory, time and space are the last three obstacles to Self-realisation.

When you wake up in the morning, you have to look at a clock in order to know what time it is. Then you think you know what time it is. But That which sees what time it is, i.e. That which is actually cognizing time, is itself *outside* of time and space. Outside of space too, for how could space be measured by space?

V: Actually, you can only perceive it in a negative sense, can't you? As, for instance, when you perceive time to be something artificial?

A: Of course! It's a trick! It is a way of thinking. Time is a function of the mind. A repetitive function. Day and night can only appear as such, because of the difference between them. Everything is an object of difference: Is anything big or small? Then you have to place it beside some other object. Both time and space are perceived by something, which is *beyond* time and space. That is the Knowing. That is also why you have the sense of eternity in you. But it is being projected onto things that are *not* eternal.

V: I find it so difficult to picture. In my view consciousness can only exist in relation to the body. Once the body has gone, then there isn't anything left. Or, for example, when I'm asleep, then there just isn't anything there.

A: That is quite an authoritative statement! For how do you really *know*, that you've had a good sleep?

V: I know it afterwards.

A: Is that so? How do you know that you *didn't* have a good sleep?

V: Because then I wake up all the time.

A: Yes, but how do you actually *know*, that you've had a peaceful and sound sleep? How do you *know* it, that you were asleep quite soundly? For there is obviously something quite curious about sleep. You may have a deep sleep, you may have a very light sleep, you may sleep like a log. But how do you *know* that you slept very deeply? What you are saying is: I know it afterwards. No! There must have been something there, which registered it—And so there is, namely that *Knowing*. And that Knowing is there in the waking state, it is there in the dream state, and it is there in deep, dreamless sleep. If not, how would you ever *know* that you had been dreaming? That Knowing or knowingness transcends the three states. He who knows That, knows everything.

Find out whether it is actually *true* what I'm saying. Investigate it. Then you will find that there is something *in* you, which *knows* that you are sleeping well or badly. Try to *see* that first moment. See how the world is born. First there is the objectless Consciousness. Next the objects appear—That is memory. So the objectless Consciousness without memory is there already, even before anything else is happening.

That Consciousness has never left you. Within That the dream appears, within That dreamless sleep appears, within That the waking state appears. If you have managed to see it in the waking state, then of course that's great! For then you are also going to see it in the dream state. And next you will see it in deep, dreamless sleep as well. Then it isn't far to go to the land of enlightenment. The land of all love.

V: Are there any conditions to 'being'?

A: No, you already *are*. What will you do in order *not* to be? You need to do an awful lot in order *not* to become enlightened. *Not* to see it—that is the biggest work. That requires an incredible lot of effort. There is no condition whatsoever in order to be what you are. *Not* to be what you are—that indeed is a hell of a job!

V: Is it any use trying to understand things at a mental level?

A: We all have been trained to think logically—men somewhat more than women. If something is logical, it gives a kind of satisfaction. For then things fit in a certain framework. It makes something fit together, it is making something whole. The puzzle fits together. However, that is not a *real* insight. Real insight often *isn't* logical for that matter. A truly profound insight in the soul has nothing to do with reason. Nor with feeling. Some people need a life-time for it, and with others it comes quickly. It is most essential that you solve your own riddle. For as long as that hasn't been solved, you will go on looking for a solution at the mental level, which ultimately is not going to give you any satisfaction.

V: Is the desire for true insight alive in every human being?

A: Among a hundred thousand people there is *one* who is asking himself why he exists. And among the hundred thousand who are asking themselves why they exist, there is *one* who attains to true Knowledge.[5]—This to encourage you...

V: What I *am*, I cannot know. But what actually happens to the *knower*?

A: The knower is that which is nearest to you, and that is why it escapes your notice. The eye is a similar case: I'm looking out through the eyes, but the eye cannot see the eye, yet seeing is there. The ear cannot hear the ear, and yet hearing is there. Similarly, knowing is there, but the knower does not know himself. Nor will he ever be able to know himself, for he cannot be made into an object. Just as the eye and the ear are not able to make themselves into an object.

V: Despite that I find that that is precisely, what I'm trying to do all the time.

A: Yes, and we strongly advise you to stop trying. That is the spiritual instruction being given here. If there is anyone who is against spirituality, then it is me. If there is anyone who is against worship and religion, then it is me. If there is anyone who is against spiritual seeking, then surely it is me. That is why I'm saying it in a straightforward and clear-cut manner. I'm a great opponent of all spirituality. The search for the Self is an absolutely absurd and perverse phenomenon. And yet searching and being spiritually occupied is considered to be something special! Not at all. Dumb misery it is!

The possibility is there, the potential is there to see the Essence. And I refuse to line up with the people who are telling that all this is so hard, and that you need a million years to do it. If *I* can do it, so can you, for most of you are more intelligent, more brilliant and more sensitive than me. So what keeps you?

V: The state of my childhood, so before I started asking myself who I was, is it actually the same as my real nature?

A: Yes, it is. But then the environment exerts pressure on you, and is trying to make you believe something else than what you as a child are seeing instantly. When I was eight years old, it was as clear to me as it is now. Only the pressure of the environment was so intense that, at a certain point, the thought came to my mind: Am *I* crazy, or are *they*? But the pressure of the environment is actually huge, because socially, emotionally, and financially, you are perfectly dependent on the satisfaction of the family, of the school, and so forth. And while the teachers at school ought to stimulate the loftiest things in us, they actually take their lowest frustrations out on the children. It can only generate frustrated politicians etc. as a result. That we are all still functioning more or less normally is a miracle to me.

V: Actually, I don't recall anything of the period before I started asking myself about the meaning of life.

A: You don't recall it, because at that age it wasn't leaving any traces. But the very moment the *self*-consciousness is born, it *is* leaving traces. All self-consciousness is leaving traces. A child which is happy, doesn't *know* it is happy. A child which is unhappy, *knows* that it is unhappy.

What is real doesn't leave any traces. Whereas traumatic experiences *will* leave their traces. After thirty years you may still recall them with tears in your eyes. On the other hand profound moments, moments of ecstasy and happiness, do not leave any traces. Because, then, *you* aren't there! If you have come here, and you no longer remember what was being said, then that's a good sign. Real communication doesn't leave any traces. For that reason I often tell you, that the things that are being said here, aren't going to bring you any profit in the sense of material profit. Here is nothing of material value which you could possibly gather in for yourself.

V: Then where does all that's being said, remain?

A: It is seen within the Consciousness. And if it is really *seen*, then Consciousness *itself* is seen, and there will be Self-realisation. Afterwards, however, each person tends to get himself snowed in again. Until that, too, won't happen any more. Then the clarity remains. And he who can listen with that clarity, is listening truly. Then you don't want anything further. Then a *true* meeting is taking place, because then there isn't really any more 'must'. That is the most wonderful thing there is.

(7th May, 1987)

34

TO BE FREE FROM CONDITIONING IS IMPOSSIBLE

Visitor: My character is largely made up of conditionings which are just there. Do they persist even after Self-realisation?

Alexander: In our tradition we leave the entire conditioning of the character completely alone. There is no interest whatsoever in such conditionings inasmuch as we do not believe in change. The real change is seeing what you *really* are, and then the conditionings won't do you any harm. Then there will be total acceptance.

V: So there is no need to put your energy in wanting to change yourself?

A: Total acceptance means that the whole question of stepping in or wanting to change is off the table and, as a result, you are connected to the big Light. Then everything will arrange itself according to your natural state. The very notion that you would have to get rid of conditionings, is itself a conditioning. It is Advaita misunderstood.

Conditioning is memory. When you are driving a car, you are conditioned. If you are a Dutchman, you are conditioned Dutch. So also in the case of a person who is suffering from loss of memory, who cannot remember that he is married, for example, or that he has got children. The logical conclusion to be drawn from this is, that love and relationships and the like are equally linked to memory. Memory is responsible for the direction and the contents of consciousness. All you can do, therefore, is to discover that there is a clarity within you, which is able to learn from the given situation. That is what I call, 'Letting things tell their story'—from that clarity. And then all the cramps—tensions, frictions, negativity—cannot but relax. In this way you may purify yourself, and you will gradually come closer to the potential which you are. At a certain point you will discover that you are no longer dependent on anybody, that everything may manifest itself, and that things may be perceived in a very natural way. Then there is a true balance, true harmony.

To be free from conditioning is impossible. You can only be free from the *notion* that a conditioning could actually bind you or make you free. No conditioning can bind you or free you. To realize *that* is true freedom. This in contrast with therapies and the like, which may lead one to a catharsis, but not to a fundamental insight.

V: Yesterday you spoke about 'the One which knows no second'. As a matter of fact, I only know the second, for the One I'm not able to see. Nor can I picture it to myself. Still that is what I'm constantly trying to do.

A: Yes, until the impossibility of it has become so obvious to you, that the phenomenon eliminates itself. Then you will stop doing it. For that reason it has to be seen again and again, it has to be repeated again and again.

Here is another such phenomenon: The majority of people imagine Self-realisation to be some kind of stroke of lightning. They are waiting for some kind of overall change to take place. But you can forget about that. It is not going to happen, because every stroke of lightning and every change is perceived by the

One that knows no change. So even if you go on changing forever, in the end you will still have to see That which remains itself *un*changed within the change. And *That* is not binding you, *That* is not something which is going to keep you out of your sleep. If it does, then things have not been grasped properly.

V: Is there really no technique needed for it?

A: A technique is a condition in order *not* to be That, which you really are. You could say that a technique acts as a sort of preservative, similar to a philosophy or a religion, which are preservatives as well. Each condition is nothing but a rationalisation in order *not* to be immediately That, which you truly *are*. In order to be yourself you don't need any techniques.

V: But at the same time a technique or a therapy could clear up certain things inside you, couldn't they?

A: No, the very idea of clearing up things is absurd. What is there in you that needs clearing up?

V: Mental blocks.

A: Mental blocks? Mental blocks are an excuse. By paying attention to mental blocks you will basically remain blocked. You are giving food to the monster, and in doing so, it will grow bigger and bigger. That is the wrong sort of attention.

V: So far that hasn't been my experience yet.

A: It will come. Learn to see the natural laws in your existence. When a child puts its hand into the fire, then the fire is not going to say, 'Oh, it's a child. I will just withdraw my heat for a moment'. No. Fire—hand—pain is a law. You only need to discover those laws. Looking from the Self, from *Atman*, you may actually become aware of all the natural laws. Then you will join in in the cadence of existence. Each time you don't join in, means resistance, defense, personality, ego, blocking. If you are going to pay attention to these mental blocks, then you will keep on feeding the monster. There is no end to thoughts, there is no end to feelings, and each stimulus that you are giving to your thoughts and feelings, is again creating new worlds of thoughts and feelings.

If you just take a close look, then you will see that the only capital you have is *here* and *now*. For the rest you are absolutely bankrupt. The greatest gift is this *here*-and-*now* moment. You just can't get out of it. People ask me sometimes: 'How do I get into the here-and-now?' Then I ask them, 'How do you get *out*?' There is no way you can get out of it. That is all you've got. Nor should you expect any Self-realisation in the future. It is *now*.

V: And yet I keep having this feeling, that there is going to be a last moment...

A: ... when you will realize that nothing is going to go anywhere, and that everything is always *here* and always *now*.

V: And for that you seem to need a teacher...

A: Not *'seem'* to—You *need* a teacher! For *he* is the man to take everything away from you, so that there is just no way you're going to escape any more. Then the *now* may reveal itself to you.

V: And yet you do sometimes speak about 'later'.

A: Yes, within time and space. But in reality there *is* no 'later'.

V: But will I then still be sitting and listening here five or eight years from now? There has to be a *last* time, or not?

A: You are *always* listening *now*. Time and space are perceived by something which is *outside* of time and space. And that something happens to be That which *I* am and which *you* are. For example, there is nothing to be found inside of me which is thirty-eight years old. Nor is there in you. Not even physically, because every seven years we have got a perfectly different body. But That which I really *am* is timeless. That is altogether spaceless even. I call it the absolute Availability or absolute Love. At the bottom of your heart you *are* that Love, that Availability. So I suggest that you behave accordingly. Or even more wonderful: Let yourself be *carried* by that Love, by that Availability. Then you will lead a truly spontaneous life. And then you just see what all is going to happen there!

(14th May, 1987)

35

LETTING GO OF THE KNOWN

Alexander: There are two kinds of knowledge: self-knowledge in the sense of knowledge of the phenomena and processes within the self-consciousness, the individual consciousness, the 'I'—and true Self-knowledge. Here we are dealing with the latter. I am saying that true Self-knowledge comes first. After that the self-knowledge in the sphere of the phenomena will automatically become clear. That's the way it is, and not the other way round. You people still want to get a clear view of all the phenomena first, but here it is exactly the other way round. When that Self-realisation has become a fact, then the world of phenomena will no longer be a problem to you. Whereas without Self-realisation you will never come to any clarity in the domain of the phenomena. For that reason I'm telling you: Self-realisation comes first. And after that the insight into the phenomena will be a gift on top of it. You are still putting the emphasis on self-knowledge in the sphere of 'knowing your own personality', and I don't see any solution there. All I can see there is *more* problems. He who invests his attention in the personality, is investing in a bankrupt property. There is no end to it.

Visitor: To me this feels like the world upside down. While you are saying it, the thought comes to my mind, 'It just isn't possible'. At the same time I do understand what you are saying.

A: You have to understand clearly that, inherent in our mind, there is a deep-rooted value-system which is continuously telling you, 'This is right, that isn't'. You will never hear me say that there would be anything wrong with the world of phenomena or with the self-consciousness. All I'm saying is, that no absolute freedom is to be found there. I also have my chocolate spread sandwich—which is the world of phenomena—but the difference is, that I don't have any conflict with it. I have no conflict with any object whatsoever. So I want it to be clear to you, that we are not dealing here with the world of phenomena. Nevertheless all the attention is going there. The world *does* require a certain amount of attention—I'm not denying that—but in that world no real solution is to be found. A real solution is only to be found in the Real. And the world of phenomena *isn't* real. Whoever has found a solution in the sphere of the Real, will no longer have any conflict with the world of phenomena. And as you are living in conflict with this world of phenomena, I'm advising you to look for something real. You will never be able to find something real by means of unreal things. He who goes on digging and romping and fighting or flirting with the world of phenomena, is never going to find a real solution. That is what I'm saying.

Conflicts take place in the world of phenomena. If you can penetrate into the Real, then a clarity is born which will also bring clarity in the world of phenomena. As a present that comes with it. But we are accustomed to look at the periphery, where only temporary solutions are to be found. I'm not saying that there *aren't* any temporary solutions, but I do say that such temporary solutions are no *real* solutions. The problem is that many people are trying to combine their objective, day-to-day life with spirituality. They try to integrate their spirituality in the world in order to bring about a change there. But the one thing has nothing to do with the other! No sensible human being would try to change the world, for it will change of itself anyway. No need to do anything for it!

Whoever is living from that clarity can no longer be manipulated nor does he have any more fear. Such a person is without concessions and therefore complete, whatever may happen! While you prefer a dull life, full of concessions. From moment to moment this whole life, this whole existence, this whole manifestation, is basically one huge school of practice, which will last until death. And even death itself will be something new, for until death is there, you don't really know what it is. One of the last 'tests' on the 'road' to Self-realisation will be, whether you are able to let go of everything voluntarily, and that *before* death has got hold of you. Even before death you should have let go of everything of your own free will. If you live intensely, you will also die intensely. 'Intensely' meaning 'without concessions'. Not without love, but without concessions.

Self-realisation is to die each moment. It means to be running perfectly synchronously with existence, with the *here*-and-*now*. Letting go of the known, letting go of everything that is tied up with the manifested. It requires total dedication. And whoever begins to see things as they really are, will become a risk to interested parties, to politicians, to society. Because such a man is totally without any concessions, nor is he in any way open to manipulation. In no way whatsoever. And all those little games of yours, all the little therapy games plus the entire consciousness-raising industry, are there to keep the nation quiet. Once you start it, it becomes a never-ending story.

Marx was right. Religion *is* opium to the people. Absolutely! I am against consciousness-expanding. I am against drugs. I am against all the things that you are for. Against religion, against philosophy, against Bhagwan, against Krishnamurti, and also against A. Smit. Why? Because you will use anything for the game of enhancing self-consciousness' glory, which means total death of the truth. There is absolutely no reason why I should take it for granted, that you won't be using me or Advaita for that purpose as well. And I won't leave anything undone to have that changed.

V: What do you mean by 'use'? As a sort of drug?

A: Yes, as a preservative. You can use Advaita Vedanta in such a way, that you actually won't have to *see* the truth. Just as you can use any religion, any philosophy, any enlightened man as a system of thought, in which you will know how to fit your own thinking—your wasted life.

V: I have the feeling that, in your case, such a thing wouldn't be possible at all.

A: We shall see. Already I hear people telling one another, 'But don't you see that you are basically Consciousness?!' Where do they get it from? They have heard it here. And the very fact that they are telling it to someone else, just shows that they haven't realized anything. Only those who become quiet at a certain point, and who remain in that quietness, recognizing the clarity there, looking from there at the manifestation, they are the truly realized ones. And they will hardly show it. There is nothing specific by which you are able to recognize it. All the rest is fake, bullshit.

V: Does one necessarily have to become quiet?

A: You don't have to anything. The effect of Self-realisation is perfect silence, *inner* silence—although sometimes it may also lead to outer silence.

V: There are times when I see it, but then it disappears again. Afterwards I'm often left with the feeling that I'm not allowed to see it. As if it is forbidden.

A: That is deep-seated. But to most people it is almost of therapeutic importance to let the manifested tell its story in a natural way. Without judging and suppressing anything. Let everything tell its story—from that solid clarity. That should come first. Realize that place of clarity. For some it is quite a job to let the manifestation tell its story, for others the story is quickly told. There are people who have gone through most horrid things, and there are those who have basically led a very quiet life. Let the body, let the mind, let feeling tell its story. Without condemning anything! Learn to look, learn to be aware indiscriminately. For that is *the* most essential thing.

V: You often speak about different levels.

A: There are two levels: an absolute level and a relative level. Looking at it from the clarity, there is no conflict with the manifestation, but from the manifestation there is quite a lot of conflict. Even *with* the clarity. And often a question is asked about the Absolute from a relative level.

From the Consciousness which you essentially *are*, you may quietly look at what is manifesting itself. But it is not possible to look from the manifestation at the Consciousness. In a sense it is the world upside down. Whoever has seen but once, that essentially he is always that Consciousness, may finally begin to look truly. Such looking truly is *jnana*. All other looking is *vijnana* or memory and conditioning. And a conditioning cannot understand anything. Nor can a thought or a feeling. For these are signals, functions, means. Only the Knowing is *im*-mediate. All the rest is mediate.

V: What does it mean to be 'in the heart'?

A: Nonsense, sentiment, bullshit, Pavlov-effects! The biggest trap you can fall into is the sentiment of the heart.

V: By 'heart' I mean the love for oneself—no conflict—the feeling of oneness with others.

A: Don't introduce the word 'heart' at all. Introduce the word 'clarity'. 'Heart' is related to warmth and friendliness, virtuousness, and so on. 'Clarity', 'presence', comes nearer to it, and it includes the heart as well. Each sensation which is manifesting itself—oneness, division, separation, warmth, cold, skating, hot chocolate—is preceded by something else. *That* is the *real* Oneness. Live from *That*, and for the rest do what you like. Live from the Oneness that *precedes* all the phenomena. Including warmth, including getting angry. If that is what you mean, then I would say, perfect! But never be satisfied with less, not even with the heart. If you mean it in a poetic sense, then that's all right. And yet, there is something fishy about it, a tricky conditioning. Because the *feeling* of oneness is *itself* also an object that is preceded by something else. That clarity, too, is the *in*-ground *in* the feeling of oneness. So don't put the emphasis on the feeling of oneness, but on that from which it proceeds, in which it is perceived, and in which it will also disappear again. That is that clarity. You may still call it the 'heart', but then in the sense of a very still centre.

Don't listen as a person, don't listen as a viewpoint. Listen as consciousness, listen as knowingness, listen as clarity. Still you will see that, somewhere, in the hidden corners of your soul, you are yet secretly waiting for some miraculous transformation to happen. And to be waiting for such a transformation is the very *postponement* of the transformation. It certainly is a matter of transformation, but that transformation does not come about through the expectation of it. That comes through direct realisation. *Now.*

As for me, I think you basically have sufficient living material in hand to get busy. And if there are any questions, then put them to the awakened and not to each other, for you will only intensify each others' projections. It is of no importance as to *who* is awakened, as long as you put your questions to the awakened.

(15th May, 1987)

KNOWING CANNOT KNOW ITSELF

Alexander: There must have been a time, when the universal Consciousness hang slumbering in the cosmos without making itself manifest. Consciousness was slumbrously conscious of itself. Of not-any-thing. Something cannot become conscious of itself, unless it has got a vehicle. That is why everything that is conscious, is a vehicle. From the flea to an elephant to a human being. The form which we have got is absolutely unique, because the human form is the most suitable instrument for returning to the essential situation. Man has got everything on hand for that realisation.

Visitor: In my view everybody is consciously or unconsciously in search of himself.

A: Everybody is in search of himself. 'Unconsciously' doesn't exist in my dictionary. Something unconscious is not known, and everything I know is known consciously. And all that I can possibly know, *is* what I know. Therefore everything is conscious. If anything 'unconscious' would exist at all, then that won't be known, until you have actually become conscious of it. So then it is no longer unconscious, but conscious. There is no such thing as 'unconscious'. I never met with an unconscious subject. It is inherent in consciousness that everything is known. There is nothing that is 'unknown'. Your ultimate guru is Consciousness itself.

V: What exactly do you mean by 'clarity'?

A: Clarity means that your fears and desires have disappeared. It is as simple as that. It may take three years or it may take thirty years. Then again, what is thirty years in eternity? The key is to return to the state of clarity over and over again—of, 'Oh yes, that's how it really is'.

In the beginning that condition is by no means steady. In the beginning it is only fragmentarily present. That is why I'm saying: Learn to perceive an immutable situation. Go back again and again to the clarity, to that force—for it actually is a huge force—which will enable you to perceive the most complex things in all their clarity. All of you did perceive it already once, no one excepted. Many people ask whether they can do anything for it. 'What should I do?' My answer is: Find yourself a place in which it is perfectly clear to you.

V: So the problem is, that we basically *are* in that clarity!

A: You are *always* in that clarity!

V: But there is a veil in between...

A: Is that so? Where is the veil? What sort of veil do you mean?

V: It's a smoke-screen.

A: Use what has been said for your self-enquiry.

V: I forget things because of the veil. Why should I forget?

A: Because you are not really interested.

V: There are also moments when I succeed though.

A: Succeed in what?

V: In looking from the consciousness. In being clear. In seeing through things, keeping a clear view of things. But after some time I relapse into my former state.

A: What did you remember?

V: The looking!

A: Then why don't you do that?

V: I don't know—That's why I'm asking.

A: Pick what you think is important. Dig it out completely, chew on it. Try to get out of it what's in there. What are the things you are interested in?

V: Music, reading, watching movies.

A: Take out the reading and the movies, then you are left with the music. That will provide a good counter-weight. Perfect. No more reading on these subjects. Just remember what is being said here. Think about it. Be serious about the matter. Concentrate on the essence. You won't find anything in books. A book may at best solve some elementary questions, but never anything fundamental. Because the fundamental things are just too subtle. You need to have personal contact with the one to whom you are putting the essential questions. You are being offered clarity, yet you embrace body, mind and feeling, and all the rubbish that goes with it.

V: The moment I have a particular feeling, should I then stay connected with the *in*-ground of feeling?

A: When a feeling is manifesting itself, then that is being *known*. Otherwise you wouldn't actually feel it. *That* is the *in*-ground. Stick to that *Knowing*. And for the rest, look closely! And to look closely means to stay with the *in*-ground, not letting yourself to be carried away by silly emotions and feelings. The moment you have a clear view of it, you will be free from it. And the moment you are free from it, you will also be able to make a conscious decision whether or not to join in something. Whereas at present you are chained by action and reaction, which is a non-acceptable situation. That is not your true nature. It is hindering your potential.

V: Does it mean that emotions will no longer manifest themselves? That I won't be jealous or angry any more?

A: At the most there will be a chemical reaction or a sign of anger that is being perceived, but for the rest nothing. And that will just wear itself out. Finished. And apart from that, it is not the intention to stop oneself in any way from becoming angry. That is more something for ex-Christians who start doing yoga. I never saw such an excited man as my teacher, Nisargadatta. He would get angry about nothing and then, a second later, all was gone, and he would just sit there laughing.

V: You are saying that fear and desire go together. I notice that in my case quite a lot of desires have actually disappeared. But along with it many incentives for living have disappeared as well. Because those incentives are based on desires. So it looks as if the basic impulses are disappearing.

A: It is possible that, in the initial phase, you will find yourself in a kind of negating sphere. That is not what we are aiming at. Work, sexuality and food are vital impulses which make you actually feel vibrant with life. In our tradition the advice is to live a normal life. Anything which tends towards exaggeration—whether in the way of taking initiatives or in rushing after impulses—means that you are out of balance. Find your natural balance, devoid of fear and desire. Lead a normal life. No imitation of anything. Just be yourself. Everyone has got his own sphere, his own mode, his own vibration. In perfect acceptance a great deal of happiness will come back to you, because then there is no longer any struggle to be anything different from what you are. As Self-realisation becomes increasingly clear, you will actually join in the manifestation with complete dedication. Then there will be a perfect acceptance of the manifestation along with all its phenomena.

V: You said that, although we *think* we have got a free will, in reality we are being lived.

A: Yes, you are being lived. You don't *look*. You organize and you force and you push.

You are born spontaneously and you will disappear spontaneously. So why should all that's lying in between *not* be spontaneous? I am saying that everything happens spontaneously. You are getting angry spontaneously and you keep it down spontaneously. Everything is happening completely of its own accord. And once you have found peace in the Knowing, then you will be able to observe everything in peace. For the nice thing about ignorance is, that it is actually being *known*. Only the Knowing itself cannot be known.

V: But I *do* have a choice, for example, whether or not to mix with other people?

A: No, that is a basic illusion. You *don't* mix with other people, not even with yourself. Things just happen, and there is nothing you can do about it. Ask anybody who is sitting here, whether they can do anything about the situation they are actually in. If they can do anything about it, then they are doing it already, in which case they can't do anything about that either. Everybody is doing his best. In the course of time many people find out that their parents, too, simply did their best, and that they couldn't do any better than they did. For, if they could have done better, then they would definitely have done so.

Realize that everything is happening spontaneously. You wake up spontaneously, you get the flu spontaneously, you get angry spontaneously, you are in search spontaneously, you are spontaneously stupid or intelligent. All happens of itself. There is nothing which isn't spontaneous. Thoughts come up, whether you like it or not, whether you want it or not. You only need to recognize the actual position in which you find yourself, and all the struggle will stop. And that is freedom. For, if there is no more struggle, if there is nothing more to fight, then there will be peace.

V: I'm still convinced though, that there is something specific in me, which gives me the sense of being '*me*'.

A: That is nothing specific. There is nothing specific to be found about you, which would answer to the sense of 'I am'. On the other hand what *is* making you interesting is the *consciousness* in you. If *that* is gone, everything is gone. There is something in you which has nothing to do with feeling, which has altogether nothing to do with thinking, which has altogether nothing to do with the intellect. It has even got nothing to do with the body. And that needs to become clear to you.

V: I still recognize this basic feeling in me, which is '*me*'.

A: That is a question of poor perception, because that feeling varies. It *isn't* a basic feeling. It *appears* to be a basic feeling, because you aren't looking any deeper.

V: Is there no entrance to it anywhere?

A: No, there is no entrance anywhere. There is neither entrance nor exit. You *think* there is an entrance. That is the delusion of being so-called spiritually occupied. I call it the 'pussy-basket-feeling'.

V: But that is how I experience it!

A: You *insist* on experiencing it that way. Because you are just not prepared to leave your pussy-basket. If I were you, I also wouldn't do it, for nobody is going to do self-enquiry from his easy chair or from his warm bed. And that is why you have to be dragged out of it. Often quite serious things will have to take place first, before somebody is going to wake up. And one of the laws is never to wake up anybody who *doesn't* want to wake up. It is at the request of the one who wants to wake up, that a start is made with a kind of awakening process. But if somebody prefers to go on sleeping, then there isn't a teacher who is going to wake you up.

V: Something is perceived. So light is thrown upon it. And that light is not limited to one person only. Is that light one with everything?

A: Consciousness is the light itself. That light falls on a form, you could say, or it assumes a form. The form is experienced as real, and then it appears as if the form is detached from the light. Then the form begins to lead a life of its own.

V: But you may have a sudden insight, in which the knowledge and the knower and the known appear to be one and the same thing.

A: Yes, you may.

V: But that is not a form.

A: No, that perception is not a form. That perception we call '*jnana*'—pure, absolute Knowing—knowingness.

There is a universal Consciousness, but we have learnt to experience that universal Consciousness as an individual consciousness. As a consequence you believe to be living in a body, as if there is an 'I' inhabiting the body. In reality it is Consciousness. We are all connected to one big Light, and that is Consciousness.

V: Which is all-knowing?

A: That's right. That is the inexhaustible source which continues to create forever. Where do all those billions of bodies come from? It is one unbroken Whole. How is Consciousness being transmitted? Through sexuality, through children. When a child is born, then it may look as if your consciousness is being transmitted to the child. Of course, that isn't really the case. It is the possibility for its *manifestation* which is being transmitted. And that is an incredible mystery. Through the fusion of the male sperm and the female egg Consciousness becomes manifest. In India it is called '*Shiva-Shakti*'. If you understand Indian symbolism properly, then the penis stands for creation, and the vagina is the place where everything begins. That is why in Sanskrit the womb is called 'bed of Consciousness'. Consciousness is being 'transmitted' through sexuality. That is why sex is so much of a taboo. 'Taboo' is an other word for 'not transparent', 'not clear'.

The sexual energy makes it possible for the Consciousness to become manifest. We are sitting here thanks to the sexual energy of our parents. Through their act of sexuality we have assumed a form.

V: And because of that there is the possibility, that all the rest may be perceived?

A: Yes, because without the manifestation, without the instruments of body, mind and feeling, Consciousness is actually not able to manifest itself. Out of love for itself it is making itself manifest within itself. And whoever has lived a complete, loving life, may at death lay down that life again in all its grandeur. He may pass away thankfully and moved even, and not cramped as it mostly happens. Although billions and billions of bodies have been there, still it is all one and the same Consciousness manifesting itself in billions of forms. Even in an insect. Even in a tree. Even in an elephant. If you just have a look at nature, then you will see the whole mystery there: manifestation, manifestation—There is no end to it! That is *Shiva-Shakti*, the creation—birth *and* death. For there is a destructive force as well. Which one always wins? Death always wins. At the same time all is being known by a power which is even bigger than both the creative and the destructive forces. That power is the Consciousness itself. That contains everything within itself.

V: Death as the destruction of the objects?

A: Yes. That in which the objects appear, can itself never be destroyed. It goes without saying that *you*, as an object, as a 'person', can never lay claim to the Impersonal. So realize yourself to be a figure *within* a Non-figure, and that at one and the same time. In our tradition we are not saying, 'You are *only* Consciousness, and all the rest is not important'. No, what we are saying is, 'Both the manifested *and* the unmanifested are there at one and the same time'. The two may appear to be at war with each other, but in reality there is no war, there is no dichotomy there. Instead there is Unity. And in that Unity you may enjoy the manifestation to the full. You only need to look at Rajneesh, for example, in order to see that he is enjoying things to the full. Whereas we are not able to enjoy, because we mistake ourselves for a small fragment. And a fragment is always colliding with some other fragment. The actual realisation of being both the manifested *and* the unmanifested Consciousness is Self-realisation. This you need to be told over and over again, and it needs to become clear to you again and again, until it won't leave you any more. Gurdjieff called it 'Self-remembrance'. In India it is called '*satsang*'.

The potential that is lying within you is unmanifested, and it wants to make itself manifest. And that is life's task. Like the semen which is pressing itself to break forth. *Shiva-Shakti* is the Force that keeps everything going. Surrender yourself to that Force. In the Chinese symbol of *Yin-Yang* you will find the whole of Advaita represented: both the manifested and the unmanifested within the infinite circle of the Emptiness. There comes a time when you will perceive that symbolism everywhere, wherever you look. The other day I saw a lemon squeezer which looked just like a *Shiva-lingam*, a phallus in a vagina. Besides the *Shiva-lingam* there is another very beautiful symbol in India: a triangle with one of its angles pointing upwards, and right across it a triangle pointing downwards, like the Star of David. So a hexagon, with in the middle a dot. Embellishments are put around it in order to divert the attention from the subject. The triangle pointing upwards is the phallus symbol, and the triangle pointing downwards symbolizes the vagina. Once you are aware of it, you will recognize that symbolism everywhere. Because such symbolism has an appeal. Why is milk poured over the *Shiva-lingam* in India? Because milk resembles the colour of the semen. Cow's milk is also poured over certain images of the Buddha. But the people who are doing these things often aren't aware themselves, why these things are actually being done.

V: Is the knowingness the same as the universal Consciousness?

A: No, the universal Consciousness is something different. The knowingness can only manifest itself *as* knowingness through the manifestation. So the knowingness needs body, mind and feeling as its instruments in order to know itself. Without body, mind and feeling the Knowing cannot know itself. It needs to have an instrument. How can a flower make itself known? The flower is potentially already present in the seed, but it has still to become manifest. The scent of the flower, too, is there in the seed already. That is why I call the body 'the scent of the Consciousness'. Speech, too, is the scent of the Consciousness. The whole of body-mind-feeling is the scent of the Consciousness. And if the Consciousness is no longer known, then the energy will go and look for a new form again, in a new human body. But if you have seen it but once, then there is nothing more to be known. Because then the Absolute is known. Then you will have stepped out of 'the wheel of rebirth', as they say in India.

V: This morning you said that the Knowing cannot possibly know itself.

A: The Knowing cannot know itself. It can only *be* known through body, mind and feeling. If you take away body, mind and feeling, then the Knowing also is gone.

(22nd May, 1987)

THE 'PERSON' IS THE PAST

Alexander: At some point in your life, probably when you were three or four years old, you began to experience yourself as something different from the perceivingness. A moment in which you made a swing-over to an 'I', that is say, to a 'person', to a *self*-consciousness.

What you know about yourself is what you *remember* about yourself. The person, the 'I', consists of nothing but memory pictures from the past. Unlike the images which you make of yourself, awareness doesn't need any memory. Therefore, all that you know about yourself, and that which you take yourself to be, is old. It is the past. Memory cannot perceive anything new, while awareness can. That which you take yourself to be, and with which you may identify yourself, are curdled experiences consisting purely and simply of memory pictures. Your so-called experiences are always the past. Necessarily the past, for what you know about yourself is derived from memory. It *is* memory. Through images memory is able to retrieve that which is past. But something that is past, is not the reality. At best it is a *mental* reality. Such reality, however, is but short-lived, as it will eventually dissolve in the awareness.

So what sort of reality does the person, composed by you from the past, actually possess? The reality that is being attributed by you to that past, consists of thoughts, mental images, ideas, concepts. And these images seem to overshadow the reality that you are actually living. Because of that you are living in a world of delusion instead of in the reality. Only through the power of discrimination you will be able to free yourself from that delusion. That is why Advaita emphasizes *viveka* so much, the ability to discriminate between what is delusion and what is reality.

This person, however, that 'somebody' which you have created, cannot be replaced by the concept of 'nobody'.

Visitor: That is precisely the point. What I have done is to replace this 'somebody' by a 'nobody'.

A: It is sufficient to see that what you call the 'somebody' or the 'person'—that is to say, all the material with which you could possibly identify yourself—is the old, memory, pictures, and that these do not have any reality. They *do* have some form of reality, but that reality in turn is being attributed by *other* images again. On the other hand the reality you are *actually* living is free from delusion.

V: I can imagine that.

A: It is not a question of your *imagining* it: You are there *already*—always.

V: I remember quite well, when I first came here, that you were saying, 'The knowing has *got* to be there'. My question is: *Who* knows that?

A: Do you need a 'who' in order to know it? At best the knowing is conscious of a 'who', but there certainly isn't a 'who' that is conscious of any knowing.

V: Such knowing happens by means of the body.

A: But then, if the body is dead, what does the body know?

V: Then the knowing also isn't there any more.

A: So the knowing *is* the body? After death the knowing has gone, but the body is still there. Although the knowing may have something to do with the body, it is not *identical* with the body.
When someone is actually dying, then the one who is afraid to die will disappear along with it. For as soon as death takes place, there won't be any further need to be afraid of it. The one who has any fear of passing away, will disappear along with the passing away. And it can never take long, so you need not be afraid of death. The fear of death will go together with death itself. If you are afraid to lose your finger, then that fear, too, will have disappeared the very moment that you have actually lost the finger. Those fears are not substantial, they are not real. In actual reality any fear will disappear. More people have died from the *fear* of death than through death itself...

V: I'm still left with the question as to whether the knowing isn't actually tied up with a 'somebody'.

A: No, it isn't.

V: What you are saying is: Things happen within the Consciousness.

A: Yes, but you can't make Consciousness into an object, into a 'thing'. By making a noun of it, it would seem as if qualities may actually be attributed to it.

V: When Self-realisation takes place, will there be a 'somebody' to know it?

A: With Self-realisation it is that very 'somebody' which is going to disappear. But there is *not* going to be a 'nobody' to take its place.

V: Then *who* actually knows it?

A: There is only the Knowing. There is neither a 'somebody' to know it, nor is there a 'nobody' to know it. There is only knowingness, Love, Consciousness. Once a person came here, and after one meeting he said, 'I know enough. I've got it.' 'All right', I said, and I never saw him again.

To see it just once is sufficient. Knowing is sufficient unto itself. *Not*-knowing is never sufficient unto itself. In that case there is always something that has to go with it—stories, dramas, ideas, philosophy, and so forth. Ignorance always needs to be supported, because it is not self-sufficient. The knowingness which you *are*, doesn't need any support. No guru, no disciple, no commentary, no confirmation, not a single reflection.

Self-realisation is self-sufficient. That is the beauty of it. The whole guru-disciple relationship, too, is transcended along with it. The reality—that which you truly *are*—is sufficient unto itself. It doesn't need anyone's confirmation, not even the confirmation of the teacher or the guru. However, until the very last you will be seeking the grace, the blessing, the approval, the confirmation of the guru as the father.

Only the reality which you are *actually* living, suffices. Self-realisation is self-sufficient. That realisation can never be confirmed by anything from outside, not by any authority, not by anybody standing outside of it. At the same time someone who is truly Self-realized is not falling into the trap of self-complacency, thinking, 'Now I'm enlightened. I no longer need anyone'. These are all very subtle things... Profound knowing will ultimately become silence.

You have to understand that this 'person' is something obsessive. You can't just tell your memory, 'Now stop producing images!' Memory is simply producing what it produces. And it is basically producing a three-dimensional delusion. There is only one thing which refuses to be part of the delusion, and that is the perceivingness. So no wonder that *that* is, where the emphasis needs to be. But from the delusion you will never be able to realize what that perceivingness really is. As a matter of fact, the will doesn't have any grip on memory's activities and, therefore, not on the 'person' either. They cannot just disappear. Memory simply continues to deliver. You may forgive, but not forget. To forget is not an act of willpower. The brains are simply doing their job. That's how it works. That is the reality.

Therefore I can see only one possibility, and so I'm asking you: Are you capable of seeing that, which refuses to be part of memory's activities? *That* is the perceivingness, the knowingness. And that is why Advaita would like to see you moving into that direction.

V: So the main thing, looking at it from the standpoint of the subject, is to shift one's point of gravity.

A: To shift one's point of gravity from constantly trying to get a grip from the delusion onto the knowingness—to the knowingness *itself*, to the *real* essence. *That* is the main thing in these meetings.

V: And then all those whirlings produced by memory are to be looked upon from the perceivingness as being more or less irrelevant.

A: No, no, no! That again would be a judgement, an undesirable involvement. The main point is the fact, that you are choicelessly aware *already*. The word 'choiceless' isn't just any word: It means to be *without* discrimination, *without* preference or aversion, *without* judgement. Because that perceivingness *is* choiceless.

V: So you let everything pass by?

A: Let me put it this way: He who realizes the perceivingness cannot but live and look *from* that perceivingness. And although the possibility for judging things will remain wholly available, to *condemn* anything will then prove to be impossible.

V: Everybody is pushing you into the reality value of the person. Is there a way to avoid that?

A: No, there isn't. Just try to see that you are not a person yourself. That is sufficient, and that will do the job.

(8th July, 1989)

WHAT YOU ARE IS NOT WHAT YOU SEEK

Alexander: Something limited will never be able to contain the unlimited or even have a conception of it. On the other hand the unlimited contains within itself all limitation. So you are conscious of any limitation from that which knows no limitations. Otherwise you wouldn't be conscious of it.

Visitor: With the body—with what I perceive to be a body—I find myself to be in duality.

A: You are perceiving duality from something which is *not* dual. That knowingness is free from duality.

V: Then why this human existence? As human beings we just can't escape duality, can we?

A: You are here because of the fact, that your parents once merged with each other. Without their merging your presence here would have been impossible. You are the remembrance of your parents.

V: If one would truly realize that non-dual knowingness, would the play of life not actually come to an end then?

A: No, it would not. As a matter of fact, that would just be the beginning! For, until then, you were living as a body, or as a thinking or sentient being, or as a combination of the three. But after Self-realisation you are living as consciousness. Then everything will only become broader and bigger. Then you will have regained your birthright.

V: The knowingness is always there, and it is that which you have to realize. Once you've realized it, you will none the less be adding qualities to the knowingness, even though as such it doesn't have any qualities. In that case what actually has changed?

A: In contrast to the knowingness which is without any qualities, objects *do* have qualities. And in order to perceive those objects you have the discriminative faculty at your disposal, so that you may actually *enjoy* the Consciousness. And it is proper to nature to have this process continued as long as possible. That is a given fact, not a problem.

V: If you realize the knowingness, then basically nothing has changed. Because the knowingness stays the same anyway. But at the same time, *because* you have realized it, *something* must have changed. Then what exactly does that change consist of?

A: As a result of Self-realisation it will no longer be possible for you to identify yourself with any object whatsoever. The fact that you have consciously realized the knowingness within yourself, will bring you immediate joy, arising from your natural state which is without any friction. Whereas as long as you remain identified with body-mind-feeling, you may be manipulated, and you will be a marionette of fears and desires. Then you are living in a cramp. For you are open to manipulation and *not* free precisely there, where you identify yourself.

V: Would it be true to say, that the knowingness actually *is* the truth?

A: Yes, you can't go any further. The definition of truth is, that it must be true for everybody, everywhere, always—irrespective of race, colour, person, age, intelligence. The knowingness is the conscious being, within which everything appears, within which everything is perceived for a moment, and within which everything disappears again.

V: Is the knowingness also beyond time and space?

A: Time and space are ideas perceived within that very knowingness. Knowingness precedes time and space.

V: The conscious being will be there, as long as you are in a body...

A: There *is* nobody in a body. That which you identify yourself with, *thinks* itself to be inhabiting a body, but in reality there is *nobody* living in a body. You are pure Consciousness. J.C. Bloem[6] says somewhere, 'Each being is created unto non-being', and it is true.

All that's being born carries within itself the tragedy of death. For all that is born must die. You can only be immortal, if you realize That which is *un*born and *un*dying. That is what you are. While you can only seek with what is mortal, it is only to be found in the Immortal. What you *are* is not what you *seek*. To identify yourself as a seeker is to identify yourself as a mortal. To know, to understand, to find, to realize, is death to the seeker. For that reason there are several gurus who will declare that they are immortal, that they were never born. Even Lou de Palingboer[7] said that he wouldn't die. His disciples, however, the so-called 'angels', interpreted this to mean that his *body* could not die. But

I'm convinced that that was not what Lou had in mind. Only if you identify yourself with body-mind-feeling, you reduce yourself to a mortal. If you identify yourself with any object, you are mortal. So the question is: *Who* dies? *Who* is born? *Who* lives? A somebody? A nobody? Spiritual seekers who have been living as a 'somebody', are inclined to go and live on as a 'nobody'. But even a 'nobody' will ultimately prove to be a 'somebody'.

V: Yes, *who* is it that knows?

A: This Knowing or knowingness which you *are*, cannot be linked to a 'somebody', nor to a 'nobody'. The absence of a 'somebody' is not the whole of Self-realisation, because such an absence will still be an object. The essence of the whole thing is the absence of the presence of the absence.

(8th July, 1989)

39

RELAX IN CONSCIOUS BEING

Alexander: Whoever closes his eyes knows himself to be aware of a space within which everything appears, and in which no particular home or place can be located: infinite space above, infinite space beneath, infinite space in front, and infinite space behind. You are the witness of that space. No knowing will ever be able to reach the limit of that space, of that availability, which must have been there even before any planets, earth and human beings had come into being. In reality this space has always been there. And just as you know yourself to be surrounded by this infinite availability outside of you, so also you are aware of that space or depth inside you. In that availability there is neither beginning nor end.

Attention is an object which gives rise to the illusion, that one would be able to focus onto anything external or anything internal. But That within which any such attention is appearing, is itself object-*less*. 'Inside' and 'outside' are apparent objects within Consciousness. 'Inside' and 'outside' are breaking-points: Consciousness made into objects. 'Life' or 'existence' arises from Consciousness, and *is* in fact Consciousness which—through existence—has become conscious of itself. As a result of the conscious 'Knowledge', which is there consequent upon the origin of life, of existence, you are invited to identify yourself with objects that owe their sole existence to the Consciousness. At one time all those objects—planets, universes, the human race, the earth—had not come into existence yet. At one time the planet earth was not there, at one time there were no human beings and, one day, no human beings *will* be there. One day this earth will not be there. The 'Knowledge' which we now have, is a Knowing full of mystery. That Knowing is the *in*-ground in everything. That Knowing is the mystery itself.

The human phenomenon has a potential of 36.500 days—36.500 days and 36.500 nights. Planetary rotations. Cycles by which to measure our so-called time. Everything consists of rounds, circles. Life is nothing but one big circle. Everything revolves in circles, and everything rotates and moves within something still.

Our time is measured by objects. Without objects there can be no time. There must have been a time, when there was *no* time, nothing by which to measure anything. Even so all the potential must have been there already—not manifest, not visible, but definitely potentially present. Omnipotent, all-mighty, all-powerful. And we, human beings, we too have come from that. The deep memory of it is still slumbering in our being. It is crystal-clear that no object whatsoever will ever be able to get at that clarity, at that potential.

In order for us to get at that clarity we must necessarily be at the deepest of the deep, the subtlest of the subtle—at That which contains everything. The only thing which contains everything is Consciousness itself. Within That everything moves, within That everything rests, within That everything passes away, within That everything is born. Within That all things are made manifest. Thus the Hindu knows three major gods—god the Creator, god the Sustainer, and god the Destroyer. These have originated from *Brahman*, while *Brahman* in turn has come from *Parabrahman*: That which precedes everything, That which is the Absolute.

The Knowing transcends every object, whether body, mind or feeling, or whatever it may be. Every object is preceded by conscious being.

Visitor: Once the body has gone, does conscious being remain then?

A: No, conscious being disappears along with the body.

V: Does the Absolute remain then?

A: It is That in which you will pass away. You were also born in something, weren't you? Conscious being will pass away along with the body. What you now call your 'consciousness' is more of a *body*-consciousness. What remains is *absolute* Consciousness: That in which everything is appearing, such as planets, earth and universes, and you too. Because of the fact that your innermost being *is* absolute Consciousness, you carry within yourself the possibility of becoming conscious of the Absolute. So you can get back to the Source. The body is just a vehicle. Dead bodies never send you any news. The dead never complain...

V: So the individual soul doesn't exist?

A: As a form of identification it does, but not in reality. There is no such thing as an 'individual' soul. Shankara devoted all his life to try and make this clear. What you call 'the individual soul' is your dissociated experience of the universal Consciousness. In its deepest sense the word 'individual' means '*un*-divided'. Nor is there any such thing as a 'mature' soul, or 'old' and 'new' souls. Gradations are only to be found in ignorance. You are absolute Consciousness.

V: Yes, ultimately...

A: No, right *now*! Not ultimately!

V: Then reincarnation doesn't exist?

A: It is ignorance which is assuming a form again and again. But that is not what you *are*. Ignorance is not what you *are*. You are *knowing*-ness. Ignorance is forever incarnating itself, seeking a form.

V: Then the individual soul should be incarnating itself forever.

A: In that case such an individual soul will be the height of ignorance. Well, if you prefer to stay in such a cramped condition... Shankara has tried to make this issue clear. This so-called 'individual' soul which is to reach maturity, has been the universal Consciousness all along! There *is* no separated soul *apart* from Consciousness. There *is* no hierarchy in Consciousness. If there were, *then* you would have found yourself a legitimate reason to be working on such an illusory soul. Then the personality—an even lower form of identification—could actually set himself to do some work on such a soul.

V: When the vehicle of the body is cast off...

A: Just hear what you're saying! Why do you use such terms?

V: As long as this consciousness is still a sticking consciousness, a consciousness which is still sticking to its contents...

A: Consciousness isn't sticking to anything!

V: But at the same time there *is* such a thing as the reincarnative course. We, the Consciousness, which finds itself...

A: That is nothing but rubbish, dreams, fantasies... The dream goes on!

V: Well, I'll just call it a sticking consciousness for now.

A: And I don't. Because it is nonsense. Consciousness *cannot* 'stick'. Call it what you like, but Consciousness just doesn't stick. As a matter of fact, everything *dissolves* in Consciousness. Including dream—your fantasies, your rubbish—and ignorance. Both dream and waking state do not have a ghost of a chance in Consciousness. So you shouldn't be attributing any qualities to Consciousness. Consciousness doesn't stick to anything, no more than I would be laying eggs.

V: Still we are sitting here, being stuck...

A: No, you are sitting here being *Self-realized*—as pure Consciousness!

V: One way to realize oneself is not to identify yourself with any thoughts. If a thought comes up in my mind, and I am able to look at it, keeping it at a distance, then I know I'm not identified with it. But there are also thoughts from which I'm not able to take a distance yet. From those I am looking at the world.

A: Realize that each thought that you are able to perceive presupposes a distance. So you need not *take* a distance, because each thought presupposes a distance *already*. If not, you just wouldn't be able to perceive that thought.

V: The thoughts which so far I haven't been able to look at with a distance...

A: That is absolutely impossible! Out of the question! I am now trying to make the heart of the matter clear to you: You are making yourself believe that you *don't* have a distance, whereas the reality is that there *is* a distance. If not, you wouldn't be able to perceive anything!

V: Even so there are certain things with which I remain identified.

A: That is what you *think*. But what I'm trying to make clear to you is, that that does not correspond with your immediate perception. You actually believe *more* than you could possibly *know*!

V: As a matter of fact, my question is exactly that: How can I detach myself from that, which I still believe to be true?

A: By realizing the knowingness.

V: It is sometimes said, that realisation will take place at the hour of death. Of what use is that?

A: That is not what our tradition says. In our tradition it is said that it only makes sense to have realisation while living. There are traditions which declare that you will see the truth at the moment of passing away. But that has never appealed to me.

V: The notion that you would realize something *after* death, would also foster the soul-concept, wouldn't it?

A: Don't compare apples with pears. I just explained that there can be no such thing as an 'individual' soul. That sort of ideas will only serve to strengthen the belief in it, with all the consequences following from it. On the other hand the knowingness *does* need a vehicle, and that vehicle is the body. Body, mind and feeling form a vehicle for the knowingness. But the knowingness itself is neutral.

V: So thoughts have no grip on it...

A: No, they haven't. The knowingness is the very light *in* the thought. It's a scary idea, because you have identified yourself, and so you have learnt to experience yourself as body, mind and feeling. Hence, too, the *fear* of losing body, mind and feeling—the fear of death. That is why nobody wants to be dead. Everybody wants to see himself continued.

V: I find myself unable to see death and the knowingness as apart from a 'who'. Who actually *is* experiencing the knowing after death?

A: You *don't* experience the knowing after death.

V: But you were saying...

A: Don't just put words into my mouth! This 'I-am-ness' will disappear at the moment of death, and the self-consciousness will disappear along with it. Thus conscious being disappears in absolute Consciousness. Even now you are this absolute Consciousness, but you don't realize it, because you are so fascinated by all that you take yourself to be. The individual *is* the universal—*That* is the pivot on which everything hinges.

There are several identifications, three in number, namely, body, mind and feeling. These are creating the 'I am'-notion, which will ultimately be transformed by the Absolute. The identification with body-mind-feeling will dissolve in the 'I-am-ness', and the 'I-am-ness' in turn will dissolve in the Absolute. But such 'de-I-ing' should be done in the right order. And don't worry about death—Be with life...

V: But you are basically saying, that all will be over with death...

A: Be with life!

V: At the risk of becoming silly, you could then say, 'In that case I might as well go and live an easy, comfortable life'. And then you could give a very personal interpretation to that—at the cost of, and things like that...

A: To live an easy, comfortable life means to live a very limited life. Live an easy life in *Consciousness*. And how would you, being anything *but* a 'person', give a *personal* interpretation to that? But you don't actually love yourself that much, because you have come to look upon yourself as a 'person'. You know very well that you are not living according to your true nature. This 'person' is a cramp within Consciousness. Relax in conscious being which you *are*.

(8th July, 1989)

EACH VISION IS A LIMITATION

Visitor: How does my vision act as a limitation upon what you are saying?

Alexander: A vision is *always* a limitation. Every vision is a limitation. What all visions have in common is conscious being. As soon as we are going to speak and act from a particular vision, then it is inevitable that we will start quarrelling with each other. Because each vision is strengthening the apparent person. Each vision is a tunnel vision.

V: It looks like a tunnel vision indeed.

A: All visions are tunnel visions. But what all visions have in common is consciousness.

V: My perceiving looks like a tunnel perceiving.

A: The perceiving itself doesn't, but that which is *being* perceived by you, and with which you may identify yourself, carries a limitation within itself.

V: Then is it a question of identification?

A: Each vision is an invitation to identify yourself. On the other hand each *real* seeing will *de*-identify you. It is inevitable that, once you start to discuss it, the real seeing will be reduced to a vision. In doing so the real seeing escapes you, because then you will identify yourself with that particular vision. However broad a vision may be, it remains a tunnel vision. Even the broadest vision is basically a limitation. Only conscious being which all visions have in common, is space itself, and is truly open.

V: But by anchoring in the 'I-am-ness' the mind may open up, and then eventually you will become broader, won't you?

A: The limitation will become broader. You may broaden your visions, but there is no such thing as an 'open mind'. The mind—thinking and feeling—is a limitation, an enclosing by definition. You may *think* to be listening with an 'open mind', but that doesn't mean anything. It's just not possible. The basic material of each vision is Consciousness.

V: Well, if that's all, then I wonder whether the tradition of Advaita has got any mission at all for man and for life.

A: Only he who separates himself from life, imagining himself to be divorced from life, will be under the impression that he has got a mission.

V: So what you find in certain traditions about a beginning and a mission and a goal to strive for—all that you may as well forget about in Advaita?

A: You *won't* forget it, if these things have been programmed into your memory. But by really *seeing* all such ideas, they will leave your conscious being. If there is any goal in life at all, then I can only picture it to myself as the potential which is able to manifest itself unhampered. So that the flower may come to bloom.

V: Actually, I do find that a bit of a problem. Because to me it doesn't seem to inspire any emotion.

A: Now, what can be more delightful than that your manifestation—body-mind-feeling—is able to manifest itself unhampered in its natural state? Is that not what is called 'freedom'?

V: In that case it won't make any difference to you, if the body were to come to an end.

A: He who knows his real nature has no need for a long, nor for a short life.
   Don't you feel unhappy, whenever your manifestation is being hampered? You sometimes notice it, for example, in a nursing home, where old people are being hampered in their ways, because nurse thinks it necessary to transport their bodies to the gym. And is a child not unhappy, when it finds itself being hampered in its urge to experience things? Almost all the problems come from that. And is deprivation of liberty not an offence? And is that very deprivation not used as a form of punishment? Is it not the highest goal of any society to enable man to develop his fullest potential? And is all the struggle in the world not directed against the obstruction of that development?

V: I was just wondering about that. I think that that very society has actually forced us into trammels.

A: Everything happens on a voluntary basis. Through unbridled greed and desires you have forged your own chains.

V: But is individual freedom actually not made impossible?!

A: The fact that it isn't a success story does not mean, that that isn't the underlying idea. Becoming manifest is not a self-chosen task—It happens forcibly. Of course, there has to be room for the manifestation to express itself at lower and higher levels. And, naturally, the most basic necessities of life such as food, clothing and shelter, need to be met first. Even so there are people who will renounce all that for the sake of that 'other'. People who suffer an entire life of privation in order to be able to express themselves, to manifest themselves. Particularly so at the level of music, dance, or some other form of art or ideal, or in the sphere of the search for truth. If I can see any purpose at all, or rather, a systematic plan with a clear structure, then it is the fact that man wants to manifest himself. And there is nothing you can do about it. Nor do I intend to go and do anything about it.

There are so many people who just don't know what to do with this life. Or people who are constantly changing direction, embarking on a new course again. These things are the result of having lost contact with the Essence. This body-mind-feeling has got its own laws for making itself manifest. It wants to gain experiences and take a certain direction. Everything is trying to find its own path. And there is no saint or enlightened man or *avatar* who can stop that. All they can do is to further awareness of the processes involved. So that any obstruction may be reduced to a minimum and the manifestation may manifest itself at its best. In a natural way.

V: But is the obstruction not the very culture, this very conditioning which is more or less being forced upon us?

A: Don't put the blame—if there is any blame at all—on somebody else nor on yourself. All this is the result of a distorted way of looking at things. Discover the Real and be happy. Re-establish contact with the Real.

V: So what really matters is not the search for a mission in life, but the search for *being*!

A: Not for *being*! The being you already *are*! What really matters is the search for the *Essence*, from which you imagine yourself to be separated because of this personality, this 'I'. And of course, it would be better, if you discover it when you are twenty instead of eighty-nine. But if you happen to be eighty-nine, then that, too, is something you can't change any more. The important thing is not to delay your realisation by rubbish and illusions and ideals.

(8th July, 1989, evening)

41

CONSCIOUSNESS IS NOT AFFECTED BY MEMORY

Alexander: The 'I'-structure derives its sole reality from the compulsory productivity of memory. Everything which you think to know about yourself is based on memory and, therefore, what you think to know is the old. And because at present the old seems to overshadow the new, you are not able to distinguish properly between the Real and the unreal. Your experience of the reality is being overshadowed. Does this insight make you free?

Visitor: Since yesterday I'm aware of the fact that this whole question of a 'somebody'—and a 'nobody' as well—in short, the question of a 'who?', is no longer an issue.

A: Do you see the consequences of such knowing? That everything with which you could possibly identify yourself, is—of necessity—memory? And, therefore, the old? And the old is always happening in the past. Even when memory is producing a picture from the past which is proving to be of service to you now, still it is the old. On the other hand the reality which you are *actually* living, is always *here* and *now*—alive. But memory, images, are always the past. Memory can only produce pictures, and those pictures in turn produce sentiments, and so forth. That is the reason why all sentiment is the old. And that is why what you call the 'I', is no more than a packet of memories. Now, how would an 'I', a packet of memories, a trick of memory, be capable of knowing the Reality? How could it ever get an insight, an understanding of the living *now*? How would the dead be able to know the living? How could something unreal know the Real? If that would be possible, then these talks would have no meaning at all.

Once I have discovered that I'm *not* an 'I', then, as a consequence, I will no longer behave as one. Then the so-called theory will have passed into practice. The question therefore is: Where *is* freedom to be found? Not in memory's domain, which is the domain of the old. Instead the search will have to be in an area, where memory cannot exercise any terror. And, in fact, that is where freedom *has* been found. What it means is, that you will need to discover something which cannot be touched, tainted or tarnished by memory. Which is not polluted by any memories, feelings and thoughts. And that can only be Awareness, conscious being *itself*.

So focus on that, which is *beyond* the reach of memory. That is why I'm telling you, that realisation cannot really be found by body, mind or feeling. Realize that each disturbance is taking place within something *un*-disturbable. And once you are living from that clarity, then it will be quite possible—necessary even—to live with memory, with conditions, with the world.

V: I think what you are saying is just fantastic! What you are saying in connection with memory is actually having a tremendous impact on me. Because I am now beginning to realize, that I do not really exist as a person.

A: Absolutely. Even the body is a packet of memories. Each cell has probably got its own memory. Within conscious being everything is ever new, like a film which is constantly illumining and dissolving itself, an infinite tape. Consciousness is erasing itself instantaneously. It is only because we have this memory, that we are able to experience an objective reality, and that we have the experience of ourselves as a person with an apparent location. It is memory which is ultimately responsible for the objective world and for what we call the 'person'. But because memory and its picture-producing capacity are perceived by something which is refusing to be affected by memory, there has got to be some *in*-ground. That *in*-ground I call awareness and, at a deeper level, consciousness; and at a still deeper level I call it absolute Consciousness.

No doubt the investigation starts from the 'person' who is on strained terms with the reality. Considering the person's interwovenness with pictures and identities and traumas and miseries become corporeal—unmistakably present in every human being and based on memory's tenacity—the case cannot be but most complex. At the same time, however, these things are forcing you to look deeper, because the situation is really untenable.

V: Despite the fact that I do not exist as a 'person', still I seem to get caught in the 'I'-illusions and memories of *others*, for example, when they are talking about me...

A: You could also ask yourself, why you are so much occupied with the fact, that others are occupied with you! The whole thing is being upheld by both sides. Get busy with the Self!

V: Why do some Self-realized men have such a wealth of memories? At least those who talk extensively about their past? While these do not appear to have any bonds with the past, there are also those who create the impression that, in their case, memories have become altogether extinct.

A: There are two traditions, roughly speaking. In the first tradition you are told extensively about the path and how it developed, while one draws on a rich source of memories, relating all the details without any hesitation. The second tradition on the other hand persists in utterances like, 'I don't exist, I was never born', etc. Or they will basically speak to you in the third person singular, using such expressions as, 'This body is hungry. This sack with bones is to be moved. This here...', and so on. The most fantastic descriptions are used...

V: How does that agree with the free production of memory images?

A: Such production is involuntary. There is a Sanskrit term for it, '*prarabdha karma*'.

V: I would just like to come back to the insight regarding this point. It looks as if there are actually *two* forms of insight. One of them seems again to be based on memory, since you have spoken to us about it earlier on. In that case it's the same song over again...

A: Quite right. Because the one insight is obtained through discrimination and intelligence *within* the manifested, that is to say, within the *contents* of Consciousness. But the *ultimate* insight—which is what finally counts here—is the real seeing itself.

V: Something which has been bothering me for some time, is this feeling of being in between two realities.

A: If I may just interrupt you here to say something else first: Since the recollections of memory are basically something involuntary, something forced, could you really say in that case, that *you* are the one who is actually responsible for what memory is coming up with? And is it therefore *worth* an identification? Is it really that *obvious* to identify yourself with that? Of course it is, considering the way in which you have conditioned yourself so far. But *not* if you are looking at it from the real insight.

V: As a matter of fact—yes. If I'm being honest, if I look at the facts, then I can see that that is true...

A: It also means, that in that case there cannot be any form of condemnation, and that the story is telling itself. And also, that things are going to be difficult, whenever any images are coming up which are born by deep feelings of sorrow. And particularly so in cases where an other person is involved, when the other, too, is being confronted with deep sorrow. But what you do *not* see at that point is, that you are not responsible, that you *can* not and *may* not be blamed for it, inasmuch as the feeling of sorrow is an involuntary product. You just can't help it. And then to actually project an 'I' into this involuntary soap bubble is showing a lack of insight. So let the story tell itself, so that things can express themselves. Then you will transcend them then and there. Do you understand what I'm saying?

V: If I look closely, then all I can see is an infinite 'here-and-now', which basically contains only this one 'thing' with memories. And that, when I close my eyes, I don't even have a body... That all there is, is only this 'here-and-now'. On the other hand there is also the impression of having actually been born, which is most powerful. As a result there now seem to be *two* realities, and I just don't know what to choose.

A: I understand what you're trying to say. As a matter of fact, there *aren't* two realities, although both phenomena are there. This is called '*maya*'.

I think the most suitable solution for this given fact is probably to hold on to a definite vision of one's own, basically because nobody can afford to do without a certain thinking order. The manifested, i.e. body-mind-feeling, is subject to laws which you simply cannot ignore. The immediate experience is always immediately present. Within that immediacy you have the pairs of opposites, because of which experience is made possible. To accept only *one* of the opposite sides as the reality is to invite *duality*. That duality can only be transformed by the awareness or consciousness, because consciousness contains *both* sides within itself. Awareness includes *both*.

V: I feel I'm oscillating.

A: That is only possible, if you are identifying yourself with an object. The awareness *itself* doesn't oscillate. Awareness is stable and centreless.

V: It appears to me, that I actually ought to have the courage to stay focussed on the direct experience itself.

A: You *won't* be able to stay focussed on the direct experience, because then you are trying *as a person*—who is *not* the direct experience—to stay with that experience. In any case, that immediacy is *always* there *already*! There is no question of your *'getting'* there! Therefore I always refer to that which is best known to you, for *that* is the location where everything happens. And since that is *you*, it is *that* which you will have to discover. *That* is *you*—All depends on *you*!

(*9th July, 1989, morning*)

NO WORLD WITHOUT CONSCIOUSNESS

Visitor: Do the 'I'-thought and the 'I'-feeling come from memory?

Alexander: They come from the illusion of the continuity of things.

V: So not directly from memory?

A: You have the ability to project continuity onto that, which is past once and for all. That *is* memory. That is how the illusion of continuity is created, and that is basically how the illusion of a 'reality' is created.

When you say that you have seen a room, because you've had a look around in it, then in fact something quite different has happened. You were seeing picture after picture after picture, onto which memory has projected continuity. And next memory goes on to claim that what you have actually been seeing is a 'room'. As a result of that process we have the experience of an 'objective' world, including an 'I' or a 'person'. To be sure, as an experience they *are* there—Please note: *as an experience*. However, for a truly deep investigation of your real nature any such experience will prove to be insufficient, nor will it be enough to be looking purely at all that's moving.

V: But do all the beads that are strung around that cord come from a registration as being 'past'?

A: Anything perceived is, necessarily, an object. And all those objects are basically 'past', old. Therefore I'm never seeing anything new, strictly speaking. And, *very* strictly speaking, I'm not even seeing 'a thing'. Because the *perceiving* of an object, does not prove the *existence* of that object. What it does prove on the other hand is the *knowing*-ness.

V: Memory's reservoir is constantly being replenished.

A: It also lets go of many things. As a matter of fact, memory is a most unreliable frame of reference. What you call 'the past' is a creative interpretation of what your memory has been telling you. Such memory is most unreliable, negligent, poor, inaccurate.

V: Still the reservoir is being replenished. For example, if you happen to be insulted or flattered, then these things are being registered. Is it in any way strategic to have this registration process, as in the case of an insult or flattery? Because the latter gets you puffed up, while the former makes you writhe. If these things were to happen, and you could just stay totally aware, would no registration take place in that case?

A: Registration will be there, but not *identification* and any consequences attached to it. If someone flatters you, then he flatters you; if someone insults you, then he insults you. Everything stands or falls with the 'person-experience'. As long as you are still in the awareness process, you will have a choice between action, reaction, and transformation. *Which* choice you are making, will depend on the quality of awareness that you have. But the registration itself precedes these three options.

The waking state, the dream state, and deep, dreamless sleep are likewise forced conditions. No wonder there is this feeling of being somehow imprisoned, whenever one is identified with one of those states—even in the case of deep, dreamless sleep which, to the person, is nearest to the unmanifested Being. Because in reality these three states stand in real contrast with your fundamental freedom. Your real, truly known Self is free from any stress or friction, whereas the objective world is a product of the waking or dream state. That world, however, doesn't have a ghost of a chance in deep, dreamless sleep, and deep, dreamless sleep disappears in the unmanifested Being again.

As long as you imagine yourself to be body, mind, or feeling, then sooner or later everything will become a problem. Even Self-realisation becomes a problem. Therefore, don't try to grasp these meetings as a body, mind, or feeling.

V: If I would now start to exalt you to the skies, then wouldn't you somehow get puffed up?

A: We shall see! Getting puffed up and getting shrunk are cramps of the apparent person. Whatever you may *think* I am, it just doesn't apply to what or who I *really* am. In any case you will basically be able to gather from the jerky movements of the self-consciousness, whether any identification has actually taken place.

The only proof of Self-realisation lies with oneself. With a bit of attention it is comparatively easy to see through this 'I'-thought. But the 'I'-*feeling* lies at a deeper level. A feeling always goes deeper and carries more conviction. Being a product of body and mind, feelings actually reinforce the body-consciousness. So, if you want to know who you really are, then you will have to go and search even deeper than feeling. Again, an objective world and feeling couldn't exist for one moment without memory. And although memory is essential and functional, it is transcended by something even more subtle and rarefied, namely Awareness or Consciousness itself. Focus on that which never leaves you.

World or no world, memory or no memory, there is something *within* you—a clear Knowing—in which the world and memory are or are not appearing. Of course, it is important that memory is functioning properly, and that it is in agreement with the reality as commonly experienced—a reality which, by the way, is also purely and simply being upheld by memory. And although there are always deviations from the natural order and norm to be found, deviations should of course never be made the norm.

V: So as long as memory is a piece of equipment to help you orient yourself, it need not be an enemy.

A: Memory is a help, a faculty to orient oneself so that you can move in a three-dimensional world. The whole problem is that, through memory, this illusory figure is created, and that you have actually come to live and feel *as* that illusory figure. As a consequence the illusion has acquired a reality value, while reality is made into an illusion. Then the self-consciousness, being a product of memory, and itself an object, is trying to get a grip on its creator, Consciousness itself! Such a situation is untenable and unsolvable.

The one faculty of man which is best developed, is his ability to fool himself...

(9th July, 1989, afternoon)

43

LOVE IS WHAT YOU ARE

Visitor: The presence, that conscious being, is that love?

Alexander: That presence is love.

V: You once said that ninety-nine percent of the problems arises, because you don't see that you *are* that love. Would you like to go a little deeper into that?

A: Wanting to be loved means, that you have altogether forgotten that you *are* that love, that presence. Then you have actually reduced yourself to a beggar.

V: So you have to realize that love.

A: All the problems will disappear, when you realize that you are not separated from love. And there is no way that the intellect can get at that. Love is what you *are*—the rest is fear. But you have actually reduced love to words and ideas. From love everything is born.

V: I think that, if I would be rooted in that love, I would be able to understand it better. How am I to take root in that love?

A: You will never be able to take root in love. The 'person' can never be rooted in love. Love is what you *are*, and the 'person' is a separation from that love. Thinking doesn't accept love, because it has no place in love; it loses its status in love. That is why thinking will never accept love.

V: Is love the same as silence?

A: Love, availability, knowingness, silence—these are all words that refer to the same thing.

V: Is any reflection possible in that silence?

A: That silence doesn't reflect. On the other hand thinking reflects in the silence. Of course it is possible to reflect in that silence, but the silence itself doesn't reflect. That is beyond everything.

V: I actually know two kinds of silence...

A: Such a thing is basically impossible. But if you can speak of two kinds of silence at all, then both of them will ultimately merge into the *real* Silence. You are probably making different concepts of that Silence or Emptiness.

V: The one form of silence tends to occur, when I'm busy talking, and then, all of a sudden, I'm stuck—things suddenly come to a halt... The other form is, that there is really nothing at all... no reflection whatsoever.

A: A 'form' of silence *isn't* silence. You must remember that realisation is not a form of contemplation or reflection. Realisation has an entirely different quality from conceptualisation. Some people stop coming here, because they can recall the talks and insights anyway. But *recalling* is something very different from *realisation*. If you have truly realized something, then you won't need to recall it, because your real nature is beyond—and precedes—any form of memory. The *knowing*-ness will be there, but not the remembrance of any insights. Insight *will* be there, but that insight is not derived from any form of memory.

To have all kinds of insights, based purely on memory and hearsay, on other people's ideas, is not the realisation we are talking about here. True realisation doesn't need the support of ideas and, therefore, of memory. And as the so-called 'person' is nothing more than a collection of memories, such a 'person' won't be able to realize and understand anything. Because that person will forever be holding on to memory, looking for support there. As a matter of fact, that phenomenon will be the last to relax. With true realisation the cramp of the person relaxes, because then something better than this 'person' has been realized. As a matter of fact, that is the true surrender. The true meaning of surrender is, that the person no longer wants to hold on to anything. What's more, this 'person' has actually vanished!

Nevertheless, even as a person you will have to be willing to let go and to learn truly. And that is where discipleship begins. Everything which may be retrieved by memory, everything which is derived from memory, is really fake. That is why the Self-realized ones express themselves in a manner which is perfectly original. Because what they say is not based on copying and imitation.

(4th August, 1989)

44

DESIRELESSNESS IS YOUR DEEPEST DESIRE

Visitor: Is it true that Consciousness has to admit you?

Alexander: There is no question of Consciousness admitting anything. The 'person' may or may not admit something, but not Consciousness. Consciousness is the very *in*-ground in everything. Admitting has to do with the person.

V: Still he, too, appears within Consciousness.

A: Yes, I know...

V: I'm actually trying to see my desire to be on the right path being endorsed.

A: A path is always leading to some place or other, but Advaita won't lead you to any place. In our circles '*to* some place' usually means '*from* some place'. But can you move away from that which you *are*?

Perhaps you would like to, but it just isn't possible. Consciousness doesn't admit or allow anything—no question about that. The conscious being is the very availability to everything. On the other hand the narrowed experience of Consciousness—that which you call 'the person'—may imagine to be admitting or not admitting things. As a matter of fact, that is pure nonsense.

V: There is something, which is still not quite clear to me. If one is established in the Being, will there still be the experience of an 'I' in that Being?

A: It much depends on how deep you go.

V: At the surface there is first still the experience...

A: Whatever it may be, the advice that is being given to you, is to establish yourself in the conscious being—not even in the sense of 'I am'. Once you persevere in staying in the conscious being, then the 'I'-sense will actually disappear; it evaporates. Most of you will get terribly frightened by any such prospect, because at present your whole location is situated in this very 'I'-sense. But if you quietly allow it to happen, then the conscious being will make itself known to you. If you pay it the right attention again and again, then at a certain point it will no longer produce any panic. Is this your experience?

V: Yes, but I'm sort of confused by it...

A: To be confused is nothing new to you, is it? That's what started your investigation in the first place!

V: No, it's nothing new, but it's just taking me a bit by surprise...

A: Actually, to be confused is something familiar to you. In fact, not seldom do you become confused, only to enable yourself to get back to the known. Dressed up under the mere pretext that now 'you just don't know it any more'. But this so-called 'being confused' suits the 'person' better than having to face the unknown instead!

V: I suppose it's desires and fears that keep us in darkness. Yet it is desire, too, which makes that I want to realize myself.

A: No, not desire. Desire is produced by dissatisfaction, which again comes from duality. It is not desire that will make you attain to realisation. It is *desirelessness*. That *is* the realisation. What you really desire is a state of desirelessness.

V: Is that the Ultimate?

A: No, that is the *Immediate*.

V: But I mean, in order to get to that point...

A: You *can't* get to that point, that's your whole problem.

V: The driving force...

A: The driving force is desire. Where does that desire come from? Desire arises, because you are dissatisfied. You are not satisfied with yourself.

V: And yet there is this desire... that you want to attain something...

A: No, it is your dissatisfaction which is first creating the desire. You are only changing names. You are changing trains all the time. You are getting from one train onto the other. But you will never reach your destination. If a desire has come up within you, then, one day, you will also be without that desire again. Yet without desires you will feel empty and unnatural as well. Then you will complain, 'Now I don't have any more desires! What's the use of it all? Am I born just to die? What can I do?' Try to understand the nature of desire. Essentially there is no difference between the desire for a man, for a woman, for a child, for a colour television set—and the desire for enlightenment. All desires hold a promise within themselves.

V: So it is dissatisfaction.

A: Yes, it is dissatisfaction. Only when dissatisfaction has gone, then you will be at peace. And what you are really seeking is *peace*. At present there is the notion that such peace is to be found outside, in the exterior world. The people who entertain such a notion are called 'materialistic'. Then there is the other notion, that it is to be found inside. Those who adhere to that notion are called 'spiritual'. However, both notions are based on illusion. It is to be found neither outside nor inside yourself.

'Peace of mind' only means that thinking and feeling are in balance with each other. And any thinking which is in balance may be brought *out* of balance quite easily. Harmony may be disturbed quite easily—but not enlightenment. Enlightenment is something quite different from harmony or 'peace of mind'. 'Peace of mind' is really a *contradictio in terminis*. As long as thinking and feeling play their terrorizing role, and you allow yourself to be affected by them, because you imagine yourself to be 'a person', there won't be any real peace. Even though it is quite possible to have harmony and a certain serenity, such harmony has always got something artificial about it. It is basically creating a balance, *without* at the same time removing duality. And that is going to be terribly monotonous. Nothing more monotonous than harmony! That is why spiritual people are the most monotonous in the world. Their monotony and limitation is kept up by a pattern of harmony.

In the approach of Advaita harmony doesn't mean anything. There 'peace of mind' is not an issue. In fact, the possibility of a war is still present there. It is lying there, waiting to explode like a time-bomb at some undesirable moment. I am telling you that your natural state is *beyond* body, mind, and feeling. Or rather, it *precedes* this body-mind-feeling. Because even before any body, mind and feelings can be there, *you are*.

V: You said 'feelings'?

A: Before any feelings are to appear, *you* have got to be there first as the possibility for them to appear in. *You* are the space within which things may take place. Objects cannot be at peace with one another. Objects are objects. By desiring peace, peace is made into an object. Do you understand that? Nobody in the world will ever be able to find 'peace of mind'—Actually, the best thing possible is naturalness. Harmony has always to be supported by rituals, talks, books. Harmony always needs to have a support. On the other hand Self-realisation doesn't need any support. If you really want to be absolutely clear, then devote yourself to Self-realisation, not to 'peace of mind'. Do you see that?

V: That's the whole point—That is the difficult part…

A: What is difficult? Just tell me, what is the difficulty about it?

V: It is difficult to be available.

A: As a person you will never be available for it. Because the 'person' *is* the resistance against the availability. If you are trying to be available as a person, you cannot but move into the direction of interested dedication and all that sort of things. Then you are going to have interests, and you will become corrupt and crafty.

As a person you can never be available—The two just don't go together.

V: You mean as an ego?

A: I said 'as a *person*'—Isn't that clear enough? Why do you play with words all the time?

V: But aren't we all *persons*?

A: Just because *you* happen to have an illness, it doesn't necessarily mean that we *all* have got that illness. If you are a thief, then you tend to think that other people are in the habit of stealing as well. Don't project your own situation onto others. And certainly not, if you want to learn something from somebody else. Look for yourself. Go on, go deeper!

V: As a body, as a person, I'm not the Real—I just *know* it. Still I try to grasp it.

A: Ultimately that 'knowledge' will pervade your being, so that it becomes a *knowing*—no longer a *grasping*.

V: I sometimes have the feeling, that the very fact that I want to see it, is standing in my way. And more in particular the concept of *not* being the body, of *not* being a person.

A: No concept is involved. If you make the fact that you are not the body into a concept, you are going to be in trouble. You are not required to have any concept about your not being a body. You just *are* not the body. That is a statement from my side. Don't make that into a concept. If you are going to make it into a concept and start repeating it to yourself like a *mantra*, you will get into trouble.

Desirelessness Is Your Deepest Desire

V: But this point of 'I'm not the body' is to be realized, not?

A: Yes, *realized—not* made into an *idea*!

V: If you know that *that* is the whole point, then what further question can there be?

A: Observe the current of your thoughts and search your heart. Don't be afraid to ask questions. As long as the questions are honest, then that's all right.

V: It's not that I'm afraid. It's just that I don't have the words now...

A: ...

V: To be established in 'Being'—to persevere in that—will lead to the evaporation of the 'person'. As a result any panic on account of the disappearing of the last bits of the 'person' is being reduced as well—Have I got that right?

A: Yes, that is what was said.

V: That is quite clarifying again.

A: Don't just collect words and beautiful statements, sir! Don't cripple yourself!

V: It is not a question of 'crippling'. It is more something like 'empty'...

A: Who is empty? *Who* is seeing this empty?

V: My awareness is seeing the empty.

A: Is there someone enjoying it?

V: It is not a question of enjoying. It's just *there*.

A: Then what does that condition of 'being empty' mean to you?

V: To me it is basically like an entrance now.

A: There *is* no entrance to awareness. Through words and ideas you think you can make progress, but you are not making any progress. You only persist in producing even *more* ideas and concepts.

V: I see...

A: Can you *admit* this emptiness? Can you be *at peace* in this silence? Do you have the courage to *invite* that peace? *That* is what matters. But as soon as this silence is making itself manifest to you, all you do is to fill yourself up with the noise of ideas and concepts. Give up trying to grasp 'yourself' with the help of words and ideas and concepts! The real question is whether you can *admit* that silence, and whether the mind will actually *stop* disturbing everything with noise, clever explanations, and all such things.

V: At this moment I know that that 'empty', that silence, is actually *there*.

A: That emptiness is still a concept, a name. It is merely the opposite of words and concepts. Suddenly, as if by some mysterious cause, there aren't any more words and concepts, you can't find any more words, and then you immediately call that 'empty'. But *that* 'empty' is still a concept.

What is meditation about? Admitting the silence. That silence is inviting you to become merged in it. So what can you do? Being silent. Don't run away from that silence, don't disturb the silence. Then you will find that you actually have a very firm base in that silence. From that silence you can live. Even with quite a bit of noise and activity around you. *That* is the silence we are talking about here. In Sanskrit it is called *'shama'*—peace. *Real* peace. Not 'peace of mind', which is the peace of the thinking mind, which is simply there whenever thinking has stopped being active for a moment—The thinking which will soon start functioning again, and with which you will identify yourself again.

If you admit that silence, if that invitation is really there and you become merged in it, then even if this so-called 'person' appears, you will not be disturbed by it. You *cannot* be disturbed any more, because then you *are* that silence. But as long as you are thinking, and the identification with the 'person' is still there, you *can* be disturbed. Because then you take yourself to be an object.

Is this clear from the 'standpoint' of the silence? I am talking to you *from* that silence, yet I'm also talking *to* that same silence. I'm not talking to you as a person. If I would be talking to you as a person, then you surely would be getting entangled in concepts. In which case glorious days would not lie ahead of you. And that is not what I wish for you. I wish you the best, because you *are* the best. You deserve the best, because you *are* the best.

So what matters is to invite this silence. Can you really *admit* this silence? You will notice that, in daily life and in meditation, you don't really want to *admit* this silence. In fact, you want to disturb that silence in all sorts of ways. You are actually *afraid* of emptiness and silence. You are *afraid* of life's availability, the root of all existence.

V: I notice that I don't feel pressed or impatient about it. At the same time there is a feeling of urgency, but not in the sense that

I'm being pressed. I feel such a great urgency, that there is just no way that this is going to leave me any more... It's an aim, without really being an aim. It's not that I'm actually striving for it, but at the same time...

A: It's all right. Now the question is...

V: I've really had enough of it!

A: Now it is up to you and to everybody else here: *Do* you or do you *not* admit this silence? That is the basic situation in which you find yourself now.

However, I'm now taking it even one step further: Is it at all possible *not* to be living from that silence? Could you actually *by-pass* that silence at all? I am telling you, that that is *not* possible. That is out of the question! Impossible! Because all you do or think or feel is *already* preceded by that silence. Just do yourself a service, and become actually *conscious* of this fact, for it will give you immediate joy, knowledge and stability. You will no longer be a burden to your environment and to yourself. And that will be a great gift to this world. Just accede to the question, look at it—with intensity and without interpreting it. *Do* I or do I *not* admit this silence? And don't blame yourself, if any thoughts or feelings are coming up, appearing to disturb that silence. No *need* even to blame yourself for it, because that silence *cannot* be disturbed!

Even if you are just a little quiet, then you will find that that silence is actually there, already waiting for you. Now it's all up to you. If you are receptive, then you are sure to become aware of this infinite silence. Perhaps you are under the impression that this silence could be conjured down or pushed away, but that is absolutely impossible.

Realisation means *admitting* this silence in every perception, so that each identification dissolves in the very Being. You have seen the impossibility of wiping out, of destroying this silence. You have seen the impossibility of filling that emptiness. *That* is realisation. Admit that silence, and then you will know what I'm talking about.

V: Is it not so, that the silence actually fades away...

A: Silence *doesn't* fade away. Only sound can fade away. Silence is your very basis. Space, silence, availability—these are all words that refer to the same thing. Don't make a formula or rubbish of it. It has to be a *genuine* realisation, or it will just be useless.

V: Is actually no description possible?

A: Many descriptions are possible. And if you are going to describe it, it will become poetry.

V: I for one would call it an 'observation-without-judgment'.

A: Wonderful! Splendid! But is that your *realisation*? You may give it any name you like, but it will not be 'It'.

(4th August, 1989)

REALITY IS NEVER A PROBLEM

Visitor: Is the full realisation attended by a feeling of excitement, by a sense of recognition, something like... 'This is what I *am*. This is what I've always been'...?

Alexander: Some people become very happy and ecstatic, while others may become very quiet instead, and with others again nothing special happens. It may be that an implosion of silence takes place. It all depends on the form of the manifestation, on the body-mind-feeling in question. Whatever it may be, you won't be intimidated by it.

V: In any case a deep sense of the familiar has to go with it.

A: You will *know* yourself to be familiar with it, because it is your natural state.

V: Because it is *me*.

A: Yes, but not as a *'person'*—This cannot be repeated enough. Because, if the 'person' imagines himself to have become 'enlightened', then megalomania will develop as a result. Then it will become an altogether different story. In that case this 'I' will actually become inflated to gigantic proportions. Therefore, before declaring the whole world except yourself to be an illusion, it is essential to recognize that you, *as a person*, are the biggest illusion of all! And that from that illusion alone the illusion of the world etc. is born. See the illusion of this 'I'-principle. If instead you first want to realize that the world is an illusion, you are only taking a roundabout way. Don't bother about the world: It is the very 'I'-principle which is the creator of the illusion.

V: Is it possible to register any change, once you have taken root in the silence?

A: I wouldn't know why it shouldn't.

V: Changes are being observed in me. But then immediately the 'I' comes in.

A: It will disappear of itself. Just anchor yourself in the silence. Shift your standpoint to the silence—That is what matters. That is also what everybody is trying to avoid.

V: I've got a bit of a problem, which is like this: When I'm taking root in the silence...

A: Now just listen to what you're saying! It may be just words, 'When I'm taking root in the silence...'

V: Wrong explanation...

A: Just try and formulate it again.

V: Once the silence is there, then at the level of the manifested a sensation of happiness arises. That is the change.

A: What of it? You wouldn't want to change anything natural!

V: I don't mean that I want to change it...

A: Then what is the problem?

V: The problem is, that 'I' am immediately *claiming* that silence, and then, at that very moment, I get disrooted from the silence.

A: There is no way you can claim that silence. This claiming is part of the 'I'. You are only playing a little game with yourself.

V: At that moment it doesn't look like a little game to me.

A: Look closely! Take off those glasses and look!

V: Do you understand what I mean?

A: It *isn't* my job to understand you! It is your job to understand *yourself*! I'm not interested in understanding you—That would only tighten the stranglehold. It would mean that I should actually take you seriously as a person, and I *don't* take you seriously as a person. Look closely for yourself, without jumping to any conclusions. Even that is probably going to be a problem, since you were trained *not* to look for yourself.

V: I'm thinking about the role which the imagination is playing in this revolution. What you are saying is all so paradoxical. I can almost touch what you are talking about, but then it seems to disappear again.

A: Be natural! Life is unfolding itself in a perfectly natural way. Be with life! Don't try to change anything. Just what exactly are all your problems about? You just don't want to accept what *is*! You want something that isn't there, and you don't want something that *is* there—That is your whole battle! How are you going to live naturally, if you keep on trying to catch the wind? You are wasting your time, you are fighting windmills! And, in the end, what will be the result of this whole battle? So many people change husbands or wives, yet in the end it is the same story all over again. Everybody just keeps on making changes, and what is the result? You end up with exactly the same situation as before or worse, so that you will be even more embittered and disappointed. You just don't want to look at the facts, though they are right there under your nose. It's a conflict between the ideas which you have collected, and that which is *really* there. Reality—that which *is*—is *never* a problem! Even death isn't a problem. Only if you want to go on living—which isn't possible once death is there—then there will be a problem. This may sound harsh, but death isn't *my* invention...

A few days ago a lady came to see me. She told me that she loved me very much. 'But that's fine!', I said. 'Now, what can I do for you?' 'Well', she said, 'that is actually a bit of a problem.' So I asked her, 'Why should it be a problem to you that you love me?' Whereupon she told me, that she wanted me to love her as well. 'Don't worry', I assured her, 'I love you with all my heart.' 'Are there any further problems?' Then the hidden motive came out, when she finally said, 'But I want to be always with you.' Now, *that* could well be a bit of a problem, even if I would agree to her wishes, and fulfil them by allowing her to stay. For to be living with me for twenty-four hours a day is not that easy. That would indeed be inviting a lot of problems! So I told her, 'Deep in your heart you must somehow have a desire to have problems. To love somebody is never a problem. But if you want to see all your desires fulfilled, then there are sure to be problems.'

V: That's wonderful, because it answers a similar question I had. But now...

A: All that you have truly understood, will no longer be questioned by you.

V: It's something I read in a book.

A: I'm not a book. I don't deal with books.

V: It says that a problem will always *give* you something.

A: Don't come to me with that New Age nonsense! A problem isn't giving you anything. At best it will deprive you of your natural state and block your potential. You don't learn anything from your so-called problems!

V: I didn't mean that I necessarily agreed…

A: You adapt yourself quite easily, don't you?

V: Because I also believe that a problem isn't giving you anything, and that you don't learn anything from it.

A: Then why start on a subject like that? I just told you, that that which has been understood truly, will not be questioned any more. And now you come up with this crap! If you need that New Age nonsense to support your half-insights, they will acquire a degree of truth, in which case you would be able to learn something from every problem that comes up. Then you will also believe that you are making progress that way. And next you will actually start *looking* for problems in order to learn something from them!

Problems tend to give you a sense of intensity, it basically reinforces the experience of being a 'person'. As a matter of fact, you are *creating* problems, because you don't *have* any real problems!

V: So you are now instructing us to accept life as it is?

A: That has *always* been the case. You are now talking as if I've just changed my way of teaching, as if yesterday I was telling the opposite!

V: The problem is that we are actually trying to flee from life.

A: Don't make it even more dramatic! Just look at what you're saying. If something is a problem to you, then it means that you just don't want to accept what *is*.

A few days back somebody was telling me, 'I want to change everything. Now, how should I set about doing that?' I said to him, 'I have been hearing that *mantra* for the past two years. It has become a *mantra* with you: I want to do this, I want to do that. Meanwhile nothing is happening at all!' All such wishing for a change doesn't lead anywhere. I can accept that this is the way you act, but I'm not going to support it. There is an ocean of difference between the way you live and all the ideas you have. Both wishing and not-wishing are mere ideas. Realisation is actualization.

I once heard an interesting story. In Korea there is a Zen monk, who is called 'the crazy monk'. He is totally unorthodox. So much unorthodox that he is, in fact, *very* orthodox. You could say that he is a walking paradox. He goes right against any tradition which, again, is actually quite traditional. He is used to drinking alcohol, and not just one small glass of wine during mealtimes—No, he drinks heavily, and *strong* drink! He makes Zen drawings, but only and exclusively when he is drunk. Only when he is totally inebriated, he will make his 'Zen creations'. His pictures are selling well for good money. And although they don't look like the old, traditional drawings, there is something original, something authentic, something refreshing about them. The crazy monk sleeps with women and men of all ages, with goats, dogs and cats, as well as with chicken and sheep. He sleeps with everything that has got the 'nature of the Buddha'. So he is quite consistent in his realisation. He doesn't make any difference between beautiful or ugly women, or between age, sex or colour. He doesn't kill any mosquitoes, because they have the 'nature of the Buddha'. He just doesn't care whether he is eaten up by the mosquitoes or not.

Now, one day this 'crazy monk' came to a particularly beautiful Zen monastery in order to secure a sleeping place. You must know that, in order to be allowed to spend the night in a Zen monastery, a certain ritual is to take place first. You have to earn a sleeping place by entering into a short philosophical discussion and thus show your insight. Now in those monasteries this has gradually become a dead ritual and, to some extent, the whole thing is just taken for granted. However, the crazy monk is an *original* crazy man. Normally you would arrive at a set hour and knock at the door. Then the door is opened, and a short discussion follows. The rest is taken for granted. You are then allowed to stay three nights in one of those beautiful Zen monasteries, after which you will have to move on again.

Instead of arriving at six o'clock in the evening, as was the custom, the crazy monk came at half past three in the morning which, even for a Zen monk, is an ungodly hour. So he knocked at the door and started shouting at the top of his voice, 'You bald-headed imbeciles, wake up, wake up! I'm standing at the door!' The monk who was on guard-duty woke up from his comfortable doze and put his bald head drowsily through the hatch, asking, 'Why are you shouting like that? Don't you have a watch? Do you know what time it is? People here are trying to sleep!' But the crazy monk replied, 'Waking state—dream state—deep, dreamless sleep: Are they not all the same?', thereby starting the discussion ritual in the middle of the night. Then the other monk at once retorted, 'If they're all the same to you, then I will go back to sleep again!' Whereupon the crazy monk replied, 'And I will start shouting again!'

Do you see the difference between the chit-chat from a book, a dead ritual or a formality—and actual reality? The real is unavoidable. In this case the shouting was the *real* situation, while the philosophy was dead and meaningless. That was the *reality* of the situation. And the crazy monk was aware of that.

The question therefore is: Do you *live* the truth or not? If you don't actually *live* the truth, then all philosophizing will just be chit-chat. In that case you are simply and solely displacing air. And that doesn't amount to much.

(4th August, 1989)

SELECTED BLOSSOMS

The result is nil

WHAT MATTERS IN THE END is, that you realize the constant factor within the inconstant. The Constant in the inconstant, the Unchangeable in the changeable, Unity within multiplicity. Otherwise you will only have multiplicity, and Unity will be a terror. That which pervades everything does not have an opposite. All the rest has got an opposite: Where there is profit, there is loss; where there is joy, there is sorrow. But within the Constant there is neither loss nor profit.

All so-called knowledge about yourself is at the level of body-mind-feeling. You may have knowledge about your body or about your so-called mind. You may even think that you have got self-knowledge. But what is That, where-*in* such self-knowledge is manifesting itself? That which knows *that*, does not have any knowledge, but is pure Consciousness. Only because the vital force is there, you are able to ask questions about yourself and about the goal of life. But is there a goal anyway? As long as the vital force is there, all will be relative. I am telling you that the sum total of everything is zero, nil, one big Zero. Within the totality *you are*, and the world is zero. The vital force is useful at a certain level. If you would really go to the root of this vital force, you will discover that the result is nil.

However, first you will have to work out everything, working your way completely through everything that is presenting itself to you, everything that is there, everything that you are, *whatever that may be.* You have to *be* that fully and fathom it completely. And once you have fully fathomed it, you will have come to the conclusion that it is '*not-any-thing*': The ultimate 'You' *cannot* be known. When there is the knowledge of '*I am*', you will have developed so-called God-knowledge. Just as '*I am*' is the first concept, so God also is a concept. But '*I am*' precedes God. If *I am not*, then God is not. God is within the reach of '*I am*'. As long as *I am*, God will be there. Whatever the dimension or criterion about yourself may be, your dimension or criterion about God will be exactly that. If *you* are, God is there. If *you* are, the world is there. First *you* have to be there, then other things may follow. If *you* are not there, nothing will be there.

That which cannot be divided, is That which you are seeking. The only thing which is wholly ever present is the *knowingness*, where-*in* each division and all differences appear. That which cannot be divided is your true nature. That is known in everything, in every object, in every feeling, in every thought. That is why it cannot be found anywhere but there where it *is*.

About bliss

'Inside' and 'outside' are really the same. The Absolute is in everything. All beings are part of the same thing. Everything exists in Consciousness, wherever you look. The Absolute is Truth, Consciousness, Bliss. Creation is there for the bliss of it. It is a play, and it is there purely *as* a play.

Man is really the Absolute, and for that reason everything he experiences (creation) is full of truth, bliss and consciousness.

Absolute Consciousness creates and experiences as a 'witness', without being involved, whereas most people prefer to experience as an 'identity', and not as a 'witness' of that 'identity'.

All these identifications are creating small bonds for man, and corresponding small blessings and experiences. Because he appropriates those identities to himself, he will go and search for *'more'* and, *'Now I've got it!'* All it leads to is even more bonds and pocketing, so that, in the end, he finds himself back in discontent and conflict.

This search for 'more' makes man hyperactive and restless, full of conflict and a saboteur of himself. Thus the true purpose of 'living' is completely lost. Somehow or other we have lost sight of the fact, that the Absolute is immanently present everywhere. The Absolute is nowhere *not*.

Once we have learned to recognize that we are undifferentiated Consciousness, we shall discover that there is neither beginning nor end, neither 'inside' nor 'outside'. It is the same Absolute which is expressing itself in multiplicity, and a real separation is nowhere to be found.

Whenever there is the experience of unity (through whatever means), it will immediately result in bliss. All unity is experienced by the one Consciousness that knows no division. In every action performed from the conscious being, you will realize the support of bliss.

Love to you all.

Consciousness

Existence is undeniably *known*. Its knowledge cannot be denied. On the other hand the world *can* be denied as is experienced in deep, dreamless sleep and in *samadhi*.

The Self, being the witness of the transitory world, cannot be transitory, for who would be there to witness its transitoriness? It is absurd to propose the possibility of its annihilation without proposing a witness at the same time.

When all form has been annihilated, formless space remains. It is clear therefore that, if name and form are discarded, formless, intransient Consciousness remains.

Only a fool will be able to sustain the idea of his own non-existence. For, in order to sustain such an idea, he himself must exist. It is as absurd to ask, 'Do I have a tongue?' as it is to declare, 'I am not aware of any knowledge' (knowledge = knowingness).

The new seeing

Thinking is a huge projection mechanism, never capable of understanding anything essential. Understanding at the level of the thinking mind takes place within the sphere of the projected: pictures, names of what we basically do not understand. No doubt thinking is absolutely indispensable for functioning in the objective world, the world of name and form. This world is really made up of name and form, it is an annexe of our senses, consisting of projections only.

The function of thinking is the ordering of the world of name and form. Body, feelings and thinking itself should also be included in that. The function of thinking is to structure, but thinking cannot understand anything, because that is beyond its reach. To understand at the level of the objective world means, that the message which has been structured by thinking, comes across as intended.

It strikes me as very important that this 'understanding' at the various levels is distinguished properly. If not, a deeper search into the more subtle layers of the psyche may give rise to confusion and chaos. After all, the thinking mind which is incapable of manifesting itself in any other way than in limitations and fragments, will never be able to include the whole, not to mention the very mystery of existence of which it is a part. Ultimately everything will disappear into that from which it has come: the conscious being itself.

Since all has come from the conscious being itself, and will also disappear into it again, that which has come from that, cannot be any other than that from which it has come. For that reason the world and the 'I' are nothing but the conscious being itself. Therefore, to declare the world to be non-existent is a precarious matter, the world being manifested consciousness, *ex*-pressed in name and form. If name and form disappear, then *conscious being* remains. To declare the world to be non-existent is actually to declare the conscious being to be non-existent. 'The world' is manifested consciousness, real as a manifestation, *not* as a real, independent world outside of you. He who sees this will abandon all attempts at wanting to understand the world or the whole, or at wanting to fathom the mystery, as being impossible.

In this new *seeing*—the true sensitivity for comprehending and understanding—the mystery reveals itself in its totality, yet within something that is completely different from thinking or feeling. Thinking and feeling are part of the seen. That of which thinking and feeling are a part, does not exclude thinking and feeling, but lovingly admits thinking and feeling within the totality. Thinking and feeling are perceived by something completely different from thinking and feeling. He who realizes this, will discover that thinking and feeling can never be a burden, for there is no dichotomy.

Within the wholeness which existence and the conscious being are, there is no place for dichotomy, and in dichotomy there is no place for wholeness.

In love.

Consciousness is looking at itself

The natural state is of a simplicity that can never be captured by thinking or feeling. To capture or grasp the natural state would imply a basic duality, namely the one who experiences and the one who describes: 'experiencing' and 'describing', the 'seeing' and the 'seen', the 'hearing' and the 'heard'. That way it becomes an explanation. The natural state, however, can never be explained.

The person who wants to change the contents of his consciousness, who wants to shape his personality or lose his ego, is seeking the impossible. One part wants to change, to remodel, to maim, to polish the other part—truly a gloomy undertaking, a desert without shade.

This is called *'the Seeking'*, a rather undesirable condition. It is said that, if one doesn't seek, then one is not truly alive—which is nonsense. To seek is to project a goal onto oneself, to try and touch the horizon, or rather, to manoeuvre oneself into an impossible situation, a situation of self-created goals and outcomes.

The outcome will be the same as the projected goal. A *tour de force* of the thinking mind. At the end of the search, if at all there is one, lies the result of your own thinking, the result of your own projections and melancholic fantasies, the regressive, infantile need for security and spatiality.

Through your uncontrollable need to identify yourself with a particular vision instead of with existence itself, you have reduced yourself. Existence has got enough room for every vision, because a vision is a *fragment* of life, *one* way of seeing, *one* way of looking at God.

On the other hand a vision has no place for existence. A vision narrows, slows down, is always too late, always *stops* to think. A vision is always a tunnel, a total vision is a very big tunnel, but a tunnel all the same. Our eyes are very big tunnels through which we perceive a world. That which is being perceived cannot see anything. Thinking divides the seeing into visions, and thus thoughts and views arise.

In its totality existence remains a mystery. It cannot be comprehended. This becomes clear at the birth of a child which comes out of the mother. The new eyes that are looking at the mother are really the Consciousness that is looking at itself. That is why birth, and everything that precedes it, is a great mystery.

The thinking mind is far too small to be able to grasp all of this. That is why it overflows at events such as birth and death. The silence of birth and the silence of death have no equal in this world. For what is really taking place then is the changing of name and form. Perhaps this is clearest at birth and at death.

The flight of an eagle

Question: *The moment your consciousness is able to admit everything about yourself and about your environment—is that 'seeing-what-is'?*

Alexander: There is no question of consciousness admitting something. The consciousness we are talking about here is not involved in your personal fears and desires. Only the person can admit something. Consciousness is the very *in*-ground of your existence. 'Admitting' is related to the person. It is the person that is always looking for a way, and a way is always going somewhere.

Consciousness does not lead anywhere to or anywhere from. Where *can* you go? Can you go away from that which you *are*? Or can you go to that which you *are*? Consciousness does not admit or cut off anything. Consciousness, or Love, is the very availability for everything. On the other hand the *narrowed* experience of the consciousness which you call 'the person', may imagine to be admitting and letting go. In reality that is nonsense.

My advice to you, if it interests you at all, is to establish yourself in the *inescapable Being*, not even in the sense of '*I am*'. When you have established yourself in the inescapable Being, and you persist in that, the sense of '*I am*' will disappear, and your true nature will make itself known. Your false location lies in the very 'I'-sense.

As an 'I' or a 'person' you will never be available. The 'I' or 'the person' is the very resistance *against* that availability. When you are trying to be available 'as a person', then that lies more in the area of devotion out of self-interest. Establish yourself in the inescapable Being. Then a Silence will come, which is no longer reflective. This non-reflective Silence is the *in*-ground of your existence. There are no questions and no answers there. All concepts are born from a desire to shape this non-reflective Silence which, however, does not allow itself to be grasped and described.

Remember, it is not a question of reflection or contemplation, but instead of realisation. Realisation is of a totally different quality than conceptualisation. Realisation is free from concepts and, as such, there is no remembering it. *Realisation is a living experience.*

Many people who come to the meetings question the use of the meetings, because they are not able to remember what was said. Others believe that they do derive some benefit from the meetings, because they *are* able to remember things, which they then make into a concept, thinking to have grasped something. But remembering is something different from realisation. If you are in contact with the Real or, to put it better even, if you are *authentic*, then that realisation does not need the support of your memory. That realisation is beyond time and space. As the person is nothing but a collection of ideas around an 'I'-notion, such an 'I' or a 'person' cannot realize anything. If you realize what I've just said, then nothing will stand in your way any more. Then you will no longer leave any traces. Then your life will be like the flight of an eagle.

Needs and desires

Man is a desiring being. At a deeper level there is the need in every human being for things he cannot do without, such as water, food, warmth, cooling, shelter and clothing. These fall under 'must', which is the characteristic of a need. Needs are absolutely fundamental, and throughout our lives they continue to assert their coercive force.

On the other hand he who has experienced love knows that love is not a need. Love cannot be reduced to a coercive force, open to repetition, and leading one to satisfaction.

Love cannot be given or received, *because it is our real nature*. At best love may be recognized, when the other is recognized as oneself, as love.

The reducing of love to a demanding need, including the hope and the expectation that, in fact, satisfaction is to be found there, is an error of the modern relationship.

Needs are physical. Love transcends physicality and reminds us that we are *spiritual* beings, longing for union in love.

Your unlimited presence

Neither head nor heart can encompass what we really are. Truth can never be found within a form, whether that form be physical, intellectual or emotional. Nor can truth be found in *ideas* of formlessness, because such ideas are nothing but subtler forms.

The body—which is really a perception—is no doubt a passing phenomenon. Whenever we consider or experience our body, we are in fact considering the *idea* that we have of it. That idea is trying to tell us that we are twenty-five, fifty or seventy-five years old. The body, however, is not an idea in that sense. It is a momentary impression of a fragment perceived by us, which—through a trick of memory—we attach onto a previously constructed image.

Generally our experience of the body is related to a smaller part of it: the feet on the ground, or an itch on our head. In case of illness, too, attention is forced to go to the unpleasant and painful area experienced by us. Although such occurrences are referred to as 'I' and 'my' body, they are in fact the ultra-quick perceptions of milder or more intense sensations.

In other words, these are sensations of things appearing within awareness. That which appears within awareness is an object or an idea. The body is perceived as a 'thing', be it a sensation, an image, or an idea, all of which is produced by memory. The same applies to all other forms of sensory perception, for these too are a form of ideas. And the story produced by us as a result of these perceptions—again, through memory—we refer to as 'the world'.

Each idea, including the sensory fragments perceived, projected together, and subsequently called 'the world' by us—*me, mine, a person, you, a tree*, or whatever it may be— is limited. The more closely you look, the more limitations you will find. A single perception may just last one thousandth of a second.

We perceive *ideas*, never a world.

Before any experience, which is the outcome of ideas, is to appear, *you*, being the conscious Presence, have to be there already *before* the idea, *during* the idea, and *after* the idea. Whether we look upon an idea as being limited by time, or by time and space, in either case it is limited. It cannot experience the Unlimited.

On the other hand the Unlimited cannot limit *itself*—It cannot come down to the level of any 'thing' in order to know that thing. Before infinite space no finite object can stand. From the standpoint of the Unlimited (if it is to be called a 'standpoint' at all), there *are* no ideas, there *is* no person having ideas, there *is* no waking state or dream state. *You*, being unlimited Awareness, *you* who are present before, during, and after any idea or perception, and therefore without any limitation, can never be bound by any form of creation whatsoever, in the same way as space can never be bound by the wind.

No thought or idea, lasting for maybe half a second, is ever capable of perceiving the Unlimited.

We are unlimited Presence, and no matter how many fragments are going to appear and disappear, there is nothing, absolutely nothing which is capable of leaving its mark on That which we *are*. What we *can* 'do' immediately though, is to become consciously aware of our habit to scatter 'I's all around. In that process *subjective awareness* will dawn.

Then we will no longer be talking of *my* freedom, *my* love, *my* enlightenment, *my* realisation, or *my* method, for we will then be integrating the whole of creation, appreciating it as an expression of unlimited Awareness. From that a deep relaxation will come, and the joy of *Being*.

Liberation or enlightenment is the total, unconditional *non-appropriation* of anything whatsoever.

The differentiation of the true principle

1

I salute my guru, Shri Nisargadatta Maharaj, by touching his feet. His one work and endeavour is to destroy the monster of ignorance.

2

This discussion on the discrimination between truth and untruth has been started in order to arrive at a correct understanding for those who, with a pure heart, approach the Guru.

3

The objects of knowledge such as sound, touch and so on, which are perceived in the waking state, are naturally different from each other. But the conscious being in which these are perceived is different from them, because it does not undergo any change.

4

In dream it is exactly the same. Although here the objects are subtler and not as permanent as in the waking state, still they too are different by nature from that in which they are perceived. So, although there is a difference, the nature of the perceiving—the conscious being—is identical in both states. It is homogeneous.

5

One who wakes up from a deep sleep, remembers an absence in his perception during that state. However, the remembrance of objects perceived earlier remains intact. Therefore it is crystal-clear that even in deep, dreamless sleep an awareness of 'knowledge' is present.

6

In deep, dreamless sleep this conscious being is detached from the objects, but not from itself. Thus it is clear that in all the three states this conscious being is homogeneous by nature and one and the same. This has always been the case.

7

Throughout time—days, months, years, centuries and world cycles, past and future—this conscious being has remained the same. It does not rise nor does it set like the sun. It is self-effulgent.

8

This conscious being which we are, is the very essence of the ultimate, permanent, restful happiness that man is searching for. It is that which is sought in love, in everything and everybody.

9

This love for the true Self may be considered to be the deepest desire of the person who says: 'May I always exist, may I never cease to exist.'

10

Others whom we call our fellow-men, we love and care for them because of this Self. But the Self loves itself as no other. That is why the love for the Self is the highest love, and we are seeking the confirmation of that love in the other who ultimately concerns ourselves. Therefore, no one loves an other, but only himself, because division is an illusion. The Self is of the nature of supreme happiness.

11

Thus it becomes clear how things are put together. The nature of the Consciousness (the supreme happiness) has three aspects: Being-Knowing-Bliss. In reality they are one. This is what is taught in the *Upanishads*.

12

If the ultimate happiness could not be known, then there also could not be any love for it. But we know very well that it is there. If it would really be known, then how could you feel attracted to lesser things (the world and matter), yet these are also there. From this it follows that the world, too, is an expression of the One. At the same time I would say: Although its presence is without a veil, it is yet to be unveiled.

Blossoms

There is no way. A way presupposes a distance between a subject and an object. In reality there is no distance between the two. Both object and subject are concepts for the perceiving of differences. Within Being, or your Presence, there is neither object nor subject.

Understanding always takes place through the intellect and is only one aspect of the totality of life. He who seeks to grasp reality through the intellect, he really is in trouble.

What we usually call 'having problems' is in ninety-nine out of a hundred times not an objective problem, but a mental attitude. Because we ourselves are the creator, a change is possible there.

Those who overemphasize the non-existence of the world are just parroting things. They usually do not live accordingly.

Positivism is just as immature an attitude as negativism. Both are born from a standpoint of what you think yourself to be. The true person is neither positive nor negative, because the true person has transformed both.

Self-consciousness is but an other word for suffering. Self-consciousness is nothing but maintaining an object-subject relationship with yourself. All struggle and dichotomy come from that relationship.

The burden of self-consciousness stands in sharp contrast with one's real nature. In order to be conscious self-consciousness is necessary, but it need not be a burden.

The witness is not an activity. He who makes the witness into an activity should not be surprised to find himself in trouble.

Anything essential is worth while. But anything that is secondhand and from hearsay will expose itself as being false and unreal in the long run.

When guilt feelings have become a strategy for 'doing good', then you are pretty hung up, twisted, and not whole.

To be a seeker is not pleasant or spiritual. It is a tragic mistake. The seeker himself is the sought. Ultimately the seeker and the sought will disappear, because then you will have found what you are.

Remember one thing: As soon as you disagree with something with regard to Self-realisation, you have reached the limit of a fear. At that point your identification with an idea is being confirmed.

There are millions of answers to millions of questions, and again each answer is food for a million new questions. Only when both the question and the answer have disappeared, then it will be clear what your true nature is.

To speak about 'my' consciousness or 'your' consciousness is complete nonsense. Even 'the' consciousness is nonsense, because that would be giving the impression that consciousness would be possessed of qualities.

However fast you may run, you will never reach the horizon. It is exactly so with the search for 'yourself'. Each time you want to get hold of that which you are seeking, it will move, for then you are mistaking it for an object.

In all religions you will find the confirmation of the same thing in the end.

If God could only be realized at the hour of death, then all our efforts would be in vain.

Meditate on what you have heard, and whenever you do not remember it, be still and stay with the sense of 'I am'.

FOOTNOTES

1. **Foreword** [p.xiii]   The term '*jnana yoga*', introduced to the West by the end of the 19th century, meaning 'the yoga of knowledge', often leads to misunderstanding. *Jnana* is not 'knowledge' in terms of the intellect (which is *vi-jnana*), nor has it anything to do with what is nowadays commonly understood by the term 'yoga'.

2. **Chapter 7** [p.47]   'Happens': i.e. according to one's expectations (*Translator's note*).

3. **Chapter 11** [p.91]   Van Kooten en De Bie: a comic, satiric duo, well-known in the Netherlands at the time (*Translator's note*).

4. **Chapter 15** [p.110]   James Warren 'Jim' Jones (1931-1978) was an American-born sect-leader, who founded a community in Guyana, where in 1978 he led some 900 of his followers into mass murder-suicide (*Translator's note*).

5. **Chapter 33** [p.277]   See: *Bhagavad Gita* VII, 3 (*Translator's note*).

6. **Chapter 38** [p.311]   J.C. Bloem: a Dutch poet who lived from 1887 to 1966 (*Translator's note*).

7. **Chapter 38** [p.311]   Lou de Palingboer (literally: 'Lou the Eel-seller'): leader of a small sect in the Netherlands, who passed away in 1968 (*Translator's note*).

ABOUT THE AUTHOR

Alexander Smit was born in 1948 in Rotterdam, Netherlands. At an early age he showed a great interest in philosophical issues as well as in music. At the age of 15 he had an extraordinary experience which changed his life completely. He came into contact with yoga and met a number of teachers, among whom J. Krishnamurti, Rama Polderman, Swami Ranganathananda, and later on Jean Klein, Douglas Harding, John Levy, Wei Wu Wei, and in particular Wolter A. Keers, who accompanied him on the classic path of Advaita.

In 1978 he met his final teacher of Advaita, Shri Nisargadatta Maharaj, from whom he received intensive training and instruction, and who directed him to instruct anyone in the West who was thirsty for 'Knowledge' on the path of Advaita. This he did extensively, particularly through his numerous talks and lectures. Alexander Smit passed away in 1998 in the Netherlands.